Envisioning Black Colleges

Envisioning Black Colleges

A History of the United Negro College Fund

Marybeth Gasman

Foreword by
John R. Thelin

The Johns Hopkins University Press
Baltimore

The Johns Hopkins University Press
2715 North Charles Street
Baltimore, Maryland 21218-4363
www.press.jhu.edu

Library of Congress Cataloging-in-Publication Data

Gasman, Marybeth.
Envisioning black colleges : a history of the United Negro College
Fund / Marybeth Gasman, foreword by John R. Thelin.
p.   cm.
Includes bibliographical references and index.
ISBN-13: 978-0-8018-8604-1 (hardcover : alk. paper)
ISBN-10: 0-8018-8604-X (hardcover : alk. paper)
1. United Negro College Fund—History. I. Title.
LB2336.G37 2007
378.73089'96073—dc22
2006023188

A catalog record for this book is available from the British Library.

To my father

James Robert Gasman
November 8, 1925–June 26, 2005

One of the first things that had to be done was to try to create the proper image of these black institutions, of these black private colleges, and to make clear the contributions made by these colleges to black people and to the American society.

—*Albert Manley, former President, Spelman College, 1987*

We've never been Democratic or Republican, and we believe that no matter who is in power, that education is a basic American need, and we thought that our responsibility was to address that need and to constantly work for equal opportunity, under whatever laws existed, whether they were laws of segregation or integration. There's no question that all of us were deeply sympathetic and committed to integration, but that was not the role of the [United Negro] College Fund.

—*Frederick D. Patterson, Founder, United Negro College Fund, 1982*

Contents

Contents

Foreword

Most American adults are familiar with the United Negro College Fund's motto, "A Mind Is a Terrible Thing to Waste." Ironically, although that masterpiece of public relations has worked its way into our national consciousness, I imagine few Americans know much about the background and workings of the United Negro College Fund since its founding in 1944. Now, thanks to Marybeth Gasman, there's no longer a good reason to plead ignorance. Finally, the UNCF has a worthy history covering more than a half century, written and analyzed by an illuminating scholar.

This book has special importance because it shows how the fusion of the study of higher education and philanthropy has come of age. For more than a decade a number of institutes and programs, including Indiana University's Center on Philanthropy, the Nonprofit Sector, and the Council for the Advancement of Support of Education, have encouraged a new generation of scholars to probe philanthropy from multidisciplinary perspectives. This book stands as Exhibit A in showing how this scholarship ought to be done. It represents what I call "horizontal history"—a focus on organizations that cut across the landscape of American higher education. As such, it provides a useful supplement to the more traditional focus on the American campus on the "vertical" institutions we associate with higher learning.

To say that *Envisioning Black Colleges* is about philanthropy is both correct and incomplete. That's a bit like saying that David Halberstam's *The Summer of '49* is about baseball. Yes, it is—but in probing that topic it provides readers with a magical mystery tour of American life after World War II. So, although one learns about the games Americans play and watch at Yankee Stadium, Ebbetts Field, and Fenway Park, the games gain in significance and stature because they are integrated into the context of such disparate settings as New York City's café society and nightclubs in an era when major league games were played in the afternoon. It is an intricate saga that also extends in a markedly different direction to the overlooked connections of major league baseball players to their homes and life in the rural South.

And so it is with Marybeth Gasman's combination of storytelling and analysis about a group of black colleges' bold venture into collective fund-raising—a venture that connected the college campuses of the segregated South with the boardrooms and corporate offices of New York City. Readers will find a particular decade that grabs their attention. For some, it will be the leadership of a Vernon Jordan who worked effectively among diverse constituencies and power groups: high-powered public relations firms of Madison Avenue, executives of major foundations, and even new ascending and prosperous African American associations. Without this book, how would one know, for example, about the ways UNCF leaders gradually yet persistently persuaded the Ford Foundation executives to shift from resistance to support for the historically black colleges?

The historical account is punctuated by critical junctures that prompted UNCF leaders to convene for serious reconsiderations of the group's policies in light of external events. Most conspicuous was the need to respond thoughtfully to the 1954 Supreme Court decision in *Brown v. Board of Education*. That landmark decision meant that the UNCF had to work through both an internal statement and a public statement about the appropriate place of black colleges in a nation where racial exclusion in public schools ostensibly had become illegal. This high stakes juncture led to a complex response from the UNCF.

For me the most original and fascinating episodes of Gasman's narrative are her accounts of African American leaders of the historically black private colleges effectively negotiating philanthropic missions and strategies in the late 1940s in partnership with New York City–based donors, including John D. Rockefeller Jr. and his contemporaries. This reconstruction reveals the unexpected and largely unnoticed work of upper-class white women in New York City who drew from their own social circles to bring the United Negro College Fund into the mainstream of large-scale donations. In effect, the New York City matrons showed how the sideshow could, indeed, run the circus of giving and spending in the metropolitan arena.

For researchers and readers, Gasman's account shows that American social history is not for the faint-hearted. By our standards of social justice today, many may find the social networks and strategies of affluent New York City immediately after World War II to be alien, perhaps odious. But that's not the appropriate litmus. The primary question for UNCF leaders of the time—and readers today—remains: Were the luncheon gatherings, the orchestrated ceremonies, awards, dinners, and the public relations events effective in building support for the black colleges? The short answer is, yes, they were. The long—and better—answer is that you should read about it in detail. In so doing you learn about not only the black colleges but also the complexities of modern American society, including the ascent of skilled public relations firms and major foundations in the business of the nonprofit sector. For example, although the South has always been an easy, obvious target for the North in exposing racism, Gasman's accounts of commercial and public life in New York City of the late 1940s illustrate well the point that segregation was a national, not a regional, failing.

Within the field of philanthropic studies, this book makes a notable contribution in its focus on fund-raising. Heretofore what I consider to be the strongest historical works on philanthropy have given first attention to donors, philanthropists, and foundations. So, we have come to know a great deal about Andrew Carnegie, John D.

Rockefeller (senior and junior), Abraham Flexner, and the great foundations. The common thread among such biographies and organizational histories has been emphasis on the problems and consequences involved in giving money away. It means that an organization such as the Carnegie Foundation for the Advancement of Teaching or the Rockefeller Foundation's General Education Board could transform the power of giving so that each could become comparable to a *de facto* national ministry of education in the first half of the twentieth century. With Gasman's study of the UNCF, the drama shifts to the other side of the stage: How do institutions go about raising funds? How do cooperative associations achieve a collective goal? So, whether it is more blessed to give than to receive becomes less important than knowing about each and all parties in the ritualized dances of American philanthropy.

Behavioral scientists often take delight in treating historical case studies to damnation with faint praise. Their predictable criticism is, "Yes, but this is limited because, after all, it is merely 'n = 1' research." Perhaps so—and the crucial corollary is to emphasize that Gasman has wisely selected an important case study that has significance in its own right. And, as part of the bargain, she has provided a model for reconstructing and telling the story of a distinctively American institution in our unique national culture of getting and giving. But, don't settle for my word on it. In a spirit appropriate for philanthropy, I can say that readers will be the richer for giving this welcome book serious reading and careful reflection.

John R. Thelin
The University of Kentucky

Acknowledgments

In 2001, I was writing an article about racial stereotyping used in fund-raising campaigns at black colleges. However, I had little success because the archival papers for the organization that I was examining, Marts and Lundy, turned up dry. In a moment of desperation, I called Kenneth W. Rose at the Rockefeller Archive Center (RAC) to see whether he had any information. John D. Rockefeller Jr. had recommended the use of Marts and Lundy's fund-raising services to many black colleges. The RAC didn't have anything, but Ken Rose suggested that I take a look at the United Negro College Fund papers at the RAC if I was interested in fund-raising. This brief conversation was the beginning of my exploration of the UNCF—an organization that I had come across many times while writing my first book, on Charles Spurgeon Johnson. With the support of a travel grant from the RAC, I began a line of research that started with an examination of fund-raising language but later expanded to become a history of private black colleges, race relations during the cold war and Civil Rights Movement, and fund-raising within the black and white communities for a black cause.

I want to take the opportunity to thank the many people who have aided me in writing this book. Since I finished my Ph.D. in 2000, many of my colleagues have supported and mentored my development as a historian. I am immensely grateful to Andrea Walton, John Thelin, Wayne Urban, and Asa Hilliard for their unending support and constructive criticism. Over the past few years, I have presented papers on the UNCF at the annual meetings of the History of Education Society and the American Educational Research Association and have always received helpful feedback from my dedicated colleagues. I am grateful to the following people for their critique of early drafts of this work. Each of these individuals has made this book much better than it would have been if I had not received their extensive commentary: Ron Butchart, James D. Anderson, Roger Geiger, Jana Nidiffer, Linda Eisenmann, Michael Katz, Peter Dobkin Hall, Theresa Richardson, Jonathan Zimmerman, Philo Hutcheson, Kate Rousmaniere, Alfred Moss, Michael Fultz, Alvin Schnexider, M. Christopher Brown, Peter Wallenstein, Michael Bieze, Charles Willie, and Marvin Lazerson. I am also thankful to Jackie Wehmueller, my editor at The Johns Hopkins University Press, for her encouragement, helpful criticism, and thoughtful advice. She, along with the anonymous reviewers of the manuscript, made it a much stronger book.

Throughout the past six years, I have been fortunate to have had wonderful research assistants who are honest with me—what more could a faculty member ask! I am immensely grateful to Kate Sedgwick, Noah Drezner, and Chris Tudico for reading drafts of this manuscript. Their comments challenged me to think about the UNCF in new ways. I am especially appreciative of Kate Sedgwick who spent hours formatting endnotes and looking for inconsistencies throughout the book. Several other research assistants also helped with this project since 2000, including Pamela Felder Thompson, Sibby Anderson-Thompkins, Kijua Sanders-McMurtry, Vida Avery, Darryl Holloman, Michael Fulford, and Nia Woods Haydel. I have also benefited greatly from the friendships of such scholars as Matt Hartley, Joy Williamson, Laura Perna, Clif Conrad, and Amy Wells. I thank them for their support and encouragement.

Since I was a small child, my mother has been a constant source of inspiration for me. Lillian M. Gasman is a rare individual who fought for her children in every situation. She is the reason I attended college, pursued a Ph.D., and completed this book. Last, I must express my love and appreciation to Edward M. Epstein, my husband, and Chloe Sarah Epstein, my daughter. Without them, life would not be fulfilling. Edward and Chloe continually motivate me to be a better person.

During the course of this research, I visited many archives. I would like to express my gratitude to the staffs of the Rockefeller Archive Center (Kenneth W. Rose), the Atlanta University Center (Karen Jefferson), the Library of Congress, the Schomburg Center for Research in Black Culture, the Columbia University Oral History Collection, the National Archives, the United Negro College Fund (Winfield Curry, Brenda Siler, Desiree Boykin, and John Donohue), the Frederick D. Patterson Research Institute (Winfield Curry), the W. E. B. Du Bois Library (Danielle Kovacs), the Bluefield State University Library (Peggy Turnbull), and the Fisk University Archives (Beth Howse). My research on the United Negro College Fund was generously supported by several research grants. I am indebted to the following organizations and institutions for their funding and confidence in my abilities as a scholar: the Spencer Foundation, the University of Pennsylvania Research Fund, the Rockefeller Archive Center, the University of Pennsylvania Center for Africana Studies, and the Georgia State University Research Fund.

INTRODUCTION

A Time for Innovation and Change

As I wrote this book, the nation was in the midst of commemorating the fiftieth anniversary of the United States Supreme Court's proclamation, in *Brown v. Board of Education*, that separate was indeed unequal. I witnessed the media, cities, and universities speaking out in celebration of this historic event. At the same time, I heard voices from various segments of the African American community and beyond discussing the limited gains afforded by *Brown v. Board*. Although there was no longing for the return of Jim Crow, some did lament the loss of the strong and cohesive black community to which segregation had given rise. These commentators included legal scholar Derrick Bell, who regretted his own efforts in conjunction with the National Association for the Advancement of Colored People (NAACP) to close segregated public schools in local black communities after *Brown*. And there were still others, myself included, who wished the High Court had used more evenhanded language when it pointed to the detrimental effects of segregation. As Derrick Bell observes in *Silent Covenants: Brown v. Board of Education and the Unfulfilled Hopes of Racial Reform* (2004), all-black institutions were pronounced substandard for their very racial makeup, but nothing was said of their all-white counterparts. Why did the Court acknowledge the negative effects of segregation only within an all-black context? The stigma of inferiority associated with segregated black institutions (whether by law or practice) has resulted in a constant

1

questioning of the rationale for the nation's black colleges. Asking whether black colleges should continue to exist in a post-*Brown* era (without asking the same question of their historically white counterparts) fails to honor the spirit of the *Brown* decision: to provide more opportunity for African Americans.

What might black colleges be like today if the *Brown* decision had been different: enforcing the "equal" portion of *Plessy v. Ferguson*, rather than mandating desegregation of public education. Perhaps these black institutions would still be producing the majority of the nation's black leaders. Perhaps, with an infusion of funds from federal and state governments, as well as contributions from an ever-expanding black middle class, most black colleges would have by now built substantial endowments. However, given the slow implementation of desegregation following *Brown* and the pervasive racism in the country prior to the decision, we can only speculate about how equal a separate society might truly have become.

Black colleges have nonetheless evolved on their own since the *Brown* decision. Although they obviously do not enjoy the monopoly on black higher education that they had under Jim Crow, they continue to educate a substantial portion of African Americans who attend college—in 2006, 16 percent. And the one institution that has done more to shape our image of black colleges than any other is the United Negro College Fund (UNCF). The story of the United Negro College Fund starts before *Brown v. Board*, in the midst of World War II, but the UNCF takes center stage right after the High Court's decision, with the effort to justify the continued existence of black colleges in light of desegregation. This book looks at the story in depth by examining the roots of the organization in the 1940s and considering the impact of the UNCF until the end of the civil rights era in the 1970s. As most archival papers for the period after 1980 are inaccessible to researchers, I conclude this story with the development of the now classic "A Mind Is a Terrible Thing to Waste" campaign. An examination of more recent developments in the UNCF will, I hope, be the subject of future scholarly research.

In many ways, the history of the UNCF is also a history of the private black colleges and universities that it represents: a chronicle of their struggles in the mid-twentieth century to break free of ties to white industrial philanthropy and to forge identities as promoters of black culture and educational opportunity. This story of black leadership and agency amidst tumultuous change in race relations in the United States crisscrosses the lives of such civil rights luminaries and black college graduates as W. E. B. Du Bois, Benjamin E. Mays, Sadie T. M. Alexander, Martin Luther King Jr., and Vernon Jordan. My research, focused on examples of independent action on the part of blacks, has always shown how African Americans have shaped their own history. Initially the UNCF seemed to be a perfect example of black agency: an organization started by blacks on behalf of black institutions. The real story is considerably more complicated.

Founded in 1944 by Frederick D. Patterson, Tuskegee University president, the UNCF is a consortium of private black colleges involved in a cooperative fund-raising effort. Its establishment represented an attempt by black colleges, "typically dependent on chance beneficence, to establish a permanent vehicle for raising money."[1] The organization's founding came during a pivotal time for blacks in the United States with the nation experiencing "intense growing pains . . . ignited by racial friction nationwide."[2] In this year Swedish sociologist Gunnar Myrdal penned, with the help of numerous black intellectuals, the classic text *An American Dilemma*. Myrdal's book brought to the forefront of the nation's consciousness the "Negro problem," and he made it nearly impossible for America's leaders to ignore the troubles that had resulted from slavery and Jim Crow.[3] In the political sphere, the Democratic Party began to splinter along North/South lines, with the southern faction bristling over northern leaders' increased support of racial change. Republicans had their own liberal-conservative differences with which to grapple as well.[4] More often than not, conservative blacks, including many black college presidents, aligned themselves with southern white liberals. Many of these black college presidents figured prominently in the efforts to improve race relations during the 1940s; in fact, they were often referred to by white southerners as "responsible Negro leaders." Instead of confronting segregation directly, these black college leaders "chipped away" at the status quo gradually; education was their preferred means.[5]

Organizations that favored direct confrontation, such as the NAACP, had established chapters in every southern state by the early 1940s.[6] While this organization's early efforts were focused on making sure that separate was indeed equal (for example, the *Missouri ex. Rel. Gaines v. Canada*, 1938), a full-fledged attempt at knocking down the wall of segregation within higher education (showing that separate could not be equal) did not come until the end of the 1940s. Some protest action occurred during this time as well; however, most took place in the North or in border areas, such as Washington, D.C. For example, in 1941, discrimination was the norm in the nation's munitions factories. Talks with President Franklin D. Roosevelt sought to secure war-related employment for blacks and desegregation of the military; when these failed, A. Philip Randolph, president of the Brotherhood of Sleeping Car Porters, began to organize a march to Washington to protest.[7] In May of that year, Randolph issued a "Call to Negro America to March on Washington for Jobs and Equal Participation in National Defense" to be held on July 1. By June estimates of the number of people expected to participate in the march reached one hundred thousand.[8] Worried about the prospect of such a demonstration in the nation's capital and its impact on the nation's international reputation with a war on the horizon, Franklin D. Roosevelt tried to convince Randolph to cancel it. Randolph did so only after Roosevelt issued Executive Order 8802, which banned discrimination in defense industries and federal bureaus; the order also established the Fair Employment Practices Committee (FEPC), an entity designed to handle discrimination complaints.[9] According to historian Joe William Trotter Jr., "Executive Order 8802 proved to be a turning point in African American history. It linked the struggle of African Americans even more closely to the Democratic Party and helped transform the federal government into a significant ally."[10] Along with the creation of the FEPC, Roosevelt established the Committee on Civil Rights whose sole purpose was to investigate civil rights issues and violations. Although Roosevelt made some concessions to Randolph's demands, he did not desegregate the military: the Marine Corps was an almost exclusively white operation, the Navy consigned its black sailors to the kitchen, the Army restricted black soldiers to all-black units with white commanders, and the Army Aircorps remained segregated, with the exception of the officer training programs, which integrated in 1942.

Another protest effort percolating in the 1940s was a campaign against segregation in public accommodations. Organized by James Farmer's Congress of Racial Equality (CORE), this campaign pioneered the use of the sit-in as a method for civil rights protest. With the help of activist Bayard Rustin (who had worked with A. Philip Randolph as well), CORE expanded nationally within a few years and became central to the 1960s Civil Rights Movement. Many UNCF member college students played a significant role in CORE, by leading sit-ins and protests as well as providing intellectual leadership for the organization's efforts.[11]

Discrimination in both the war effort and public accommodations was part of a broader pattern of hostility toward blacks throughout the country during this time. By the early 1940s, the promise of war-related employment was an impetus for black migration to the North; the percentage of blacks residing in urban areas increased from less than 50 percent in 1940 to more than 65 percent by 1944. According to Katrina Sanders-Cassell, unlike the black migration associated with World War I, this instance "was different as blacks fervently pushed to obtain a piece of World War II's economic pie. Blacks were fully aware of the opportunities associated with this war and did not plan to miss out."[12] For the first time, blacks and whites were in direct competition for jobs. Tensions in cities throughout the country grew high, with riots breaking out in Detroit and Harlem as well as Los Angeles, San Diego, and Philadelphia. Throughout the United States, African Americans were expressing outrage at the discrimination they experienced and its economic repercussions.[13] Moreover, the federal government's support of black civil rights (for example, Roosevelt's efforts in 1944 to end poll taxes and eliminate all-white primaries) caused deep agitation among whites. In typical response, whites fell back on "their old social methods of fear, hatred, and violence to control blacks."[14]

As higher education for whites expanded through the mid-1940s, so too did it expand for blacks; the 1944 G.I. Bill contributed greatly to this growth. Black soldiers coming home from World War II enrolled in colleges and universities; some enrolled in schools scattered throughout the United States, but the majority entered black colleges in the South. With an aim to exercise their rights at home after fighting for democracy abroad, the veterans began to compare segregation at home to the fascism they had defeated in Europe.[15] For instance, one black soldier from Alabama, speaking on behalf of his colleagues in the Army, described his feelings: "I spent four years in the army to free a bunch of Dutchmen and Frenchmen, and I'm hanged if I'm going to let the Alabama version of the Germans kick me around when I get home. No sirree-bob! I went into the Army a nigger; I'm comin' out a man."[16] Veterans, constituting an important influence on black college campuses, sometimes sowed the seeds of activism among students. In the words of Walter White, executive director of the NAACP, "World War II has given to the Negro a sense of kinship with other colored—and also oppressed— peoples of the world."[17] According to Gunnar Myrdal, "the present War is of tremendous importance to the Negro in all respects. He has seen his strategic position strengthened not only because of the desperate scarcity of labor but also because of revitalization of the democratic Creed."[18] But another decade would pass before blacks initiated the highly publicized actions of the civil rights era, beginning with the heroic 1955 Montgomery bus boycott.[19]

During the mid-1940s, a time of great expectation created by the imminent victory against fascism, Frederick D. Patterson developed the idea for the United Negro College Fund. From the start, Patterson wanted to create an organization led by blacks working on behalf of black institutions. During its early years, however, the

UNCF was merely a new face on early twentieth-century industrial philanthropy. Philanthropies such as the Julius Rosenwald Fund and John D. Rockefeller Jr.'s General Education Board provided seed money for the organization—Rockefeller Jr. maintained a tight grip on its everyday activities for many years. But was it possible for the organization to operate in any other way? According to Gunnar Myrdal, "The selection and the behavior of Negro leaders in the South is an outcome of this fact, that practically all the economic and political powers are concentrated in the white caste while the small amount of influence, status, and wealth that there is in the Negro community is derivative and dependent."[20] Furthermore, Myrdal explained, "The Negro masses are well aware of this situation. They need Negro leaders who can get things from whites. They know that a Negro leader who starts to act aggressively is not only losing his own power and often his livelihood but might endanger the welfare of the whole Negro community."[21]

In the case of private black colleges, whites held the purse strings even after the formation of the UNCF. Although Patterson and his black colleagues were the "leaders" of the organization, the rules were crafted by those whites who, with their money, made the Fund possible during the early days. In the mid-1940s, the UNCF publicly represented itself in a conservative manner and portrayed African American college students as loyal, patriotic, hardworking citizens—precisely the image that Rockefeller Jr. needed to bring in large sums of philanthropic support from his business colleagues. Behind the scenes, the African American leaders desired integration and equality of all kinds—economic, political, and social. This two-sided character—what W. E. B. Du Bois termed a "double consciousness"—defined early UNCF activities.[22] In the words of Du Bois,

the Negro is a sort of seventh son, born with a veil, and gifted with second-sight in this American world,—a world which yields him no true self-consciousness, but only lets him see himself through the revelation of the other world. It is a peculiar sensation, this double-consciousness, this sense of always looking at one's self through the eyes of others, of measuring one's soul by the tape of a world that looks on in amused contempt and pity. One ever feels his twoness,—an American, a Negro; two souls, two thoughts, two unreconciled strivings; two warring ideals in one dark body, whose dogged strength alone keeps it from being torn asunder.[23]

In the early years, the African American leaders of the UNCF operated behind a veil within the confines of a white world. During this same time, the UNCF built its infrastructure and fund-raising base. In particular, the National Women's Committee made strides in the New York City area. The committee raised funds while also challenging societal taboos and pushing the boundaries on interracial socializing.

With the Supreme Court's landmark *Brown v. Board* decision in 1954, the UNCF began to change its public image. In light of the Court's pronouncement that segregated environments were inferior, the organization faced the dilemma of advocating for its all-black campuses without seeming opposed to integration. At this time the UNCF's African American leadership changed the images and language used in publicity and focused on the benefits of attending black colleges as well as the possibility that these institutions might integrate.

By the 1960s several philanthropic organizations, including the Ford and the Carnegie foundations, started questioning whether black colleges should exist at all. In cooperation with prominent researchers, these foundations attempted to evaluate the performance of the black institutions. Some of their reports contained blistering attacks, denigrating the colleges for mismanagement and low academic standards. As part of the UNCF's robust defense, the Fund began to change the way it presented black colleges to the public. Combined with more militant students on black college campuses, the outside attacks forced the UNCF to embrace a new black-centered image and to become more activist in its public stances. The images used to represent the thirty-nine member colleges were no longer conservative and docile; instead, they became assertive, active, and spirited. These changes also reflected a shift in black consciousness throughout the country—a veritable groundswell within the UNCF leadership. Black leaders of the organization, now at the helm, proactively represented the colleges to the public by, for example, meeting with United States presidents, making public appearances, and advertising.

Spurred by a growing black middle class, the 1970s ushered in an era of change and greater national presence for the UNCF. At this time the National Ad Council, in conjunction with the UNCF, coined the phrase "A Mind Is a Terrible Thing to Waste"—a slogan that invoked a sense of compassion and obligation in many Americans who might not have previously donated to black education. No longer relying entirely on money from large corporate philanthropies, the UNCF began to draw from a broader national donor pool. According to the Ad Council, the "A Mind Is a Terrible Thing to Waste" effort, one of the most effective campaigns in history, made the UNCF a household name.

By considering the changes that have taken place in the UNCF over the years, I aim to answer several central questions. First, if the UNCF started as an auxiliary of industrial philanthropy, how has it evolved and what progress has it made toward independence? How did the Fund use language and images to shape the public's understanding of black colleges? How did the UNCF, an organization rooted in capitalism, push for social equality? In the face of a changing society, how did the UNCF justify the continued existence of black colleges? How did the UNCF deal with pressure from within the black community to become more open and honest about its goals? With black colleges often under attack, how did the UNCF move from mere fund-raiser to an advocate for and an authority on black colleges? Last, given the many changes during the second half of the twentieth century—in society, race relations, and the organization itself—how did the UNCF's fund-raising publicity evolve over the years? This book is more than a history of people and events; it is an account of the words and images—and the messages imbedded in them—used to convince people to give to the cause of African American higher education in general and black private colleges in particular.

Note: I refer to either the black or the white leaders of the Fund, depending on the situation or action. When I refer to the United Negro College Fund, as a whole, I am referring to both the black and the white leaders of the Fund.

CHAPTER 1

Black Colleges and the Origins of the United Negro College Fund

From the time of their forced arrival in North America, black people have thirsted for knowledge and viewed education as the key to freedom.[1] In the South under the cruel subjugation of slavery and the unfair imposition of the laws that forbade them to read and write, African Americans nonetheless pursued their education.[2] In the North just prior to the Civil War a few colleges for free blacks appeared, universities such as Lincoln (1854) and Cheyney (1837) in Pennsylvania and Wilberforce (1856) in Ohio.[3] With the end of the war the daunting task of providing education to more than four million formerly enslaved people was shouldered by both the federal government (through the Freedmen's Bureau) and many northern church missionary associations. As early as 1865, the Freedmen's Bureau began establishing black colleges, drawing in staff and teachers fresh from the ranks of the Civil War military. During the postbellum period most black colleges were colleges in name only; these institutions generally provided primary and secondary education, a feature that was also prevalent during the first decades of existence among most historically white colleges, including Harvard.[4]

Religious missionaries—some affiliated with northern white denominations such as the Baptists and Congregationalists and some with black churches such as the African Methodist Episcopal and the African Methodist Episcopal Zion—were actively working with the Freedmen's Bureau. Two of the most prominent white

11

organizations were the American Baptist Home Mission Society and the American Missionary Association. White northern missionary societies founded black colleges such as Fisk University in Nashville, Tennessee, and Spelman College in Atlanta, Georgia. However, the benevolence of the missionaries was tinged with self-interest and racism. The missionaries' stated goals in establishing these colleges were to Christianize the freedmen (that is, convert formerly enslaved people to their brand of Christianity) and to rid the country of the "menace" of uneducated African Americans.[5] In fact, this notion of a "Black menace," often at the center of white hatred toward African Americans, had been a chief justification for perpetuating the slave system prior to the Civil War. Among the colleges founded by black denominations were Morris Brown in Georgia, Paul Quinn in Texas, and Allen University in South Carolina. Unique among American colleges, these institutions were founded by African Americans for African Americans.[6] Because these colleges relied on less support from whites, they designed their own curricula with less outside influence; they were, however, also more vulnerable to economic instability.

An entirely different type of black college was established with the help of the federal government in 1890. In the second Morrill Land Grant Act, Congress provided additional funds for expanding education. Because whites benefited from the Morrill Act funds, Congress demanded that blacks benefit as well. However, states were permitted to provide education in separate institutions. Determined to maintain a segregated system of education, southern and border states established public black colleges. In practice, none of these institutions was equal to its white counterpart with regard to facilities and resources. Through the 1890 Morrill Act, seventeen black institutions were funded. Six of these were actually newly established colleges, which resulted directly from the federal government's funds. Rather than spending the additional state funds needed to establish separate, fully functioning, black public institutions, most southern states chose to allot the monies from the Morrill Act to colleges that were already included in the state budget; in a few cases they annexed private institutions and changed the colleges' status to public. The curricula at all these 1890 land grant institutions focused on agricultural and mechanical arts, the English language, math, and the physical and natural sciences.[7] Because they were public institutions, none of the black colleges established at this time was eligible for membership in the United Negro College Fund when it was founded in 1944.

At the end of the nineteenth century, private black colleges had exhausted funding from missionaries, which had limited financial resources. Simultaneously, a new form of support emerged—white northern industrial philanthropy. Among the industrial leaders who initiated this type of support were John D. Rockefeller, Andrew Carnegie, Julius Rosenwald, George Peabody, and John Slater. Although these captains of industry professed a deep commitment to Christian benevolence, it is easy to see that their philanthropic activity dovetailed neatly with their desire to control industrial enterprises nationwide.[8] The organization making the largest contribution to black education was the General Education Board (GEB), a conglomeration of northern white philanthropists established by John D. Rockefeller Sr. but spearheaded by his son, John D. Rockefeller Jr. Between 1903 and 1964, GEB gifts to black colleges exceeded $63 million—an impressive figure, but only about a fifth of what it gave to white institutions.[9]

The funding system created by these industrial moguls showed a strong tendency to control black education for their own benefit. For example, the curriculum they favored produced graduates who were skilled in the trades that served their own enterprises. Black colleges such as Tuskegee and Hampton showcased such industrial education.[10] At these institutions students learned how to shoe horses, make dresses, cook, and clean under the leadership of individuals like Samuel Chapman Armstrong (Hampton) and Booker T. Washington (Tuskegee).[11] Above all, the educational institutions receiving the industrialists' support were extremely careful not to upset the segregationist power structure that ruled the South by the 1890s.

The philanthropists' support of industrial education was in direct conflict with the path prescribed by many black intellectuals, who favored a liberal arts curriculum.[12] Institutions such as Fisk, Dillard, Howard, Spelman, and Morehouse focused on the classical liberal arts training favored by W. E. B. Du Bois rather than the skills developed through labor and self-sufficiency favored by Booker T. Washington.[13] Although the two educational giants were sometimes depicted as having diametrically opposed philosophies, they in fact shared the goals of educating African Americans and uplifting their race. Their differing approaches might be summarized as follows: Washington favored educating blacks in the industrial arts so they might become self-sufficient as individuals, whereas Du Bois wanted to create an intellectual elite among the top 10 percent of the black population (the "talented tenth") to lead the race as a whole toward self-determination. Both men favored training teachers, who would then go out and educate the race, according to these different philosophies.[14]

Beginning around 1915, the attitude of the industrial philanthropists shifted; they started to turn their attention to those black colleges that emphasized the liberal arts. Realizing that industrial education could coexist with a more academic curriculum, the philanthropists opted to spread their money (and therefore their influence) throughout the educational system.[15] According to James D. Anderson, the GEB wanted to orchestrate the "systematic development of a few select institutions of black higher education."[16] These institutions would "produce college-bred leaders to acculturate black Americans into the values and mores of southern society. Second, it was very important that black leaders be trained in the South by institutions 'in touch with the conditions to be faced by the young people in later life rather than in the North by institutions . . . out of touch with southern life.' Third, and most important, the development of a few strong institutions was viewed as a strategic means to reduce the number of existing black colleges."[17]

The pervasive influence of industrial philanthropy in the early twentieth century fostered a conservative environment on many black college campuses. Not wishing to jeopardize their business interests, the industrial philanthropists favored leaders (typically white men) who upheld southern social norms. But attention from the industrial philanthropists was not necessarily welcomed at institutions like Fisk and Howard, where rebellions ensued against autocratic presidents, whom students assumed to be puppets of the philanthropists.[18] In spite of these conflicts, industrial philanthropists provided the major support that kept individual private black colleges afloat until the late 1930s.

The Beginnings of the United Negro College Fund

In 1935, at the young age of 34, Frederick D. Patterson became president of historically black Tuskegee Institute in Tuskegee, Alabama.[19] A graduate of Iowa State College's veterinary science program in 1923 and the chair of Tuskegee Institute's Department of Agriculture, Patterson was not aware that then-president Robert Moton was considering him for the role of president.[20] Regardless, when Moton retired, Patterson eagerly stepped into the position (and married Moton's daughter as well). In the first few years of his presidency, he became aware of the troubles the institution faced. Unbeknownst to him when he took the job, Tuskegee was running a deficit of $50,000 a year. According to UNCF historian Lewis W. Jones, "he was faced with the demand for a cut in the institution's budget of $90,000" the first year and $60,000 the next year. Patterson quickly acknowledged that he lacked the fund-raising skills and personal ties of past Tuskegee presidents Booker T. Washington and Moton—skills necessary to turn the institution around.

Washington had been a master at fund-raising; Moton, traveling with him and the institute's choir, raised funds along the way. Thus, Moton acquired many keen public relations and fund-raising skills needed by a college president. Typically, a new president would look to the trustees of an institution for assistance with fund-raising, but Tuskegee's trustees, given the strong abilities of both Washington and Moton, had become accustomed to a more passive

Frederick D. Patterson. Used with permission from the United Negro College Fund, Fairfax, Virginia.

role. Without either well-honed personal skills or well-established institutional connections, Patterson found it difficult to run Tuskegee in an efficient manner while meeting the needs of poor black college students, many of whom could not afford tuition.[21]

Unlike his predecessors Washington and Moton, Patterson, a highly educated scientist, a veterinarian, was deeply committed to black academic and intellectual accomplishment. Like Washington and Moton, he was regarded as a conservative by many and chose to work within the system.[22] He believed that funding black educa-

16

tion was a method by which blacks could achieve full rights as citizens. According to historian John Egerton, Patterson was the kind of black leader who avoided the "confrontational exposure" sought by organizations like James Farmer's Congress of Racial Equality or A. Philip Randolph's March on Washington.[23] However, his actual views were not that different from those of Randolph, W. E. B. Du Bois, or Langston Hughes (all considered radicals during the 1940s). For example, when asked to write an essay for Rayford Logan's *What the Negro Wants* (1944), Patterson wrote, "Any form of segregation based on race, creed or color is discriminatory and imposes a penalty inconsistent with the guaranties of American democracy." Moreover, he added, "The more conservative element of Negroes differ from those who hold the most radical views in opposition to segregation only in terms of time and technique of its elimination. In any statement which attempts to speak unequivocally in terms of ultimates, all Negroes must condemn any form of segregation based on race, creed or color anywhere in the nation."[24]

According to Egerton, African Americans everywhere, regardless of political persuasion, opposed segregation. This view was evidenced by Logan's book, which included five essays by radicals, five by moderates, and five by conservatives.[25] Each and every one of these individuals, Patterson included, called for an end to segregation and a beginning of full American citizenship for blacks.[26] This stance was not atypical for Patterson. According to Charles Stephens, the UNCF national campaign director from 1973 to 1976, Patterson "walked around mad as hell most of the time." He usually did not agree with white leadership, but he knew what had to be done to save black colleges; as such, he did it. In Stephens's words, whites viewed Patterson as a conservative, but "he was really a Roosevelt Democrat."[27]

Among the problems Patterson confronted was the state of wealth in America. According to historian Scott Cutlip, "'the golden age of fund-raising,' came crashing down in economic ruin and social chaos as the Great Depression followed in the wake of the Stock Market crash of October, 1929. This bitter climax to the false prosperity of the 1920's brought an end to 'the greatest era of voluntary giving any nation has ever witnessed.'"[28] Many wealthy people who had given to Tuskegee under presidents Washington and Moton, having lost their money in the Great Depression, had not yet found ways to recover. Others had died, and their children lacked the philanthropic interests of their parents. Moreover, many wealthy donors were angry with the Roosevelt administration for its increased taxation of the rich. These conservative donors typically argued that private philanthropy, rather than the federal government, should provide relief for the poor.[29] However, President Roosevelt thought different: "One of these duties of the State is that of caring for those of its citizens who find themselves the victims of such adverse circumstances as to make them unable to obtain even the necessities for mere existence without the aid of others. . . . To these unfortunate citizens aid must be extended by Government, not as a matter of charity, but as a matter of social duty."[30] When black college presidents approached wealthy individuals, their response was predictable: Roosevelt "took our money, you go and ask him for your support. Don't come back to us."[31] In actuality, Roosevelt's New Deal policies were hardly equitable in the assistance they provided to black Americans. Most blacks were not covered by the Social Security Act, and many rural blacks lost their jobs owing to the enforcement of the Triple A acreage reduction contract, which paid farmers to decrease their crops in order to push up product demand—in effect, forcing thousands of tenant farmers into a jobless state.[32] According to sociologist Gunnar Myrdal, "unemployed Negroes, unlike unemployed whites, had no savings upon which they could fall back in the crisis."[33]

Patterson could see the writing on the wall: black colleges were in dire financial trouble. His predictions for black colleges were borne out by financial data published by the United States Office of Education in 1943, as part of a study that analyzed private giving to black colleges. The study found that between 1930 and 1943 the overall income of black colleges decreased 15 percent and income from private gifts decreased 50 percent.[34] Among the nation's white colleges and universities, the situation was similarly dismal. According to a study conducted by John Price Jones, which reported the results of forty-six white colleges' fund-raising efforts, these institutions received $77,867,380 in gifts and bequests in 1930, much less than they received in 1935.[35] As a result of the financial difficulties throughout the nation, between 1930 and 1940 several better known small black colleges—including Roger Williams, Mary Allen, Walden, and Howe Institute—closed their doors. Some of the more nationally known black colleges were merging to ensure survival. Under the guidance of John Hope, Atlanta University had become the graduate university of the Atlanta University Center, which included Spelman, Morehouse, and Atlanta University. Likewise, New Orleans and Straight colleges merged to form Dillard University. State governments took over grounds and facilities of other, once private, institutions in still further survival measures; these "new" state institutions included Fort Valley State, North Carolina College, and Jackson State.[36]

After much frustration with the fund-raising situation, Patterson began to correspond with a cadre of black college presidents about the challenges of raising money and possible solutions to these problems. The majority of college presidents wrote back to him with details of their similarly bleak financial situations and anecdotes about the difficulty of approaching foundations for funds. From his correspondence Patterson realized that black college presidents were competing for the same small pool of funds; everyone was soliciting the same organizations and the same donors.[37] In fact, in his autobiography, Frederick D. Patterson noted, "I can recall bumping into some of the presidents of other black colleges in the offices of the General Education Board. Our meeting wasn't intentional; it was just happenstance. They were going for their interests, and I was going for mine. There was no secret about who was donating what: reports were usually available indicating the gifts a particular foundation had made to various colleges."[38] Many college presidents who responded to Patterson's query thought he was assessing their situation to assist in their fund-raising connections with major philanthropists, something that Booker T. Washington had done when he was president of Tuskegee. The presidents were most likely under this impression because Tuskegee, considered one of the philanthropists' favored institutions, was thought to be the least likely to have financial problems.[39]

Meanwhile, in the late 1930s and early 1940s two of the largest supporters of black higher education—the General Education Board and the Julius Rosenwald Fund—were turning their attention to other projects.[40] Their contributions to black colleges, as well as those of other large philanthropic organizations, waned. Some foundations were liquidated; others turned their attention to special ventures in black affairs such as Gunner Myrdal's *An American Dilemma*; still others were directing money toward white education.[41] In addition, philanthropists were calling for more support from the black community itself; philanthropists wanted to see contributions from individual alumni, organizations, and churches.[42] According to James P. Brawley, president of Clark College, foundations and corporations were asking pointed questions: "How much do your alumni give?" "Where are your alumni, and what are they doing?"[43] Although many alumni gave what they could, most did not have any extra income. At this point the majority of alumni, teachers and college professors at black schools, were being paid only one-fourth of their white counterparts' salaries.[44] Meanwhile, black colleges were faced with students who could not afford to pay tuition and church boards that were reluctant to increase their contributions; most churches supported more than one institution and did not have enough money to spread large donations among multiple institutions. These factors combined to produce near-impossible financial hurdles for black colleges; their budgets were running substantial deficits, and they were unable to keep up with operating costs. Without the support of the foundations and affiliated churches, black colleges needed to broaden their search for funds. Therefore, the task of fund-raising for individual colleges could not be left solely to the president.

In 1943, in response to this critical situation, Patterson crafted the idea of a united appeal for private black colleges carried out by an organization specifically created for fund-raising.[45] Among the models Patterson looked to in developing his idea was the March of Dimes' National Foundation for Infantile Paralysis. This campaign pushed charitable giving in a new direction by reaching out to the average citizen rather than focusing exclusively on a small number of wealthy donors.[46] According to Patterson, "The idea occurred [to me] that this was the direction of national philanthropy, with the masses brought together to contribute. Only by going beyond any immediate constituency such as alumni and trustees could a campaign have a national appeal."[47] The UNCF campaign also provided a mechanism for businesses to give to higher education in a systematic and continual fashion rather than for individual projects, as they had done in the past. According to a UNCF statement, "By making it possible for a corporation to channel its gift through an agency for a group of colleges, the Fund made the task easier for the business man. He was not called upon to choose among a number of institutions."[48]

Also in 1943, Patterson called an exploratory meeting to measure the feasibility of a combined appeal for black colleges. His public call, published in the black-owned Pittsburgh *Courier*, clearly articulated his original vision to create an organization similar in nature to the March of Dimes, one that would reach out for support to the general public—both white and black.[49] However, his immediate goal was to begin with his own people. In 1943, Patterson wrote: "The question remains as to whether or not these institutions have sufficiently impressed their worth on the general public and there has been sufficient growth in the public conscience to permit the quality of widespread, if small, individual generosity that is necessary to offset the substantial gifts of the past. . . . Such a campaign might well begin with Negro people in America."[50] Because he liked what he read, the president of the Pittsburgh *Courier*, Ira F. Lewis, offered Patterson the editorial support of the paper: "I think your column of last week strikes a very happy chord, and we are going to support the idea editorially. It is my further belief that a national committee should be formed of colored men of all walks of life. This same committee's work to be dedicated to raising funds among

Negroes for a general education fund. . . . I certainly would like to see that idea go over."[51]

Patterson's comments in the Pittsburgh *Courier* provided the guiding words for the establishment of the United Negro College Fund. According to Patterson, "The coming together of the private Black colleges out of concern for our needs; the fact that we were not going to get the amount of money we had been receiving from our former sources; and the innovative fundraising practices of other organizations—all of these factors contributed to the formation of the UNCF."[52] Patterson also thought it was important to reach out to those who were interested in educating black youth but who did not know about black colleges. In the early 1940s, most whites in the North had little idea that private black colleges existed.[53] With the UNCF, the presidents had an opportunity to educate the public about black colleges—a task that became central to the organization's success. By working together, the presidents had many more connections and greater influence than when they worked individually.[54]

Eighteen black college presidents came to the initial meeting of the United Negro College Fund, including Dillard University's Albert Dent, Spelman College's Florence Read, Atlanta University's Rufus Clement, LeMoyne Owen College's Hollis Price, and Morehouse College's Benjamin Mays. Patterson invited the college leaders to meet with a representative from the John Price Jones fund-raising firm, a firm with which Tuskegee had worked in 1925 when it joined the Hampton Institute for a joint campaign that raised 4 million dollars. It is interesting to note that John Price Jones was recommended by Rockefeller Jr. and his associates. Some college presidents thought the idea of the UNCF would not work. Buell Gallagher of Talladega College, for example, came to the meeting with a paper in hand that detailed the myriad reasons the idea was flawed. Thomas Elsa Jones, then president of Fisk University, was highly skeptical but eventually became one of the Fund's most valued participants.[55] Jones's main concern was the inevitable distance between the individual black colleges and donors when the UNCF served as the intermediary. In a letter to Patterson, Jones outlined his concerns: "There are many difficulties of which I am sure you are aware, in conducting a financial campaign for several colleges. The greatest difficulty is that experienced by private agencies in the Community Chest movement [the forerunner of the United Way]. The unification of the appeal is sometimes weakened by the distance that develops between the donor and the particular problem or institution which secures his interest. I recognize that the Presbyterian church colleges were able to overcome these handicaps."[56] President Gallagher decided not to join because he thought the combined fund-raising effort would weaken the strength of the individual colleges. However, after the UNCF had a successful first year, he changed his mind.[57]

In the words of the founders, one of the most important goals for the UNCF was to help provide funds for operating budgets—that is, 10 percent of each member college's budget.[58] Even more important was educating the American public about the significant contributions that black colleges and their graduates had made throughout the nation.[59] Because the monetary goal was to be achieved through public relations, publicity and the establishment of a national presence became the major concerns of the organization.[60] Specifically the UNCF sought to:

1. Raise funds for member colleges.
2. Promote better public understanding and appreciation of the needs and problems of Negroes through fundraising.
3. Set an example of interracial cooperation in [the Fund's] national campaign.[61]

Of course, the organization had a daunting task ahead of it in a time of uncertainty throughout a country in the midst of World War II. In addition, the new concept of raising funds through interracial cooperation would not be welcomed by everyone.

When the whole group of twenty-seven colleges was finally assembled in 1944, Patterson referred to it as "the greatest bunch of organized poverty in the U. S."[62] The poverty-stricken colleges had a difficult time raising funds precisely because they were poor. Prior to the existence of the UNCF, a black college president convention-ally raised funds by showing need and pointing to the institutional deficit as rationales for individuals and foundations to give money. The president justified the deficit by noting the number of poor people served by black colleges. According to Patterson, the deficit approach appealed to individual donors, "but the foundations be-gan to take a different point of view, and to summarize the change, they said, to a college, well, a deficit is not the basis of an appeal that we are willing to respond to. We think a deficit is evidence of poor management, and therefore we are more interested in new initia-tives. We are interested in improving your program, but we're not in-terested in picking up your deficit."[63] Despite Patterson's objection to the deficit approach, the UNCF leaders did, on occasion, use pub-licity that spoke to physical needs or the poor facilities of their col-lective institutions. In time they began to emphasize the accomplish-ments of their graduates and the rigor of their academic programs.[64]

As a result of his previous interactions as a college president with the General Education Board, Patterson was easily able to convince John D. Rockefeller Jr. to publicly endorse and financially support the UNCF.[65] This, according to Patterson, was important to the UNCF's fund-raising success: "Leadership is the key to any cam-paign. If the top one or two or three people in the community iden-tify themselves with it, their endorsement will make an important difference in its success."[66] Rockefeller Jr. was intrigued by the idea because it was consistent with his family's perspective as well as his politics. Patterson sold him on the UNCF by couching it in the framework of black self-help. The industrialist came to the en-deavor with a background that lauded "pulling oneself up by the bootstraps" and evidenced an obsession to convince the public that capitalism was benign. Rockefeller Jr., therefore, was persuaded that the UNCF was a good idea and confident he could persuade others to back the cause. Almost immediately, he convinced the Julius Rosenwald Fund to join him in supporting the UNCF through a $25,000 donation.

Given his role in creating the UNCF, Patterson became the organization's first president. However, because Patterson was simultaneously the president of Tuskegee Institute, William Trent Jr. was chosen to be the first executive director of the Fund.[67] Trent was the son of William Trent, the president of Livingstone College. After graduating with business degrees from Livingstone as well as the Wharton School at the University of Pennsylvania, Trent Jr. was unable to secure a job with a large company owing to the racist conditions of the South. With his father's help Trent Jr. secured a job at Livingstone, where he taught economics in 1932. After a few years, he moved to Bennett College in North Carolina where he taught and served as acting dean for one year. In 1939, Trent Jr. started to work with Harold Ickes for the Federal Works Agency, where he was the race relations officer. At this time Patterson approached him about the position at the UNCF. Trent Jr. was interested, but he had one problem; he had just been examined for the draft, and he would probably be called to serve.

In 1981 Trent recalled the developments that prompted his appointment at the UNCF:

> Then Pat . . . said, well, if you can get released from that, will you take it? I said, well, yes, sure. So he [Patterson] went to call on the draft director in Washington, D.C., and when he walked in and announced that he was the President of Tuskegee Institute, the draft director said, oh, Booker T. Washington delivered my commencement address when I graduated from Iowa State. So they talked about it and Pat told him about the needs of the colleges and he said well, I think he ought to be deferred. So Pat [credits] Booker T. Washington with getting me deferred from the Army, so I could come with the United Negro College Fund.[68]

Trent began at the UNCF in January 1944 and stayed through 1964, when he was offered a position at *Time* magazine as an assistant personnel director.

William J. Trent Jr. Used with permission from the Special Collections Department, W. E. B. Du Bois Library, University of Massachusetts Amherst.

One of the first items of business for Patterson, Trent, and the twenty-seven member college presidents was to gauge the assets of the colleges and design a formula for distributing the money they planned to raise in the upcoming years. Based on self-reported data from the member colleges, the Fund determined that the combined average annual income from endowments was $1,345,600. According to UNCF historian Lewis W. Jones,

> Two-thirds of the colleges had no invested funds or such small investments as to yield less than $25,000 per year. These 15 colleges were apparently dependent on gifts and grants. Yet, the combined annual average of gifts and grants was approximately half the amount of the return from invested funds—$630,043. Two-thirds of the colleges received gifts and grants of less than $25,000 per year. Three institutions had more than $100,000 annual income from endowment and also received more than $50,000 a year in gifts and grants. Two other colleges with endowment incomes of more than $100,000 secured $1100 and $2900 yearly in gifts or grants. Two institutions secured more than $50,000 annually in gifts and grants—one had no endowment income, and the other $1600 annual endowment.[69]

Although their situation was grimmer, black colleges, in fact, faced the same general pattern of financial problems that plagued many private white colleges at that time. According to a 1952 article in the *New York Times,* which presented data from a ten-year study of small private colleges, "The independent liberal arts college is in serious financial trouble. Fifty per cent of these institutions are operating on a deficit. Many are on the verge of bankruptcy."[70]

The UNCF distribution formula was created to favor the weaker colleges by taking into account the average five-year income from endowment gifts and grants.[71] The presidents also decided that *a percentage* of the money raised would be divided equally among the schools, regardless of institutional size. This policy meant that the smaller and generally weaker colleges received a proportionately larger share of the funds raised. According to Patterson, "we took into account the base of support which each college had, and that was what we called the endowment or its equivalent. And then the least factor was the size of the student body. We thought sometimes a college might take more students than it could afford to take, so we didn't make that a rigid determination, but we did think the size of the student body had to reflect to some degree the size of the institution's obligations."[72]

Along with the distribution formula, the staff and member college presidents established a solicitation policy stipulating that member colleges could only raise funds on their own college's behalf during specific times of the year. During the remainder of the year in assigned cities, the presidents acted on behalf of the UNCF and raised funds for the good of the group. From time to time, Patterson and Trent had trouble with presidents not following this rule. For example, Patterson had to rebuke Mary Mcleod Bethune, president of Bethune Cookman, on several occasions. According to Patterson, "Calling on Mrs. Bethune was hard. She was a person of great stature [having a close friendship with Eleanor Roosevelt], but we didn't go to anyone about infractions of the solicitation policy unless we knew they were violating the policy."[73] When a member college was in violation, Patterson explained the problem to the president:

And if you go to the donor ahead of the College Fund, he may give you five dollars or five thousand dollars, when he would give the College Fund a hundred thousand dollars, because the cause is a bigger cause. Now, the only reason for you to have membership in the College Fund is because you believe you can do better as a member of the Fund than you can by yourself. You're not bound. You come in here. You ask for membership. You get it. You can get out of it any time you feel that membership in the Fund is not valuable to you as what you can do for yourself outside the Fund.[74]

In addition to violating the solicitation policy, many member college presidents were reluctant to share their donor contact lists with the group, although each benefited from the contacts of other members. It was initially difficult for the individual college presidents to trust one another; moreover, they were skeptical that their work for the whole group would benefit their individual colleges.[75] Betty

Betty Stebman, 1950. Used with permission from the United Negro College Fund, Fairfax, Virginia.

Stebman, the long-time secretary of the UNCF, described the problem of sharing names: "I can tell you that that was the hardest thing the colleges had to do . . . they did not want to part with their names . . . some of them would send us their list and it would be a very small list, and we would look at it and say, so where's the rest of it? Which they eventually came through with."

Paul Franklin, a representative of the John Price Jones fundraising firm and the Fund's first campaign director, recruited Stebman, a white woman, to the Fund in 1944. Before she came to the organization, Stebman had worked for a number of years with the National War Fund. Although she was originally hired for a five-month stint, Stebman stayed with the organization in various capacities for more than twenty-five years and had a profound impact on its inner workings.

The Fund established two requirements for membership in the

UNCF: accreditation by the Southern Association of Colleges and Schools (or the equivalent for those colleges in the North) and private status. To date, there have not been any public members of the Fund. Some institutions, such as Lincoln University in Pennsylvania, were members when they were private institutions, but they were dropped from the Fund once they affiliated with the state.[76]

Prior to beginning any serious work, Patterson and the member college presidents incorporated the organization and elected Arthur B. Brenner as chairman and George H. Burchum as secretary. According to UNCF historian Lewis W. Jones, "These two gentlemen were destined to have a continuing interest and influence on the affairs of the corporation. Mr. Brenner, of the legal firm Von Vorst, Seagel and Smith, had served as the attorney and legal advisor in effecting the incorporation and Mr. Burchum of the Chase National Bank had been named assistant Treasurer."[77] The work of Brenner and Burchum was behind the scenes. They essentially held these positions in name only; in actuality, they legitimized the organization in the eyes of white financial entities. It is important to note that Brenner worked for Rockefeller Jr.'s legal firm and Burchum worked directly for Winthrop Aldrich, Rockefeller Jr.'s brother-in-law and the president of the Chase National Bank.

From its beginnings, the UNCF was tightly connected to the Rockefeller family and its associates. At the time of the incorporation, the board of the UNCF was established with Frederick D. Patterson as president, Thomas Elsa Jones of Fisk as vice president, and Florence Reed of Spelman as secretary. Of the three officers, only Patterson was African American. To celebrate the incorporation, Rockefeller Jr. gave $25,000, the Julius Rosenwald Fund donated $25,000, and the black college presidents "taxed" themselves a combined total of $50,000. The twenty-seven member colleges pieced together every bit of money they could find within their colleges, their local communities, and their church communities to establish and secure the Fund.[78]

As the Second World War reached a climax, the organization charged Betty Stebman with finding a space to locate the Fund near its strongest donor base. The new secretary sought an office on New York City's upper west side. But racism was alive and well in New York City at that time, and de facto segregation ruled the day. As such, Stebman's task proved more difficult than she imagined. Everyone she visited was eager to show her office space, but once they heard what it was for, they quickly changed their demeanor and asked her to leave: "We can't. This space is not available to you."[79] Eventually, she found an office at the posh address of 38 East 57th Street. Upon hearing that Stebman needed the space for "a group of private Negro colleges that are coming together to form an organization to raise money," the owner, Mr. Briscoe said, "Isn't that interesting? Is Hampton one of them?" According to Stebman, the "world looked brighter" because Mr. Briscoe's father had been on the board of Hampton. Based on the reputation of one member college, the UNCF was granted an office.[80] One can imagine how much trouble there would have been if a black UNCF officer, and not Mrs. Stebman, had been given the task of securing a headquarters. In this context of racial intolerance the Fund began raising money and shaping the country's understanding of black colleges.

The UNCF's first campaign, solely focused on raising operating funds, aimed to raise $1,500,000. However, after viewing the situation from a more realistic angle that considered the war and the national mood, Patterson and the UNCF staff halved the goal to $750,000.[81] During 1944, the final tally of funds raised was $765,000:

Corporations	$228,831
Foundations	$113,055
Individual Negroes	$106,000
Southern Individual	$111,000
Northeast Individuals	$196,114
Labor Unions	$10,000[82]

Prior to the fund's formation, the combined UNCF colleges received slightly more than $250,000 from public gifts and grants. In this new cooperative effort, they raised three times as much in their first campaign. Moreover, the total overhead costs for the first campaign were $116,866, or 15.4 percent of the monies raised, a percentage ranging from one-half to two-thirds less than the individual colleges spent when raising money.[83] In addition, the colleges raised considerably more from the black population for the cause of black education as a whole rather than in support of an individual institution. For example, in 1944 groups of black soldiers stationed in Europe, upon finding out about the UNCF's efforts, pooled the money they had won in card games and sent it to the Fund in support of scholarships.

Prior to 1944 and the efforts of the UNCF, relationships between black colleges and their alumni were loosely organized and sometimes nonexistent. Most UNCF colleges did not have alumni offices on campus; only three had full-time alumni secretaries. Some colleges had a few alumni clubs, but most did not have any organized alumni activities. Few colleges kept records of their graduates' whereabouts. This lack of communication between black colleges and their alumni led to low morale and considerable tension between alumni and college administration. The member colleges' failure over time to cultivate support from the alumni had a negative impact on their fund-raising ability within the black community.[84] Upon discovering this problem, the UNCF leadership immediately sought its remedy through cultivating alumni and forming alumni organizations. In addition, the Fund, providing consultant services for alumni affairs to the individual colleges, eventually formed the Inter-Alumni Council through which member colleges could gain support in their efforts to raise funds from graduates.

With improved relations with the black alumni community, it was time to charm the white business community, and no one could do this better than a Rockefeller. His name alone carried enormous sway because the average businessmen wanted to be connected with anything Rockefeller. During the early years, Rockefeller Jr. and his white associates performed the fund-raising work of the UNCF. Frederick D. Patterson and the member college presidents were involved, but not in the organization's daily decisions.

CHAPTER 2

Bringing the Millionaires on Board

In 1944, John D. Rockefeller Jr., the seventy-year-old son of billionaire oil magnate John D. Rockefeller Sr. and Laura Spelman Rockefeller, led the hugely influential Rockefeller Foundation and General Education Board. With millions invested in areas ranging from medical research to international human welfare to higher education to historic preservation, the Rockefeller family held enormous sway over many fields of public endeavor at that time. Committed to black education and determined to put a more human face on his family's monopolistic reputation, Rockefeller was willing to lend his name and financially support the UNCF campaign. Above all, he was willing to write letters and speak publicly on its behalf.[1] Rockefeller's participation in the UNCF campaigns resulted in a generous response. Many people wanted to be in his good graces; thus, they were willing to contribute when a letter arrived over his signature.[2] However, along with Rockefeller Jr.'s involvement came his tight grip on the Fund's operations.[3] When the philanthropist was involved in a project, he wanted to guarantee its success. This may be the reason that he handpicked the early key players in the UNCF, all of whom, except Patterson and Trent, were white.

According to Patterson, Rockefeller Jr. knew that his "name and his standing in the field of philanthropy would be a great asset" to the UNCF.[4] His involvement assuaged the fears of more conservative donors. In a time of legalized segregation and newly emerging

John D. Rockefeller Jr., ca.1940. Used with permission from the Rockefeller Archive Center, Sleepy Hollow, New York.

fears of Soviet domination, these donors were less likely to question the black college curriculum, to accuse black colleges of Communist affiliation, or to worry about these institutions supporting "radical" solutions to the race problem; they knew Rockefeller Jr. was involved.[5] As a strong supporter of the Republican Party, he was able to convince many of his friends in the party to support the UNCF.

Rockefeller Jr.'s backing did more than raise funds for the UNCF. It lent fiscal credibility to the cause by attracting to the campaign some of the most prominent contemporary business leaders, such as Alfred P. Sloan, Harvey S. Firestone, Richard K. Mellon, and Robert Woodruff.[6] According to the UNCF's executive director, William J. Trent Jr., "This was important because northern philanthropists and individuals generally had been 'mulcted' out of huge sums of money by fraudulent solicitors who claimed to represent some poor struggling Negro college or secondary school. This had led them to be wary of even legitimate appeals; they had no way of knowing which warranted their support. The Fund in the very beginning gave assurance to those who had a genuine interest in Negro education but who wanted also to be sure their fund[s] were being used wisely."[7] The involvement of prominent business leaders was integral to the success of the Fund, and Rockefeller Jr.'s connections made their involvement both possible and enthusiastic.

Examining Rockefeller Jr.'s Motivations

John D. Rockefeller Jr. was the 1944 honorary national campaign advisory board chairman for the United Negro College Fund. He stepped up to this task armed with a long and complex history of working with blacks and their educational needs. His involvement had begun forty-three years earlier, when he attended Robert C. Ogden's 1901 "millionaire's special" tour of black colleges in the South.[8] Ogden, a northern philanthropist, organized railway excursions for wealthy, prominent northerners, "visiting white and black schools in order to see the needs of the region firsthand."[9] Shortly after participating in the tour, in 1902, with the assistance of Rockefeller Foundation members Frederick T. Gates and Wallace Buttrick,[10] Rockefeller Jr. convinced his aging billionaire father to create the General Education Board. Not only did his father pledge $1 million, but the son also persuaded his father to give an additional $42 million to the GEB.[11]

Despite his incredible generosity, the Rockefeller name was synonymous with oligarchy. John D. Rockefeller Sr., much maligned in the press for his monopolistic practices, became the target of government antitrust actions. Rockefeller Jr. himself was scarred by a 1915 labor confrontation at his Ludlow, Colorado, mining company. A week-old strike erupted in violence when Colorado militiamen were called in at the request of Governor Teller Ammons. In the end, forty people, including two women and eleven children, were killed, and countless others wounded.

Despite the Rockefeller family's controversial business exploits, Rockefeller Jr. was determined to generate respect for his family's name.[12] He "threw himself into the task of mobilizing the philanthropic community."[13] He rallied support for and poured money into war relief efforts, medical research, historic preservation, the Interchurch World Movement, and the arts.[14] Rockefeller Jr. may have described his efforts as "bring[ing] men and nations closer together, consolidat[ing] important but disorganized social fields, and build[ing] . . . landmarks that great numbers of people could enjoy and learn from," according to Rockefeller Jr. biographers Peter Collier and David Horowitz, but underneath his altruism and philanthropic endeavors a practical element flourished in which "good works interfaced smoothly with power and a sense of control."[15] Even endeavors such as the construction of New York City's Rockefeller Center in the late 1930s were tinged with a concern for his family's reputation: "[Rockefeller Jr.] has tried to show that the wealth was only entrusted to his family to invest in the well-being of mankind. They had said that the name Rockefeller was synonymous with irresponsible power and privilege; Junior had tried to prove that it was the embodiment of responsibility and obligation."[16]

Rockefeller Jr. brought this perspective to his role in the United Negro College Fund. The Fund epitomized consolidation—another key aspect of the Rockefeller approach. To eliminate rival competition John D. Rockefeller Sr. had made an art form out of consolidating the businesses of others. Rockefeller family practices in education funding mirrored those of their business interests. The family and its foundations sponsored or supported several studies that favored either eliminating weaker institutions or merging them into larger ones. This was the case in 1907, when Hampton Insti-

tute's W. T. B. Williams, conducting a study of black higher education, eventually recommended that a small number of strong black
colleges be developed in the South.[17] This was also the case in 1910,
when Rockefeller associate Abraham Flexner inspected 155 medical
schools and determined that only 31 should continue to exist.[18]
Thus, the UNCF strategy mirrored the Rockefeller way of viewing
education and business: consolidation was efficient and effective.[19]

Rockefeller Jr.'s publicly-stated reasons for supporting the Fund
were much different, of course. During a 1944 NBC radio broadcast
on behalf of the newly formed UNCF, he discussed his reasons for
involvement with the organization:

1. My maternal grandparents were all their lives the friends and
   ardent supporters of the Negro.
2. Spelman College . . . was named after my grandmother and
   has been aided by three generations of her descendents.
3. The General Education Board was established and financed
   . . . having largely in mind the promotion of Negro education.
4. Many, if not all, of the institutions in the Negro College
   Fund have been studied, helped and aided financially by the
   General Education Board, a sympathetic but discriminating
   and critical organization.[20]
5. I, myself, have visited and contributed to many of these
   institutions and have known and counted among my valued
   friends numbers of their leaders.[21]

True enough: Rockefeller Jr.'s grandparents were abolitionists, and
Spelman College had been named after his grandmother. But, in
contrast to these liberal-sounding justifications, an excerpt from a
letter to his nephew Fowler McCormick shows that he may also
have had a hint of typically racist fears of a "Black menace":[22]
"Because I believe so fully in these Negro Colleges, in their importance to our educational system, and because educated Negro leadership seems to me so greatly needed if this Negro tenth of our pop-

ulation is to take its rightful place in the United States and make its contribution to the progress of the country instead of being a drag and a menace in our social and economic life, I have been glad to contribute . . . to the Fund."[23] Of course, the idea of a black menace had a long history in the United States.[24] Rockefeller Jr.'s sentiments in the letter to Fowler McCormick were also expressed in a "Discussion Guide on What the Negro Problem Means to You," which the Fund gave to those whites interested in supporting the UNCF. Specifically, potential donors were alerted to the *fact* that "since the last war the Negro has grown more militantly race conscious and more aggressive in the fight for his civil liberties." They were also made aware of the solution: "In communities where Negro leaders have emerged in civic and inter-racial affairs, conflict ended and attitudes between white and colored have vastly improved. Multiplied widely, the community development would provide a national solution."[25] According to Rockefeller Jr. and the UNCF, supporting black colleges was the key to solving the "Negro Problem."

Rockefeller had another motivation for supporting the Fund: timing. The Rosenwald Fund was set to terminate in 1948, and the General Education Board increasingly turned its attention away from higher education, Rockefeller Jr. knew that the existing philanthropies could not sustain the future of black colleges.[26] On behalf of the UNCF, he cited the need to promote independence and bolster race relations: "the Negroes are themselves in considerable numbers contributing substantial sums to the support of these institutions" and "it has seemed to me that nothing could do more to promote the spirit of friendliness and tolerance between our white and colored citizens than such a joint effort."[27] Reflecting his belief that "in order for corporations or people of great wealth to take [the] campaign seriously, we had to have a lead gift," Rockefeller Jr. inaugurated the campaign with a $25,000 contribution of his own.[28] He had the power both to bring people together and to convince them to cast aside their hesitancies about giving to a black cause. Of course, the billionaire philanthropist's power and financial support accompanied his presence in the UNCF overall.

An Overarching Philosophy

Although UNCF Executive Director William J. Trent handled the logistical activities of the Fund, Rockefeller Jr. and his designee Lindsley Kimball were heavily involved from their New York posts. Kimball, a white associate of Rockefeller Jr. and close confidant, was also the president of the United Service Organization (USO) from 1945 to 1949. As Rockefeller's direct line to the UNCF, Kimball held no official position within the organization but nonetheless wielded enormous influence. Rockefeller Jr. chose leaders like Kimball who, despite their personal conservative views about social equality and desegregation, believed adamantly in advancement through self-help. For instance, Walter Hoving became the National Campaign Chairman and assisted Rockefeller Jr. with efforts to attract funds for the UNCF.[29] Hoving, a graduate of Brown University who worked his way up quickly in the department store business, became the president of Lord & Taylor Department Store in 1936.[30] Under Hoving's leadership, Lord & Taylor had taken progressive steps to bring blacks into the company as salespeople. According to Frederick D. Patterson, Hoving accepted the position with the UNCF not only because Rockefeller Jr. asked him personally but also because the idea for the Fund had come from black leaders. Said Patterson, "It was not an idea that somebody else had thought up and had given us as Blacks."[31] For Rockefeller Jr., Hoving, and other like-minded business people, the UNCF represented the right kind of black self-help. It was an example of black people acting on their own behalf without overturning the existing social order. An oft-repeated phrase in Rockefeller Jr.'s letters was: "[The UNCF is] the most promising, non-controversial approach to the solution of the whole perplexing problem of race-relations."[32]

Hoving's views were, in fact, much more conservative than those of Rockefeller Jr. Betty Stebman characterized Hoving as a "Godsend" and said "if it hadn't been for Walter Hoving in that first year, there may never have been a second year for the United Negro College Fund." Her assessment of Hoving was realistic:

His politics were . . . revolting. I mean he really was politically on the other side of the fence from most of us. But he was so much the right man to get this thing off the ground. Because at that point, you know, Communism was so much associated with anybody black that you really had to be terribly, terribly careful that you were absolutely clean, and not get involved with anybody who might be too liberal. After all, our allies— we were still fighting a war, and our ally was the Soviet Union, and it was a very tricky business. And to have a conservative Republican, who hated Roosevelt's guts, and boy, did he hate Roosevelt's guts—that man in the White House! You know. And every time he would say anything, I would get sick inside, and say, ugh, I can't stand this man's politics, but God thank You for letting us have him.[33]

Despite his politics, Hoving committed himself to the cause of black colleges, most likely in an effort to establish a good relationship with Rockefeller Jr. He came in every morning before going to work at Lord & Taylor and typically stayed an hour or more. He even came in on Saturdays "in his country clothes" before heading out of the city with his wife and family.[34]

Although Walter Hoving served as the national campaign chair, the bulk of the public speaking and letter writing on behalf of the Fund came from Rockefeller Jr. Hoving was not a household name and lacked the influence that the nationally known philanthropist enjoyed. Of course, this arrangement was fine with Hoving, who considered his role a favor to Rockefeller and happily accepted all the help he could get from the philanthropist. As the UNCF approached its first national campaign, it was important that a national figure set the stage, generally among the American public and specifically among the white business community. With this idea in mind, Rockefeller Jr. elaborated on the Fund's "non-controversial" approach in a 1944 radio address:

Some people are seeking to solve this problem [the Negro problem] exclusively by law, or by pressure methods. There are many others, however, of both races who, fully conscious of the colored man's right to fair treatment, of the injustices that have too often been done him, the inequalities to which he has long been subjected, are likewise conscious of the phenomenal progress he has made as compared with other races. This large group believes that through mutual understanding, forebearance [sic] and progress by agreement, supplemented by law when necessary, the solution of the problem can be most wisely approached.[35]

Such talk as this, coming from a successful white businessman, was designed to reassure white America that the aims of the UNCF were neither radical nor militant. Rockefeller's communications on behalf of the Fund consistently express the idea that the Fund was the all-purpose solution to the "Negro problem." At times, the oratorical maneuverings necessary to say this were curiously contradictory, as evidenced by this 1946 letter to Howard Pew, president and chairman of Sun Oil Company: "While it is true as you say, that many institutions, however admirable in other ways, often permit in their liberality the teaching of a 'philosophy contrary to our American way of life,' one reason why I have been so interested in the United Negro College Fund is that, by and large, the institutions which it represents are, I believe, exceptionally sound and conservative although, at the same time, open-minded and progressive."[36]

From the outset, Rockefeller Jr. anticipated potential donors' reactions to the UNCF fund-raising appeals. This is exemplified in the handwritten notes he used to prepare for a speech given at a UNCF fund-raising luncheon; he framed both the problem and the solution for the audience. In Rockefeller Jr.'s mind, the Negro problem was urgent. In his notes he emphasized that the problem could neither solve itself nor be neglected, not only for economic reasons but also for fear of leftist political exploitation, which would spread like an infection. Leftists might point to the deficiencies of capitalism, specifically how it exploits racial divisions to prevent social justice. But to underscore the reasonableness of the UNCF approach, Rockefeller Jr. dealt in turn with alternatives, all of which he considered unable to fully solve the Negro problem: "returning blacks to Africa," the "southern 'laissez fair'" [sic] method of gradual change, and the "radical approach of equality" involving legislative action and force. After dismissing these "solutions," he offered the "conservative approach," which, he contended, was based on "good will," "mutual understanding," and "cooperation." Of course, this reasonable course could be supplemented by judicial "legislation" and "force" if needed—but only if needed.[37] Rockefeller had the ability to anticipate the objections of donors. His influence among whites, crucial for the UNCF, stands out as one of the most important strategies for garnering funds in the minds of the Fund's white leaders. According to Lindsley Kimball, "The best examples of genuine persuasion are to be found in the . . . personal correspondence of Mr. John D. Rockefeller Jr. Starting from scratch, Mr. Rockefeller personally dealt with 91 corporations and their executive heads."[38]

Although generally supportive of Rockefeller Jr.'s and his designees' characterization of the Fund, the African American members of the UNCF staff and the member college presidents saw the organization as having a much deeper purpose. They believed they were working toward the more far-reaching goals of social equality and integration. These goals became more evident as the Fund matured in the coming decades.

Recruiting UNCF Leadership

One of the first tasks that the UNCF and Rockefeller pursued was recruiting local campaign chairs. Much different from the member college presidents who also campaigned in local areas and cities throughout the country, these individuals were the white corporate leaders of the campaign in key cities—typically well-known, wealthy businessmen who held enormous sway in their local communities. Because of this influence, these men were easily able to raise funds for black education by convincing friends and admirers to give to the Fund. In many ways, they represented lesser versions of Rockefeller Jr. in their own cities.

Rockefeller Jr.'s recruiting focused on people who either felt "a kinship with the Negro race" or craved a solution to the "Negro problem."[39] For Rockefeller Jr. "feeling a kinship" had less to do with manifesting personal interaction and sympathy for blacks and more to do with understanding how race problems in America affected the nation's socioeconomic structure. Specifically, he sought individuals who, like himself, saw the UNCF as a solution that neither undermined capitalism nor involved government intervention. A letter Rockefeller Jr. wrote to Bayard Pope of the Marine Midland Corporation demonstrates Rockefeller's outlook. In 1950 he asked Pope to become the chair of the New York UNCF campaign: "Because the Negro problem concerns a tenth of our population, because it is one of our most important national problems—a problem, that successful handling of which is of vital significance to all citizens and corporations, whether they happen to be personally interested in it or not . . . [we should support it]."[40] Rockefeller Jr. spoke of race relations as not only a regional issue but also one with national implications, particularly during the Cold War. A letter asking financier and government advisor Bernard Baruch in 1951 to serve as a local chair speaks of a "time of uncertainty": "You know, of course, of my conviction of the Fund's great value in approaching the whole vital problem of better race relations, and its particular value in this time of uncertainty as a means of strengthening the country's basic educational structure."[41]

As a man of business, he understood that "the average business leader naturally hesitates about involving [himself] in any of the more radical approaches to the [problem]."[42] He also stressed that the UNCF was a way for business leaders to advocate a free-market rather than a tax-supported solution. Rockefeller Jr. was pushing the buttons of those who were still angry about the Roosevelt administration's approach to handling societal problems. Gifts to the UNCF supported the positive uplift and contributions of hardworking

African Americans who wanted to help themselves without advancing radical black factions. This belief is consistent with the themes of his "I Believe" creed, first uttered in a radio address supporting the United Service Organization and the National War Fund: "I believe in the dignity of labor, whether with head or hand; that the world owes no man a living but that it owes every man an opportunity to make a living."[43] It was particularly important for Rockefeller Jr. to deemphasize radical behavior among blacks during the postwar period. Many potential donors had bad memories of the violence that emerged throughout the country after World War I, "when cities in the North witnessed race riots and there was an upsurge of lynching and interracial disorder in the South."[44] With Rockefeller Jr.'s backing, people who were wary of supporting the National Urban League or the legal efforts of the NAACP found a cause that would enable them to advance race relations without making an overt political statement.

Another way in which Rockefeller Jr. spoke to Cold War concerns—in particular, the loyalty of blacks—was by focusing on the "heroic efforts of our Negro citizens" and the fact that black colleges had been "a national asset [during World War II]."[45] According to Rockefeller Jr., black colleges furnished both a basic educational background for blacks and the leadership skills necessary for them to serve their country as both officers and other military personnel. In addition, the colleges served as "direct training grounds for the various military services of the United States."[46] Thus, according to Rockefeller Jr.'s fund-raising rhetoric, the black colleges created loyal United States citizens.

This theme was also prevalent in the UNCF's fund-raising brochure images, designed by the publicity firm handpicked by Rockefeller Jr.'s associates. The connection between UNCF colleges and themes of freedom and democracy was most apparent in the inclusion of photographs of black students in uniform. Pictures of blacks serving in various capacities of the military were spread throughout the pages of "Thirty-two Steps Toward a Better America"—a publi-

A group of black airmen in front of a bomber. Photographs like this one were used by the UNCF to convince the public that blacks were patriotic and contributed to the war effort. "America is Free to Choose," 1944, General Education Board Papers, Record Group 5235–5240, series 1, sub-series 3, box 491, folder 5338, Rockefeller Archive Center.

cation that appeared near the end of World War II.[47] Likewise, the 1944 publication "America is Free to Choose" featured a row of black airmen in front of a bomber with the caption, "The Negro is making a substantial contribution to the war effort."[48] After the end of the war, UNCF photographs, continuing to suggest that activities at black colleges were contributing to America's interests, showed that civilian efforts worked hand in hand with those of the military. The 1950 publication, "A Significant Adventure," depicted a black man in uniform on the left with a group of young black nursing students on the right; the caption underneath the image and enclosed in a stylized coat of arms, read "Loyal citizens serving their country."[49]

A young man in uniform addressing a group of nurses. This photograph was among the many that the UNCF used to shape public opinion about black students. Here they are portrayed as loyal and patriotic. "A Significant Adventure" [1950], General Education Board Papers, Record Group 5235–5240, Series 1, sub-series 3, box 491, folder 5240, Rockefeller Archive Center.

This implicit message suggested that service to the United States could come in either the military or any form of hard work.

Numerous titles, headings, and captions in UNCF pamphlets advertised the link between the organization's goals and those of "the free world": "The Tools of Freedom"; "America is Free to Choose"; "Education Means Progress"; and "Living Democracy." It is significant that these UNCF publications appeared at the same time that accusations of disloyalty were being made against many figures in higher education, government, and the media.[50] In certain cases, the House Un-American Activities Committee (HUAC), including southern conservative members such as Senator Martin Dies Jr. of Texas, brought charges against educators because they had shown support for the black cause.[51] Whereas segregationists sought to show that the black cause was connected to communism, the UNCF sought to align it with democracy and free enterprise. UNCF leadership necessarily advertised to all citizens that its member colleges were on the right side in the struggle against communism.

By knowing his audience so well, Rockefeller urged the UNCF leadership to design their fund-raising publicity to appeal to the corporate leaders that he was trying to recruit. Examples of this can be seen in the 1952 UNCF report entitled "What are the Answers?" which pertained to the "Negro problem." This piece presented itself as a casual exchange of information between two corporate leaders, who just happened to be members of the UNCF board: Alfred P. Sloan Jr. of General Motors and Devereux C. Josephs of New York Life Insurance. The publication featured each correspondents' letters, reproduced as if photographed directly from the desk top: off-centered, slanted, with the original letterhead, signature, and typewriter print. The following pages gave "scientific" answers to the questions raised by Sloan to Josephs. Each page had a visual presentation of quantitative data, with multiple pictograph figures, maps, and bar and line graphs. The publication culminated in a table, which laid out the financial needs of the UNCF member colleges.[52] In fact, "What are the Answers?" displayed quasiscientific information about complex issues, the type that had become standard fare in corporate presentations and annual reports.[53] By adopting a corporate style of design and, in particular, mimicking the annual report, the UNCF's "What are the Answers?" appealed to the targeted readers as if they were shareholders in a company rather than donors to colleges.

The Millionaires Head South

In recruiting the white campaign leadership of the Fund, Rockefeller Jr. and his associates realized that many of these men had never been on a black college campus. Believing that personal familiarity with the colleges would help make the campaign leaders more effective, they organized a plane flight and subsequent train ride South to remedy this deficiency; the trip was much like the one on which Rockefeller Jr. had embarked many years earlier. In 1952, Lindsley Kimball, Rockefeller Jr.'s associate, made the arrangements. It was not an easy task to bring people together, however, and many influential people throughout the country assisted. According to Kimball,

> I got Winthrop Aldrich to take the Chase [National Bank] plane and to invite a whole plane load to go down to Atlanta University where they could meet men and women. . . . That made a social event of it. They all accepted. About eight or ten of the top people in New York. I got the Chairman of [the] Board of Standard Oil of Indiana whom I knew very well. He took a plane load down from Chicago, with all the prominent people. I got Bob Woodruff, who was everything in the South, . . . owner of Coca-Cola. . . . All the power structure in the South he heads. I got Harvey Firestone to fly in from Ohio. We landed there and had a meeting in the auditorium of Spelman, which was wildly enthusiastic. About half of them got on a special train that we had arranged and went from Atlanta down to Tuskegee. As a matter of fact we got Woodruff to host that party so we had a private train and held up the Southern Limited because we couldn't get the guests to finish cocktails and dinner. . . . We really developed some interest, seeing the thing right on the ground.[54]

The fact that a regularly scheduled train was held up to accommodate the group indicated the amount of power Woodruff held throughout the South. Having his involvement was essential to the

Fund's success. Frederick D. Patterson commended the visit to the black colleges as the natural thing to do. Unlike the first campaign that barely raised $750,000 and focused specifically on operating expenses, "We were asking for twenty-five million dollars and asking them to be endorsers of the appeal." Therefore, in Patterson's mind, the "people themselves ought to be educated about the colleges."[55] It was unlikely that the businessmen would give unless they had some evidence of the education taking place at black colleges. The students at Atlanta's black colleges and those at Tuskegee Institute referred to the visit as "Millionaire Day," and so it was. Among the guests were Devereux Josephs, John D. Rockefeller III, and Richard Mellon. Most students were familiar with the surnames of these individuals because many campus buildings were named to honor them.

During "Millionaire Day" there was much interaction between blacks and whites. All participated in convocations in the chapels of the colleges involved, and there was even interracial dining, something that was considered highly taboo throughout the South. Although the businessmen from the North did not object to eating with black students and staff in the college cafeterias, those men who accompanied Robert Woodruff from the Atlanta area considered it a practice beneath them and a violation of social norms. According to William Trent Jr., the UNCF "had this luncheon out at Atlanta University and some of the Atlanta businessmen were in the group also. And some of them weren't sure they wanted to go to the luncheon out there, because they'd be eating with Negroes. So Bob Woodruff just said, yes, you come out there. It ain't gonna hurt you, Goddamn it. That was it."[56] Although Woodruff could appear to have liberal tendencies, he was merely pragmatic. The goal of the southern trip was to acquaint donors with black colleges; thus, it was important for the black college personnel and students to interact socially with the donors.

Despite these tensions, the Fund leadership considered the plane/train "Millionaire Day" a successful part of their first capital campaign. According to Patterson, the Fund leadership wanted the "millionaires" to "catch something of the atmosphere and the spirit" of black colleges: "I think it made those persons permanent friends of the cause of black higher education. I think they saw what Tuskegee represented, they saw what the Atlanta group of colleges represented and they took that to be more or less typical of all that had membership in the UNCF. And so, . . . it gave them a degree of understanding where they felt they not only could give, but they could sponsor. They could endorse to their friends this program of service to black youth."[57]

Different Messages for Different Groups

After bringing together a group of leaders who shared his vision for the organization, Rockefeller Jr.'s work on behalf of the Fund turned to soliciting specific individuals for donations. For each individual he asked, the message changed slightly. For example, requests to industrial leaders focused on the impact that educated blacks could have on industry: "support of this effort can be justified not only in terms of a significant contribution to the national good, but in terms of direct and indirect benefits to the corporations themselves."[58] He promised industry leaders that the UNCF colleges would provide "a great reservoir of untapped manpower which is bound to bring its reward in increasing efficiency and productivity for industry in particular and for America in general."[59]

Rockefeller Jr.'s words were reinforced by the images of students on black college campuses used by the UNCF in fund-raising brochures. Students were shown as productive and hardworking. In the publication "America is Free to Choose," for example, the words "The Negro prefers to live by the American traditions of independence, thrift and self-help" appeared under a photograph of a young black man, presumably a student, driving a tractor.[60]

Another page in the same publication included a collage of photos of black students engaged in activities ranging from machine work to agriculture to medicine. The idea of productivity ap-

The early UNCF often used pictures of black students doing industrial and farm work in their publicity. This image was included in a cluster of photographs depicting the kinds of jobs that black college graduates could perform to make a living. Under this photograph appeared the words, "The Negro prefers to live by the American traditions of independence, thrift and self-help." "America is Free to Choose," 1944, General Education Board Papers, Record Group 5235–5240, series 1, sub-series 3, box 491, folder 5338, Rockefeller Archive Center.

peared so often in the publication as to draw attention to itself. If not by the traditions of "independence, thrift, and self-help," what other tradition would the "Negro" prefer to live by? Accompanied by these photographs, the text seemed to assume that part of the audience needed evidence to refute the racist myths of dependence and sloth. According to Fund secretary Betty Stebman, this brochure was specifically focused on asking the question, "What do you prefer?" "Riots and horror" or "educated people"? Supporting the UNCF was a way to ensure that blacks would be hardworking individuals guided by leadership from within their own race, not rebellious, "lazy" members of society dependent upon the government for their welfare.[61]

Another curious aspect of the brochures during Rockefeller Jr.'s time of influence were the photographs of students at work and the continued prevalence of industrial and agricultural occupations. By the time these publications appeared, in 1944, the debate over liberal arts versus industrial curricula had all but ended.[62] Although at some black colleges industrial and liberal arts curricula existed side by side, according to Henry Drewry and Humphrey Doermann, "Industrial education lost much of its attraction well before World War II."[63] By 1915 northern philanthropists began to shift their donations from industrial to liberal arts colleges, and of the 27 colleges on the Fund's 1944 membership roster, only a few were known for their industrial curricula.[64] True, UNCF founder Frederick D. Patterson was also the president of Tuskegee—a noted center of industrial education—but as a veterinary scientist his idea of "industrial" included medical technology and aeronautics (programs he had supported), not plowing and making bricks.[65] But of the nine photographs that depict work in the 1944 "America is Free to Choose" pamphlet, four are of occupations generally considered manual: machine work, milking cows, driving tractors, and operating sewing machines.[66] In all of the photographs, there seems to be a deliberate selection of activities that emphasize making or doing as opposed to simply thinking. Given the opportunity to present its own picture of the activities at member colleges, the UNCF chose to showcase the colleges' past rather than their future.[67]

Of course, an obvious reason for the persistence of photographs of industrial occupations is that the UNCF wanted to avoid challenging the accepted social status of blacks in the South in order to garner funds from more conservative donors. The photos reinforced the sense of productivity and industry that a student acquired as the result of a UNCF member college education—precisely the message that Rockefeller Jr. was highlighting in his correspondence with potential donors.

Rockefeller Jr. was successful in getting white northern support for the UNCF's activities. But it was much more difficult to garner interest from the white southern community. First, the Rockefeller name did not carry the same clout in the southern states as in the North. Many southern whites associated it with the carpetbaggers who, as they viewed the matter, came south after the Civil War to exploit the region for their own financial gain. Second, many southern whites felt that it was unnecessary or inappropriate to educate blacks. They had grown up in a two-tiered society that ensured that they would always enjoy a higher status than blacks. Why do anything to upset a status quo that benefited them?[68] Given the persistent and sometimes unabashed expression of racism in the South, Rockefeller Jr.'s strategy to attract prominent whites from the region to raise funds in their local communities on behalf of the UNCF put an arduous task ahead of him.

Raising funds among southern whites, Rockefeller Jr.'s rhetoric changed from that which he used among northern industrialists. His communication with this group of potential donors showed awareness of their prejudices and of the history of relations between the southern society and northern capital. For example, in a 1945 letter to Governor J. Melville Broughton of North Carolina, Rockefeller was almost syrupy in his grateful words toward one of the few southern supporters of the UNCF campaign:

As one who believes so thoroughly in the United Negro College Fund and all that it stands for, I want you to know how grateful we here in the north are to you for being willing to cooperate with the fund along the lines proposed. Your own position of leadership in the south, the high regard in which you are held throughout the land and your sympathetic and understanding attitude toward the Negro problem will enable you to render a service in this connection that will be of the utmost significance and value.[69]

Perhaps Rockefeller Jr. was grateful that Broughton was willing to "cooperate" because he knew that many southern whites were contemptuous of anything from the North and were unwilling to support even the most cautious efforts in the area of race relations.

In 1946, Rockefeller Jr. wrote to Governor Colgate W. Darden of Virginia to ask that he act as a representative of the Fund in that state. He couched his solicitation in language that appealed to Darden's southern perspective, reminding the governor of previous Rockefeller contributions that specifically benefited southern whites as well as blacks: "Practically all of the institutions in the United Negro College Fund have been individually visited by and are currently under review by the General Education Board which my father established nearly a half a century ago to aid in the improvement of both negro and white education and economic betterment throughout the country but primarily in the South."[70] Rockefeller Jr. also suggested that the only sensible method of alleviating racial tension was through "a long period of effort on both sides to understand each other, to develop sympathy with and appreciation of each others problems and to work out through growing goodwill and mutual consent improved conditions."[71] Gradualism, or the idea that race-related change should proceed slowly, a notion typically advocated by moderate southern whites, was at the center of Rockefeller Jr.'s comments.[72]

Challenges to Black Leadership under Rockefeller

Rockefeller Jr.'s influence on southern whites was particularly important as the black leaders and member college presidents had difficulty raising money on behalf of the Fund in southern cities. For example, although Atlanta, Georgia, was listed as a key campaign city for the Fund, it was initially a campaign city for black donors only. Blacks working in the public schools and alumni of the Atlanta black colleges consistently gave money, but whites rarely contributed to the cause.[73] With the goal of associating more wealthy men with the black colleges, Rockefeller Jr. and his associates spent time reconfiguring the boards of several of the colleges in Atlanta. According to Lindsley Kimball,

> One of the colleges in the Atlanta group . . . had a board of directors that [was] nothing but ministers. I went down and had lunch with my good friend Robert Woodruff from Coca-Cola and we brought in the Mayor and the president of the bank and Paul Austin who was just retired as president . . . of Coca-Cola. We said that what we need down here is some weight on the board. They don't represent anything. They can't raise any money because ministers can't raise money and can't organize. They don't know how. They said, "We'll help you. We'll pick out some citizens, you okay them, and we'll go get them. Tell them it's their civic duty." I built that board up to a real good looking board.[74]

Although made as late as 1981, Kimball's commentary overflowed with the kind of condescension toward black college leaders typical of Rockefeller and his associates. His belief that ministers could not raise money and could not organize was as arrogant as it was insulting, especially when one considers the influence of ministers during the Civil Rights Movement in the areas of organizing and fundraising. According to biographer David Garrow, part of Rev. Martin Luther King Jr.'s success as a civil rights leader was due to his ability as a fund raiser.[75] Despite Rockefeller Jr.'s efforts to change the boards of many black colleges, most southern cities did not become major fund-raising hubs for the UNCF; racism was too deeply imbedded in the culture.

In Birmingham, Alabama, much like Atlanta, the black UNCF representatives faced discrimination in all areas, including being left off the UNCF letterhead or being relegated to a segregated section of the letterhead when it was sent to potential white donors. According the UNCF secretary Betty Stebman,

> in 1945 I opened a piece of mail from Birmingham, Alabama United Negro College Fund . . . there was the United Negro College Fund letterhead, and on the side it had a listing of the Chairman and Vice-Chairman and Executive Committee, and underneath it had the Negro Committee listed. And I saw this thing and it really infuriated me. I walked into Bill Trent's office and I said, look at this, just look at this, just look at this terrible thing. He said, take it easy, take it easy. Last year we didn't even have any Negroes on the committee. They wouldn't put them on the same piece of paper. We're making progress.[76]

In the beginning, the only people who gave money to the Fund in Birmingham were blacks and those rare whites who believed that the black colleges were doing a good job educating students. Without a strong white donor base, the campaigns centered on friends of Tuskegee, Miles, and Talladega colleges (all located within Alabama).[77] Rockefeller and his closest associate, Lindsley Kimball, changed the conditions. Referring to their transformation of the situation for black colleges near Birmingham, Kimball remarked boastfully,

> I did it in Birmingham where they had a ridiculous situation. Providing all the [Black] teachers for the whole state with no support. We decided we had to get some more support for the college there, poor little Miles College. One of the poorest and doing a heroic piece of work. I tried to get them some money and found out that nobody would write them a check because they didn't want to see the check for a Black college go through the bank. We had to raise the money in cash. That one I got changed and got some good people on the board.[78]

Despite the Fund's willingness to publicly acquiesce to the southern norms in most cases during the period of Rockefeller Jr.'s involvement, none of the southern campaigns were as strong as those in the Northeast or Midwest.

Although Rockefeller Jr.'s willingness to exert influence in difficult situations worked to the benefit of the Fund in most cases, he also used this power in a way that worked against the cultivation of leadership among the black members of the Fund. He had very little trust in the ability of the black leaders of the UNCF and his actions, on occasion, expressed these feelings. According to Morehouse College president Benjamin Mays speaking in 1987, "you've still got to convince white people that Negroes can handle big money. . . . They think a white man can handle it better. . . . In so many of the [black] state schools there's a white man who handles the money."[79] This lack of trust on the part of Rockefeller Jr. and his associates may explain why the treasury for the UNCF was held by the Chase National Bank under the direction of a white treasurer. Up until the presidency of Stephen Wright in 1967, the UNCF president could not write a check for over $200 without the permission of the Chase National Bank and Rockefeller associates.

Rockefeller Jr.'s mistrust was very much in evidence when, shortly after the founding of the UNCF, he asked Lindsley Kimball to conduct a study of the organization. He was unhappy with its performance, and felt that the organization's lack of cohesion led to inefficient operations, something no Rockefeller would tolerate. One of the study's first recommendations was the dismissal of Paul Franklin, the white fund-raising professional from John Price Jones. According to Kimball, "Mr. Rockefeller called him [Bill Trent] on the telephone and suggested that they would get more money if they got a better professional to work on it. [Franklin] was a sort of worn out individual that knew how to raise money by sitting on his tail and writing on a piece of paper but didn't get out and organize anything. Didn't have any proper committees. You can't get money by writing letters. You've got to meet people face to face."[80] Although Rockefeller Jr. left the final decision regarding Franklin to Bill Trent, the Executive Director had little choice but to fire the John Price Jones fundraiser. A second recommendation based on the study pertained to the relationships between the UNCF college presidents. The study seemed to show that years of competing for the same funds had led to a lack of trust between them. Using an awkward metaphor for black college presidents, Kimball described this problem:

> I think that every one of those puddings, if you could call them a pudding, is made of several ingredients. They had almost divine trust in Mr. Rockefeller. It wasn't just his money. They knew him, he met with them. They had such an admiration for him that it wasn't believable. I think they put a lot of trust in me. They would do anything, almost, that I asked them to do. I think it's hard for a college president who has to get along. He can't run a deficit, he doesn't have a big endowment. He has to break even or go bust. So I can't blame them for being jealous of the amount of money the next one gets. They had quite a time for trying to arrive at the formula for distributing the money.[81]

In an effort to garner the support of the member college presidents for the results of the study, Kimball asked a few of them to participate in its design and implementation. Kimball spoke of this process in a tone similar to that of a parent speaking to a child: "That was done because when the doctor prescribes medicine for the patient and the patient isn't a part of the prescription, the patient may not swallow the medicine. If you make it a participating study you sell it as you go along." As a result of the study, the UNCF drew "up finer ground rules as to how they could raise money on their own" in an effort to streamline the fund-raising process and limit the jealousy on the part of some presidents.[82] In addition, Rockefeller Jr. and his associates kept a closer eye on the operations of the Fund, effectively cementing the white control of the organization during this time.

A Brush with Social Equality in the Northeast

Out of sheer pragmatism, the UNCF did much during the early years to change the social mores of some of New York City's most "elite" establishments. Often times, it was the Rockefeller name that helped to open doors that might otherwise be closed to mixed-race organizations. For example, in 1944, UNCF chairman Walter Hoving and secretary Betty Stebman were planning a meeting at which they wished to launch the national campaign. Hoving suggested the Perroquet Suite at the Waldorf Astoria. Hoving and his business colleagues had met there often in the past so he asked Betty Stebman to call and reserve the suite. According to Stebman, "I picked up the phone and called the Waldorf and I said I'd like to reserve the Perroquet Suite for the 14th of March . . . And what is it for? They asked. It's for the United Negro College Fund. Just a minute, please. I'm sorry that suite is booked for the day."[83] Stebman had several dates that were possibilities and thus she asked about these but the Waldorf was booked for all of the dates she proposed. At that point she went back to Hoving and informed him that the Perroquet Suite was unavailable on all three days. Hoving suggested that they look for an alternative suite, prompting Stebman to call the Waldorf once more only to be turned down once again. At that point, according to Stebman,

> I said, you know, Mr. Hoving, they're not going to give us any room at the Waldorf, and I can tell you that I know from my own experience in trying to find this office. I've already learned, and they're not going to give us this room. They're not going to have the United Negro College Fund in the Waldorf. And he said, "What do you mean, they're not going to have the United Negro College Fund in the Waldorf? Get me Lucius Boomer." Lucius Boomer was the manager of the Waldorf, a very important man around town. . . . Mr. Hoving . . . said, Lucius, John Rockefeller and I are planning a meeting for a group that we're both involved in, the United Negro College Fund, and we've

tried to get a suite at—the Perroquet Suite is what we wanted
. . . and it seems that you people are all booked up. Would you
see what you can do for us? So Boomer said, "Oh certainly, Walter, I'll call you back." That afternoon Mr. Boomer called back
and said, I can make the Perroquet Suite available to you. We
had a temporary booking on it, but they've taken another date
and it's perfectly okay, you can have the Perroquet Suite on the
date that you asked for. And we all had big smiles on our faces.
You know, we'd licked it.[84]

Of course, the "it" was segregation and discrimination rearing their
ugly heads in the North. However, not even the Rockefeller name
could curb all of the insidious strategies that racists generated to rob
people of their dignity. When the day of the meeting came, instead
of "United Negro College Fund" on the sign outside the room, it read
"Hoving-Rockefeller Education Meeting." When Walter Hoving saw
the sign, he tore it in two. According to Stebman, "And that was the
first meeting of the United Negro College Fund. It was at the Waldorf, but there was no name . . . And it was the *first time* that they
had Negroes at a meeting at the Waldorf."[85] After several more meetings, the name of the organization appeared on the sign outside the
meeting room.[86] Ironically, the UNCF sent press releases to all of
the major media outlets publicizing the event at the Waldorf, resulting in a substantial write up in the *New York Times*.[87] The secret was
out—the hotel whose name was synonymous with upper-crust
white America was now hosting a meeting about the future of black
colleges.

Although Rockefeller Jr.'s associates at the UNCF knew they could
use his name to open some doors, they also knew that there were
limits. Rockefeller Jr. made it very clear that he did not want his involvement in the UNCF to be seen as a personal quest for black
equality. Despite his efforts to disguise the exact purpose of the
organization, the appearance of promoting social equality was almost impossible to avoid. For instance, he received much criticism
when he made even the smallest humane gesture toward a black

child. During a 1944 UNCF radio broadcast, he was photographed holding a little black girl, Marietta Dockery, on his lap. After the photo appeared in newspapers across the country, Rockefeller received angry letters from citizens who disapproved of his actions. He was extremely careful in his responses to the letters. Consider this exchange, beginning with a hate-filled letter from Buford G. Lincoln of Los Angeles, California:

> Your name stands for the best in America and the effect of this picture . . . on the minds of the average colored person is impossible to understand by one in your station of life. . . . [T]he average colored person fails to comprehend your feelings towards education of the race but consider it an approval of their licentious acts. They seldom bear any respect to the northern white and drop their religious habits of the south. With money in their pocket and sated with food and liquor their morals would shock the wild man of a few generations back.[88]

In this message Lincoln alluded to the "Black menace" feared by many whites, claiming that any retreat from the policies of segregation was an invitation to violence and sexual perversion. Choosing to ignore this idea, Rockefeller Jr. merely explained the situation with the little girl and shared his overarching philosophy, hoping that "the facts will help you to a different interpretation of this picture and a better understanding of my attitude toward the Negro race."[89] He noted that he was asked to have his picture taken receiving a dollar bill from a child making a contribution to the UNCF on behalf of her school. "The child became frightened by the clicking of the cameras and the snapping of the bulbs and began to cry. Her mother was unable to pacify her. . . . The photographers were anxious to get the picture in the interest of the Fund." Hoping that the child would stop crying, Rockefeller put her on his knee, as captured in the photograph. In Rockefeller's words, "The value of the picture to the Fund, and its only purpose, was to indicate thus dramatically that the Negroes themselves were contributing to the

John D. Rockefeller Jr. holding Marietta Dockery on his lap. During a UNCF photo shoot, Dockery was to give Rockefeller Jr. a dollar bill to show that blacks were doing their share to support black colleges. When the little girl became frightened by the lights and cameras, Rockefeller Jr. tried to comfort her. John D. Rockefeller Jr. and Marietta Dockery, 1944, Photo found in Buford G. Lincoln to John D. Rockefeller Jr., 3 June 1944, Messrs Rockefeller—Education, III 2G, box 96, folder 6620, Rockefeller Archive Center.

Fund."[90] In other words, he did not intentionally promote social equality.

However, accounts by UNCF staff show that there was more to the story than Rockefeller Jr. related to Mr. Lincoln. When the little girl was crying, he "took charge asking the others to let him handle it. He took from his pocket a six-foot folded carpenter's rule and proceeded to manipulate it into shapes that fascinated Marietta, who dried her tears and soon found herself sitting on Mr. Rockefeller's knee. The philanthropist silenced the surprised onlookers by his reminder, 'Remember, I have grandchildren.'"[91] In essence, Rockefeller Jr. was showing the black child the same kind of care that he would his own grandchildren. But when confronted with Lincoln's blatantly racist comments, Rockefeller refrained from preaching and instead validated the critic's perspective. He went on to assert that both men were interested in a "reasonable position" and that his detractor's views and those of the Fund were not all that different. Rockefeller Jr. said of the Fund's perspective on race, "I think you will agree that it is a fair and wise position. It is a constructive, middle-of-the-road position which seems to me the only position that can lead to a just and right solution of this great problem."[92] Rather than being a window through which to view the true purpose and ideals of black education, Rockefeller Jr.'s rhetoric became a mirror in which each recipient of a solicitation could see his or her own racial perspective reflected.

The UNCF also avoided issues of social equality in its fundraising materials used to solicit white businessmen. At a time when legalized segregation was still intact, the placement of blacks and whites together in a photograph was a delicate undertaking. Any image that suggested that the races were equal on a social level and that they were free to mix in all situations was likely to spark controversy. In film and on television, black characters were almost always stereotyped.[93] Roles were usually subservient (for example, maids, butlers, and gardeners); black characters were portrayed as less intelligent, shiftless, and were often the object of ridicule.[94] Even the suggestion of familiarity between blacks and whites was

A group of black college presidents and white philanthropists. This photograph was typical of the kind used in newsletters by the UNCF when soliciting corporate executives. The pose is formal, and there is no body contact. This image was considered acceptable as a representation of an interracial gathering. "America is Free to Choose," 1944, General Education Board Papers, Record Group 5235–5240, series 1, sub-series 3, box 491, folder 5338, Rockefeller Archive Center.

enough to cause an outrage. Where mixed groupings were depicted in UNCF publicity photos, the images were either formally composed, collaged, or the white figure was shown in a dominant position. One such mixed group appears in the publication "America is Free to Choose" over the caption, "The Educated are Tolerant."[95] The grouping of white UNCF supporters with black college leaders was shown standing in a line—there was no body contact and each member had his hands at his side. Although the message might have referred to toleration as a quality of liberal democratic society—a quality desired by both potential black and white donors—it may also have been read as a reference to the supposed lawlessness of blacks. To at least part of the audience, the interpretation of the caption might have been "The educated behave themselves," a message that was nicely reinforced by blacks standing in line with their white benefactors.

Another photograph that showed the "correct" relationship between blacks and whites was on the cover of the June 1953 publication, *The Mobilizer,* a monthly newsletter distributed to UNCF donors and campaign directors.[96] The subordinate role of the black participant was carefully constructed as to obscure the true meaning of the image. In the photograph, Frederick D. Patterson, the president of the UNCF, was shaking the hand of a much taller John D. Rockefeller III, while Rockefeller held an award certificate; Dwight D. Eisenhower was standing behind the handshake but on the same side as Rockefeller, smiling. The slightly angled and more active stance of Rockefeller as he leaned over toward the stiffer figure of Patterson suggested that the philanthropist was giving an award when, according to the headline, he was actually the recipient of a citation from the UNCF.

Evidence shows that the selection of a photo like this was not mere coincidence. According to Lindsley Kimball, the positioning of whites and blacks in public gatherings and the posing of photographs was something to which great attention was paid. During a 1981 interview, he offered an example to oral historian Marcia Goodson. He had this to say about the difficulties of planning social events (and taking photos) where the black college presidents were present:

I went down to visit one of the Black colleges at the request of its president. He said come down and spend the day if you want. We'll have lunch with the Board of Directors [many of whom raised funds for the UNCF]. I met in the morning in the president's office and the whole board gathered there. He said, "Let's adjourn for lunch and have lunch at my home." We all walked down to his home right on the campus. The door opened, his wife was there to meet us too, and he turned and said, "Would anybody like to wash up?" The chairman of his board shook his head to me, meaning you don't use the facilities of a Black man. So, of course, I said I would. I was the sole one that went in and washed. We came out and sat down at the table. His wife waited on us. He walked in the garden. He couldn't sit at his own table, in his own home. When we had our picture taken afterwards he had to stand one step lower than anybody else. That's where we started from back then.[97]

Other UNCF brochures included photographs that seemed to be included to reinforce a sense of self importance among the white benefactors. *The Mobilizer* had pages of photographs of corporate executives and their wives dining together; black college leaders, if included at all, were relegated to a secondary role. In one particularly telling photograph, guests seated at a head table included John D. Rockefeller III, General Motors Chairman Alfred P. Sloan, and numerous other executives who were conversing with one another. Seated in the center of the head table was Morehouse College president Benjamin E. Mays, whose gaze was focused on the table; none of the other guests were talking with him, and their backs were turned away.[98] The message seemed to be that social interaction between whites and blacks did not happen at these dinners. *The Mobilizer* clearly belonged to a genre of donor publicity that supplied extrinsic rewards to the donor—showing them at the center of social networks.[99] That blacks, with few exceptions, were not included in these networks was conveyed by the pictures.

Whatever his personal beliefs, Rockefeller Jr. distanced the UNCF from a perception of advocating for social equality. This was essential, he felt, in order to gain the support of the business community. It was as if he ignored the underlying purpose of the UNCF—

John D. Rockefeller III receiving an award from UNCF President Frederick D. Patterson, with Dwight D. Eisenhower presiding over the exchange. This picture shows an acceptable interaction between blacks and whites. Patterson is positioned lower than Rockefeller III. It was typical for the early white leaders of the UNCF to ask the black leaders to stand on a lower step when photographed. Frederick D. Patterson, Dwight D. Eisenhower, and John D. Rockefeller III, *The Mobilizer*, June 1953, Rockefeller—Education, III 2G, Box 96, folder 664, Rockefeller Archive Center.

support of black colleges as a means of social and racial uplift. It was, in fact, the UNCF colleges that would produce key leaders in the ensuing Civil Rights Movement. These institutions emerged as places of ferment for civil rights in spite of early efforts by white funders to dilute their curricula. As James D. Anderson shows, previous industrial philanthropy was not interested in improving race relations, but in training a labor force and creating a pliable environment in the South for investment. In later years, under the

Rockefeller-sponsored GEB, the reason for supporting black colleges shifted from crafting a workforce to crafting a better public image. As the GEB moved, around 1914, from a focus on industrial education to higher education for blacks, there was a corresponding change in the reason for giving. It was no longer solely to fulfill a specific business purpose, but rather to boost the Rockefeller family's prestige and perhaps to promote the idea that Rockefeller-style capitalism was good.[100] The advent of the UNCF, in 1944, brought no additional clarity to the question of whether philanthropy was really interested in supporting racial uplift. For Rockefeller Jr. the UNCF was clearly a winning idea—but not necessarily because it helped blacks. Although he showed himself to be a strong supporter of black colleges, and brought up much evidence of previous support by his family, he stopped short of endorsing a future in which blacks and whites could freely interact on all levels. Rockefeller spoke to the economic advantages of supporting black higher education, but not to the economic or social advancement of blacks themselves; he referred to "better race relations," but not to a better status for blacks in relation to whites.

Thus, in spite of the fact that Rockefeller Jr.'s words were extremely convincing, they did not necessarily paint a picture of black colleges that was true to life. Or rather, he allowed each potential donor to conjure up his or her own image of black higher education, and he encouraged UNCF staff to do the same in the official publicity. Rockefeller Jr.'s efforts on behalf of the UNCF point us to the age-old division between persuasion and truth.[101] Like other types of rhetoric, fund-raising language easily slips into a condition where it exists to support itself, rather than a concrete cause. In the case of the UNCF, Rockefeller Jr.'s ambiguous language, and that of the Fund's leadership as a whole, successfully raised money and helped get the colleges through the tumultuous years following World War II. However, the question remains as to what would have resulted had Rockefeller fully supported social equality. What would have happened if the UNCF itself had pushed for greater change and social equality among its donors?

CHAPTER 3

Flirting with Social Equality
New York's Elite Women Raise Funds

At the same time that John D. Rockefeller Jr. was working with white male leadership across the country, another fund-raising arm of the United Negro College Fund—the New York Women's Division—mobilized. Beginning in 1944, under the direction of Betty Stebman, several wealthy white women began to raise funds for black colleges to create a "parallel power structure."[1] This was precisely the kind of situation described by scholars Kathleen McCarthy and David Hammack: women used their connections with other women and their social privilege to broaden public interest in various social causes.[2]

When Walter Hoving began the business of organizing the Fund in New York City, he had difficulty recruiting people who were committed to putting consistent effort into the organization's day-to-day activities. Because most men associated with the Fund held full-time jobs, these daily responsibilities fell to their wives.[3] In fact, the inclusion of women in the Fund's work was seen as essential; not only were they the true "workers" of the organization, but they also had the closest connections to the wealthy businessmen who would be its financial mainstay. First, Hoving asked Rockefeller Jr.'s wife if she would head a women's committee, but she declined. Out of desperation, Hoving asked his own wife.[4] With her help and the staff support of Betty Stebman, the UNCF's Women's Division was born. Knowing that fund-raising among society women required well-

Catherine Waddell, 1945. Used with permission from the United Negro College Fund, Fairfax, Virginia.

connected individuals at the center of the campaign, Mrs. Hoving recruited Catherine Hughes Waddell, who eventually assumed the responsibilities of the Women's Division in 1946.

Catherine Waddell was the daughter of Supreme Court Chief Justice Charles Evans Hughes and was married to Chauncey L. Waddell, the chairman of Waddell & Reed, principal underwriters of United Funds, Inc. Prior to coming to the UNCF, Catherine Waddell served on the National Board of the YWCA and as a board member of the New York City Metropolitan Opera.[5] When first approached by Mrs. Hoving, Waddell refused the invitation. However, "upon reflection, she decided that her strong feelings about equal opportunity for all were not sufficient—here she had a chance to act in support of those feelings."[6] Waddell became one of the most active volunteers for the

UNCF. In the words of Betty Stebman, "she was just remarkable . . . she would never stop working. . . . Wherever she went, [the UNCF] was the number one thing."[7] When interest in the Fund died down on occasion, Waddell was able to ignite a fire underneath the cause; putting it in the sexist terms of the day, Lindsley Kimball said "she did all that she could do for a lady."[8]

In fact, as a lady, Waddell could do quite a bit. Knowing her influence and importance to the Fund, from time to time she would threaten to leave the organization if things were not done her way.[9] And she got her way because she was very well connected and had a way of making the UNCF's work appear glamorous. She saw to it that the women associated with the Fund were featured in newspaper society columns where they were tying their names to the support of education for future black doctors, lawyers, and teachers.[10] To Waddell and the other women associated with the Fund, voluntarism was "more lovely" than being paid for their service. According to historian Dorothy Becker, volunteer women "cherished [the] belief . . . that volunteer effort, by definition, was superior to paid work. Charity, like love, could not be purchased."[11] These attitudes, of course, were made possible by the women's privileged position; moreover, these women "could exist only in a society in which status was fixed and the upper classes were not self-conscious about their superiority and their obligation to help the less fortunate."[12]

Realizing that she needed additional help, Waddell asked Mrs. Marjorie Loengard, a college classmate from Wellesley, to join her at the UNCF. According to Betty Stebman, Waddell was the chief fund-raiser in the group (the "money person") while Loengard "was the intellectual," who helped bring the UNCF story to the public.[13] Through their links with the Seven Sister Colleges, they recruited an active and well-connected group of women.[14] In addition to the black cause, most of these women also volunteered on behalf of women's education. Their involvement with the UNCF showed them that the two issues went hand in hand. By paying particular attention to Spelman and Bennett colleges, the two historically black women's colleges, the women found connections between their own advancement and that of other oppressed groups.[15] Eventually more than one hundred of New York's wealthy women donated either money or time to the Fund.

With money and volunteer power at their disposal, the Women's Division planned their first formal fund-raising affair in 1947—a symposium at Hunter College that featured General George C. Marshall, former secretary of state and author of the Marshall Plan. At this time, with the exception of President Truman, Marshall was the most sought-after public statesman. His presence drew large audiences across the country. The Fund secured General Marshall, despite his public proclamation that he would no longer do any public speaking, because he owed Frederick D. Patterson a favor. During the war, Patterson had helped him out of a politically sensitive situation involving "Negro troops" and "Negro Air service" by housing a unit at Tuskegee. Before 1940, African Americans were barred from flying for the United States military. Pressure from civil rights organizations and the African American press resulted in the formation of an all-black squadron in 1941—the famed "Tuskegee Airmen."[16] The Tuskegee Airmen overcame prejudice to become one of the most highly respected fighter pilot groups of the Second World War, in which they demonstrated to the nation that African Americans could fly advanced combat aircraft. In fact, the Tuskegee Airmen's achievements paved the way for full integration of the United States military.

In addition to discussing foreign affairs, the Hunter College symposium was carefully planned to educate its audience about the UNCF. The event started with dinners at the homes of the women involved in the project. The strategy was to use these elegant affairs as an enticement to potential white donors and their wives to attend the Hunter College symposium.[17] This strategy resulted in a "handpicked audience" of 2,300 people listening to General Marshall, but more importantly they also listened to Morehouse College president Benjamin Mays telling the story of the UNCF.[18] The following year, under the guidance of Waddell, the Women's Division held a similar symposium featuring Madame Vijayalakshmi

Pandit, India's first female ambassador to the United Nations. Again they drew an enormous crowd and created a tradition that New York's elite looked forward to year after year.[19] Although these events drew unprecedented interest in a black organization, the Women's Division was careful not to upset the racial status quo in New York City. Racially mixed audiences listened to a formal address by a black college leader at the symposium, but the preceding, more intimate gatherings were strictly segregated.

In planning for the third annual event, Betty Stebman and the Women's Division wanted to "drum up" a "little controversy." It was decided that the Fund would participate in a town meeting broadcast throughout the country via the "George Denny Show." NBC's George Denny hosted one of the nation's most popular radio programs, "America's Town Meeting of the Air," which was "dedicated to the advancement of an honestly informed public opinion."[20] The typical program included a debate on a specific subject and questions from a live audience. This was a way to get the message of the UNCF out to an enormous audience in a time before "television was universal."[21] Stebman went to see George Denny, who was immediately interested and agreed to host the UNCF, asking the Fund itself to decide on the topic. In Stebman's words,

Well, heck, the United Negro College Fund was not a controversial subject, and the one thing that we always used to say is "this non-controversial organization." And here I am, getting us into a controversy on this thing. . . . I wanted real controversy, but I knew it wasn't a good thing to have. I would have loved to have had somebody take sides against the United Negro College Fund, or Negro education, or education for Negroes. . . . But what we came up with, and what Mr. Denny accepted, a really waffley kind of thing, which was "Are We Close to Solving Our Race Problem?" So you got two sides. No, we're not close. Yes, we are close. And that was about as much of a controversy as the UNCF could take at that point.[22]

On one side of the debate was George Schuyler, an "ultra-conservative, right wing black writer" for the *New York Times* as well as many of the black newspapers.[23] On the other side was Philadelphia lawyer Sadie Alexander. The first black female graduate of the University of Pennsylvania School of Law, Alexander held a Ph.D. in economics and was an active civil rights crusader. She and her husband integrated the movie theaters of Philadelphia in the early 1930s. Sadie Alexander took the perspective that "we were not close to solving the problem," and George Schuyler held the opinion that "we were."[24]

On November 27, 1949, in front of a live audience of 2,300 people in Hunter College's auditorium, the debate began on national radio. With George Denny as the moderator, Sadie Alexander and George Schuyler started to debate the subject at hand. According to Betty Stebman, "it was a very, very interesting program and Mrs. Alexander was terrific. . . . She made her point magnificently, and of course, that was the point *we* were taking, that we are certainly not close to solving our race problem. And Mr. Schuyler was somebody whom we didn't particularly like . . . Mr. Schuyler made his case well." However, during the question-and-answer period, Alexander broke down, responding in a way that was too emotional. She did a fine job answering the first few questions, "but then she began to lose herself and . . . [got] too emotional and said harsh things. . . . I mean, I sat there in a corner dying. Here we were, losing our side of the argument."[25] In Stebman's opinion, Schuyler should not have won despite the fact that he was composed and made his points clearly.

Although the UNCF was not the main topic of the debate, the Women's Division had planted questions among those asked by George Denny so that the Fund's name would be raised throughout the evening. In addition, Denny would occasionally remind the audience, both at Hunter College and across the nation, that the event was sponsored by the United Negro College Fund. Although the debate failed to convey the UNCF's perspective, it succeeded in getting the organization's name out to the American public.

The Alexander/Schuyler debate was not the only time that the Women's Division attempted to challenge conventions by sprinkling some controversy on the UNCF's squeaky clean image. A few years earlier, Catherine Waddell endeavored to make change. Although she herself was a product of privilege, she was intent on pushing the nation when it came to segregation, which she considered "obnoxious," a "weak spot in the vision of democracy America presents."[26] An incident in 1947 illustrates her willingness to force Rockefeller Jr.'s hand on the idea of social equality. In November that year, Waddell wrote to Rockefeller Jr. with the idea of hosting an interracial reception and dinner to honor the presidents of the UNCF colleges.[27] She had rallied the support of William Trent Jr. and Frederick D. Patterson for the dinner. She envisioned a reception followed by small, intimate dinners at the homes of prominent New Yorkers. Knowing that this type of gathering might cause a stir by its embrace of social equality, Waddell proposed a cautious, low-key plan. The dinners would appear to be unplanned and spontaneous—a mere outgrowth of the reception. She assured Rockefeller Jr. that the "right people" would be invited and that the event would present the UNCF in the most favorable light.

Upon receipt of Waddell's letter Rockefeller met with Kimball and Hoving, his male associates at the UNCF in New York, to discuss the ramifications of an interracial reception and dinner. In the eyes of her male counterparts, even Waddell's carefully planned strategy was viewed as too radical. After much thought, Rockefeller Jr. wrote back to Waddell:

The dinners which you speak of would seem to me dangerous. You and I may hold such views as we see fit regarding social equality between the races. If you ask one of these college presidents to dine with you, or I do, when they happen to be in the city, as we would ask any other friend and as I have done in the past with Booker Washington or Major Moton, that is no one's concern except our own and is made nothing of. If, on the other hand, by common agreement, three or four or half a dozen or, as is now planned, twelve different families invite various of these college presidents to dinners, it would seem to me utterly impossible for the fact not to become known to the newspapers, with the result that some thoughtless although well meaning reporter would come out with some such headline as "the Negro College Fund is seeking to establish social equality of the races."[28]

Rockefeller Jr. had concluded that such an emphasis on social equality would not bode well for the UNCF's "fund-raising task."[29] So reluctant, in fact, was the UNCF to allow interracial dining among the men attending its staff and board meetings that it declined to serve food at these events. According to Betty Stebman,

In the early years of the College Fund, meetings of blacks and whites were looked upon with some question. And you had to question that. What were these people doing? Because the only people really that were doing it in big public ways were the Communists, and we were very, very frightened that we would be tarred with the same brush. We had to keep it on a very high level, and constantly we had to think how this would be looked upon . . . we avoided big things of this nature at that time. But we always had integrated audiences, and we always had an integrated organization.[30]

Thus, meetings and symposiums were acceptable, but interracial dining and socializing in white homes and white establishments during the 1940s and early 1950s were out of the question. Waddell would not see any kind of social integration, especially over meals, for years. It was a sign of the times that the most civilized and diplomatic of acts—strangers publicly breaking bread together—was highly frowned upon among people of different races in the United States.

Mrs. McCullough's Luncheons

In the 1950s, the Women's Division of the Fund began a series of lunches sponsored by Mrs. Hall Park McCullough (also known as Edith Arthur McCullough), who had substantial experience in fundraising among the elite. According to Betty Stebman, "Mrs. McCullough . . . had married a man whose family had a pre-Revolutionary house in Bennington, Vermont. And she and one or two other women . . . became involved in starting [Bennington College]. The land and some buildings were given for the use of a college, and that was about 1926. And they began to raise the money, these women began to raise the money to create this women's college, that was to be an extraordinary institution. . . . Mrs. McCullough had tremendous power."[31]

Hall Park McCullough was an attorney with the Davis Polk Law Firm.[32] At the time that she was recruited to help with the UNCF, Mrs. McCullough and her husband were doing very well financially and owned a home at 1035 Fifth Avenue. According to Betty Stebman, "she was absolutely fascinated with the whole idea of the United Negro College Fund."[33] Having dedicated years to the support of Bennington College, in 1950 she approached the UNCF and said, "What can I do for you?" After some conversation, she decided that the best thing she could do was to place her elegant home at their disposal. Stebman remembered their exchange: "I said . . . if you would invite people to come to your home, we could tell you whom to invite and you could invite your own friends too. If they could come to your home for lunch and we could have Mr. Trent, whom she had met and fallen in love with, speak to them and tell them about the College Fund. Let them ask questions."[34] McCullough was "delighted" to oblige Betty Stebman's request and as a result, Mrs. McCullough's luncheons began.

McCullough took the planning of the luncheons very seriously, as her reputation as a hostess was on the line. She was following in the traditions of eighteenth- and nineteenth-century society women, who according to historian Cameron Binkley "had long used their credentials as homemakers to convey the propriety of their opinions on social issues."[35] Betty Stebman spent much time on the telephone debating with McCullough over who should be invited to the ever-so-elite engagements. For example, Stebman recollected one conversation: "We'd have a luncheon. I'd say, 'How about Mrs. So-and-So?' [And she'd say] 'Well, I don't think she's ever met a Negro.' 'I think it would be good to have her.' [I'd say] 'Well, you think we ought to put her next to Mr. Trent?' [And she'd say] 'Oh no, I wouldn't do that. No I think that's going a little far. I'd put her at Table Three in the next room and then maybe we could ask her again some time later, and we'd see what her reaction is.'"[36]

Inviting some of the most elite people in New York sometimes meant inviting some of the "most biased people, really biased people, who never knew a Negro except the woman who worked in the house or the elevator, black elevator man."[37] However, these luncheons soon became the place to be seen in New York City, and supporting the United Negro College Fund became the thing to do among society ladies. Members of New York's high society were vying for positions on the UNCF women's committee.[38] These women became the "inner circle" of professional volunteers in New York City.[39] According to Betty Stebman, "And they came to Mrs. McCullough's luncheons. Elegant Mrs. McCullough, who really was elegant. She was a wonderful, tall, stately, beautiful woman. And they'd come to Mrs. McCullough's lovely apartment and she'd have her two maids, all in their nice uniforms, and everything was done just right. We had as many as thirty or thirty-two people at a time, because they [the luncheons] got to be very fashionable. I mean, it was a question of did you get invited to Mrs. McCullough's luncheon?"[40] The centerpiece of the luncheons was an informal talk by William Trent. In Stebman's words, "He came to these luncheons . . . and he spoke beautifully." After their lunch, all of the ladies would gather together in McCullough's huge living room, "this beautiful living room overlooking [Central] Park, with the fire going in the wintertime in the fireplace, and people would just sit around this lovely room, and Bill would get up and just absolutely charm the pants off everyone. He would tell the story of the College Fund. He would answer questions."[41] Some of the women asked rather sophisticated questions. They were well informed about education in general and, because many of them had gone to women's colleges themselves, were interested in Spelman and Bennett in particular. So sheltered were the attendees at these affairs that they would sometimes unwittingly make racist comments. According to Betty Stebman, they might say they "never in their lives had met a Negro, and it was a fantastic experience for them." They would say, upon meeting Bill Trent, "isn't it fascinating that a Negro could be that educated, a Negro." "And people would go away saying, oh-h-h, Mr. Trent is so marvelous." Knowing Bill Trent became fashionable. "And before you knew it, Mr. Trent was invited to go on the Board of this organization, on the Board of that organization. Mr. Trent became *the* Negro." "You really had to know Bill Trent. Otherwise, you know, you didn't know anybody. And, of course, my friend Bill Trent. I know a Negro. His name's Bill Trent. Well, that was all part of this whole thing."[42]

Much like the women mentioned in historian Beverly Gordon's *Bazaars and Fair Ladies,* who, although "always mindful of their domestic public image, often sought out the titillating and sensual," the ladies at McCullough's luncheons found it exciting to flirt with societal taboos, chief among which was fraternizing with a "Negro."[43] Of course, whites in New York City had a history of "craving" interaction with the "Negro." This was the case during the 1920s Harlem Renaissance when whites, going "uptown" to visit jazz clubs, found it exotic and risky. There, as with McCullough's luncheons, blacks were the entertainment.[44] Although Betty Stebman found the exploitation of Trent distasteful, she believed that his presence at the luncheons moved the UNCF ahead and helped it gain access to the "right" circles. Moreover, because many of the ladies attending the lunches were connected to wealthy individuals in other cities, these events had nationwide ramifications for the Fund. After the first few luncheons, the Women's Division also solicited the help of other black college presidents, including Benjamin Mays of Morehouse and Rufus Clement of Atlanta University. Mays, much like Trent, would eventually become, in Lindsley Kimball's words, "exhibit A" of the UNCF.[45] Over the course of a few years, McCullough gave more than one hundred luncheons for the UNCF and reached nearly three thousand women.[46] Her luncheons were an "institution" that continued until her old age prevented her from hosting them.[47]

Lady Bountiful?

According to some contemporary critics, McCullough and her friends could be easily characterized as "Ladies Bountiful"—women who used giving to the poor on occasion to enhance their own social standing and build feelings of self-righteousness.[48] These UNCF Women's Division members vehemently denied the title, of course. In their minds, giving to the UNCF was no shallow, attention-getting act, but an effort to change race relations throughout the country. To reinforce the women's sense of seriousness about their activities, the organizers assigned serious-sounding topics to luncheon discussions. These included "The Role of the Negro College in American Education," "The Problems of Negro Colleges," "The Economics of the Negro College," and "The Future of the Negro Colleges."[49] On many occasions, the women who attended the luncheons would communicate these issues to their husbands, with the goal of securing a donation for the Fund. Above all, challenging material presented at the luncheons gave everyone involved the sense that they were tackling the important issues of the day.

Although she herself gave much credit to the volunteers in the Women's Division, according to Lindsley Kimball, Betty Stebman did "all the work for the women's committee and kept it quite separate from the rest of the campaign, just turning in a final amount" raised at the end of the year. The women would quietly "go forth and work among their friends." According to Kimball, the Women's Division became a very important part of the total effort. "Some of the women were so dedicated," in Kimball's opinion, "that it [the

UNCF] was practically their mission in life." Betty Stebman served them, pulled them together, and kept after them.[50]

The approach to fund-raising used by the women's committee was different in character from that used by the men in the Fund.[51] The leading women, including Waddell, Loengard, and McCullough, aimed to touch the heart strings of potential donors. They pointed to the personal impact that their circle could have on black individuals and used phrases such as, "Look what you can do for these people. Look at the career that you can make possible."[52] The Women's Division brochures pointed to the history of volunteerism among New York City's women (with the USO, the Museum of Modern Art, and the Metropolitan Opera House) and how these women had made a difference to various organizations. In many ways, the work of the Women's Division seemed to anticipate the underlying ideas of the much later "A Mind Is a Terrible Thing to Waste" campaign by cultivating African American individuals rather than keeping them in their place. For the first time, a brochure mentioned equality:

Whether you G I V E

Because so much remains to be done to equalize the educational opportunities for Negroes . . . or

Because more doctors, dentists, nurses and social workers are needed to improve health conditions for Negroes—and indirectly for the entire nation . . . or

Because the Negro colleges stress character building and citizenship, and work to improve race relations throughout the country . . .

Your gift will help America to realize her destiny and responsibility as a leader of free peoples throughout the world.[53]

Although it did touch on the tried and true themes used by the UNCF, such as morality, leadership, and Cold War fears, the Women's Division also relied on the old maxim that "people don't give money to causes . . . they give it to other people." The Division's success came from the fact that these women saw each other socially all the time; they played bridge together and attended the same dinner parties. It became very hard to say no to a friend regardless of whether you believed in the cause of black education.[54]

According to Lindsley Kimball, the approach used in the male world was more focused on the success of the potential donor's company than on that of an individual African American. Kimball would approach a Con Edison (New York's electrical company) executive, for example, and say "how many blacks are in your employ." And the executive would say, "I don't dare tell the public, but more than half of them." To that Kimball would respond, "Well, do you want them with leadership or do you want them without leadership." According to Kimball, it was impossible for the chairman of a company to answer with anything other than yes; it was like saying, "Do you want them just a rabble or do you want them with educated leadership?" The heads of companies "couldn't stand them [blacks] if they didn't have some leadership." Supporting the UNCF was the way to gain leadership for the blacks in one's company. This kind of approach was obviously quite different from that of the women's committee.[55]

Integrating the Colony Club

One of New York City's most exclusive social clubs during the 1940s and 1950s was the Colony Club located at the corner of Park Avenue and 62nd Street. It was "the last word in women's clubs," "a very, 400 Social Register-type club."[56] Admission was granted only by the proper pedigree. When, in 1946, the Golden Rule Foundation chose Mrs. Clarissa Clement, the mother of Rufus Clement, as "National Mother of the Year"—the first time that an African American woman was chosen for the award—the UNCF's women's committee decided to use the occasion to pry open the doors of this exclusive club.[57] Clement had one son who was a diplomat in Africa, her other son Rufus was president of Atlanta University, and her daughter was active in government circles. The Clement family was considered quite distinguished by the white members of the UNCF, and as such, the Women's Division thought it was an opportune time to garner publicity for the organization. Clement agreed to participate in any festivities planned by the Fund.

According to Betty Stebman, Waddell's choice of the Colony Club for such an event was strategic. Said Stebman, "She and Mrs. Loengard and many of our other women were members of the Cosmopolitan club . . . which is also a women's club and a very fine one, but it's a much more intellectual kind of setting—the Cosmopolitan Club—as [compared to] the Colony Club, which is very social."[58] Having decided on the Colony Club, the women had to find a member who would be their entry ticket to the exclusive organization. The only Colony Club member who was within reach of the Women's Division was Mrs. John D. Rockefeller Jr., who was not active with the UNCF and had earlier declined an invitation for involvement. Waddell, who had a close relationship with Rockefeller Jr., called and asked for his assistance in securing the use of his wife's name. He thought this was a fine idea and said that he and his wife would gladly sponsor the event. In the words of Betty Stebman,

> I think probably Mr. Rockefeller regretted that action of his, because it involved him in innumerable conversations on the telephone. They [the Colony Club] wanted to know who these people were. You could just imagine from the conversations— and I had a number of them—they could see [the] hordes of Harlem marching into the Colony Club, you know. It was really a terrifying prospect for them . . . we went through this whole horror and Mr. Rockefeller was a darling about the whole thing, and he kept saying that he had to provide all kinds of information. About Mrs. Rockefeller and about himself.[59]

The event turned into a "lovely day, with tea at the Colony Club, and Mrs. Clement was presented, and all these ladies, very nice ladies, were there . . . a lot of black ladies and a lot of white ladies, but they were all very, very elegant ladies." According to Stebman, when the event was over, the "people at the Colony Club . . . were just absolutely on the edge of their seats." Surprised that it didn't turn out to be as "wild and exotic" as they envisioned, the Colony Club leaders were touting it as a "lovely affair."[60] The Women's Division's activities at the Colony Club were one more important step in creating a more socially integrated environment.

According to Hollis Price, president of LeMoyne-Owen College, "the whole idea of the organization of women's groups had never caught on in the College Fund nationally to the same degree that it caught on in New York City, and I think that you've got to give Catherine Waddell credit for her great interest, great drive and the responsibility for getting that off the ground, because this was her whole life devotion."[61] In fact, Price noted that "the men in New York and the men's committee never paid the women's committee any attention . . . they just operated, they raised money and so forth, but so far as any type of cooperation activity or working with the women's committee in New York, they apparently didn't even deign to notice that the women's committee existed."[62] The Women's Division was what philanthropic scholars Kathleen McCarthy and David Hammack have referred to as a "parallel power structure," promoting reform in subtle ways.[63] While the white males involved with the UNCF were operating on one plane, the white women were acquiring fund-raising clout on another. Although the women did much to undermine social segregation in New York City, in many ways the work of the Women's Division still played into the "double consciousness" of the UNCF. By and large, the Women's Division events still presented the UNCF from a privileged white woman's perspective. Aside from the occasional involvement of a member college president at one of McCullough's luncheons, most fund-raising activities of the Division were events that were the norm for white society women—events that failed to move them out of their comfort zones. This changed in 1955 when, as a response to the *Brown v. Board* decision, the Women's Division planned an extravagant affair, which aimed to tell the nation that black colleges were still needed and relevant even after the end of legalized segregation.

By the early 1970s, Betty Stebman had left the Fund, and the Women's Division "had just about petered out." According to Vernon Jordan, the new president of the UNCF, "She was the sole force behind it, and Betty had some very determined attitudes about the College Fund and how it ought to operate." Moreover, "the College Fund was changing—or had changed—in the sense that historically it was white people who had access to the doors of philanthropy, and therefore the staff was largely white."[64] In an era of increased black consciousness, nearly thirty years after the inception of the Women's Division, a group of older white ladies sponsoring society teas was no longer the right approach to promote the goals of the UNCF.

CHAPTER 4

A Stigma of Inferiority
The Effect of *Brown v. Board*

In spite of the immediate euphoria of the *Brown* decision outlawing legalized segregation, black leaders and presidents of the member colleges of the United Negro College Fund understood that this critical point in history could bring drawbacks as well as benefits to black higher education.[1] If integration was now mandated by law, what was the purpose of a black college? Was it desirable for black colleges to become mainstream institutions in order to survive? The UNCF and its member colleges faced a difficult task: supporting integration while also showing commitment to the continuation of their unique institutions. They believed both goals to be essential to the advancement of blacks.[2] Seeing the slowness of the federal and state responses to *Brown* during the 1950s, scholars who study the contemporary time realize that dismantling segregation required a process, not just a proclamation. Yet for UNCF leaders of the day, it may have seemed that the end of black colleges was imminent.[3] Foundations, philanthropists, the NAACP, and many of the more liberal members of academe, both black and white, were questioning the future of black colleges. In the opinions of some, black colleges really stood in the way of integration.[4]

Part of the UNCF's response to *Brown* was to announce a shift in its goals to encourage whites to attend black colleges, although even the UNCF recognized at the time that such a shift was unlikely. In spite of this professed change in their mission, the actions of the

UNCF and its member college presidents expressed a desire to continue as they had been. They realized, as W. E. B. Du Bois had realized earlier in the century, that these black institutions were essential to the educational advancement of blacks, even if blacks were not banned from attending predominantly white institutions, by either law or practice: "The Negro college has done a great work. It has given us . . . intelligent leaders. Doubtless, without these colleges the American Negro would scarcely have attained his present position. The chief thing that distinguishes the American Negro . . . is the number of men that we have trained in modern education, able to cope with the white world on its own ground and in its own thought, method, and language."[5] Of course, in reality, historically white institutions did not open their doors to black students until the early 1970s and then only by the force of law. However, this did not preclude the UNCF and its member college presidents from contemplating the future of their institutions.

The 1954 decision came just as the Fund was coming into its own. The UNCF had raised more than $14 million in its first decade. These monies were used for training better African American teachers, updating classrooms and lab equipment, providing scholarships for emerging black leaders, and funding new buildings.[6] By 1954, the united appeal of the thirty-one member colleges had led to much more financial success than the institutions could have achieved on their own.[7] Thus, at the very moment that the UNCF was reaching its goals, the ongoing legitimacy of its member institutions was being questioned.

The Court's proclamation that separate schools were inherently unequal and its call for dismantling segregated public school systems were welcomed by civil rights leaders and enlightened citizens across the country.[8] However, in 1955 the Court still had to convene to discuss the implementation of its new constitutional mandates. Chief Justice Earl Warren placed great responsibility on the local schools and courts that originally heard the school segregation cases. In a May 1955 decision, later known as *Brown II*, these institutions were to implement a plan for desegregation. Warren instructed localities to act quickly and to move toward full compliance "with all deliberate speed." Unfortunately, the interpretation of "all deliberate speed" was left to state governments and local schools; as a result, segregation remained intact for years after the landmark decision of 1954. Despite the slowness of implementing the *Brown* decision and regardless of the fact that it dealt specifically with primary and secondary schools, in the minds of the UNCF leadership, the historic case offered potential for change at the higher education level. *Brown* provided an occasion for black college leaders to assess the role of their institutions in the larger society.[9] In fact, they had been thinking about this question in a systematic fashion since the early 1950s.

Preparing for the *Brown* Decision

Prior to the *Brown* decision, the NAACP had staged a carefully planned series of legal battles against Jim Crow education at the graduate school level.[10] In each case, a black graduate applicant challenged the notion of "separate but equal education."[11] Although southern states claimed that a black student could receive an equal education in any field in a separate institution, this was clearly not the case. A black student wanting to be educated in law, for example, might either be sent to another state or made to attend a makeshift "law school" that was created solely for the purpose of compliance and without any real intent to provide equal education. Two particularly important cases were *Sipuel v. Board of Regents* (1948) and *Sweatt v. Painter* (1950). In the first case, Ada Sipuel applied to the University of Oklahoma law school and was denied admission based on her race. With the help of the NAACP, Sipuel sued the state, and the case eventually reached the Supreme Court. Based on the 14th amendment, the Court held that states must provide equal graduate education for blacks. At first, however, the ruling did not specify how that education was to be provided. Thus, rather than admitting Ada Sipuel to the University of Oklahoma, the state's Board of Regents roped off an area in the state capitol building, designated the area as the "Negro law school," and hired three black lawyers to serve as the faculty. Eventually in 1948, the Supreme Court decided that this practice was unconstitutional, and Ada Sipuel was allowed to enroll at the University of Oklahoma.[12] The *Sweatt v. Painter* case involved Heman Sweatt, a black man who in 1946 applied for admission to the law school at the University of Texas. Citing the fact that it was a segregated institution, the school rejected Sweatt's application. With the assistance of NAACP attorneys, Sweatt sued the university. Although he lost his case at the state level, the U.S. Supreme Court, finding that equal education had been denied, forced the University of Texas law school and the institution's graduate school to open its doors to all students, regardless of race, in 1950. This case, in particular, was a vital predecessor to *Brown v. Board* because in it the Court unanimously decided that "separate but equal" was not, in fact, equal.[13]

Notably, the court declared in these cases that the states not only had an obligation to provide graduate education for blacks but also that the education must replicate the intellectual level experienced by whites. These cases established the role of the environment (for example, the facilities, traditions, and faculty) in the student's experience at a college or university. To receive an equal education, a student not only needed to learn the same material but also to receive the same institutional support while on campus. Because, in most cases, this could only be achieved by sending blacks to the same schools as whites, these decisions made it almost inevitable that segregation would be overturned.

In addition to paving the way for the ultimate challenge to segregation, the pre-*Brown* cases raised some important issues surrounding both black colleges in general and the UNCF in particular. If, as the *Sweatt* and *Sipuel* decisions held, the traditions and culture that made up the college environment were important, did not the unique traditions of black colleges provide an educational environment that was, for some students, more suitable than that of predominantly white institutions? With their black-oriented curricula and scholarship (already well-established at universities like Fisk and Atlanta) did black institutions not offer a better choice to some students?[14]

The fact that the plaintiffs in these cases were hand-picked raised another issue important to the black college environment.[15] All these court decisions involved students whose academic preparation was excellent, and who would easily have been admitted to predominantly white institutions had race not been used to exclude them. Knowing these facts, UNCF leaders began to ask themselves what would happen when the larger segment of the black student population, which came from unequally funded secondary schools and consisted of first-generation college students, moved into predominantly white institutions. Would they receive an "equal" education? Was it possible that a separate, identically funded environment could better provide an equal education—one that was caring, black-centered, and successful at raising the expectations of black students?[16] Of course, this question was hypothetical because black colleges had never been funded at a level equal to white colleges. Chronic underfunding, in fact, had created the need for the UNCF consortium in the first place. Nevertheless, factors were present at black colleges that could not be duplicated at wealthy white institutions. According to Frederick D. Patterson, black colleges provided "(a) congenial social atmosphere, (b) lower costs, (c) greater concern for [the] limitations of [the] academic background of Negro youth and (d) participation in extra-curricular activities."[17] Although intended to advance the cause of black education, the desegregation cases posed an ideological problem for the UNCF leadership and all those interested in the education of blacks.

John S. Lash, in "The Umpteenth Crisis in Negro Higher Education"(1951), provided a pointed description of the problem that lay ahead as a result of the NAACP's success in the higher education desegregation cases and in the event of a positive decision in the *Brown* case. Specifically, Lash stated,

If Negro colleges are to retain a place in an integrated educational system, immediate and drastic changes must be made. . . . Administrative theories must be revamped; the training, efficiency, and productivity of teaching personnel must be increased; physical facilities must be greatly enlarged and improved; curriculums must be modernized and effectively handled. In a word, the Negro colleges must accomplish in a comparatively brief time what the courts have decreed has not been accomplished in some fifty years: they must bring themselves into substantial equality with erstwhile "white" institutions.[18]

In 1952, based on the legal victories in the *Sweatt* and *Sipuel* cases, UNCF leaders displayed increased confidence that the Supreme Court would overturn segregation in the pending *Brown* case. As a result, UNCF Executive Director William J. Trent Jr. held both formal and informal discussions with leaders and supporters of black colleges pertaining to black higher education after desegregation. Some initial statements made by Trent and others indicated an understanding that the unique role of black colleges made them useful in the years after Jim Crow. In an interview with Rockefeller Foundation staff member Yorke Allen Jr., Trent noted that the Fund and its member colleges would survive, regardless of a positive decision by the Court based on their past service to black students and their families. He predicted that integration would be slow moving and that black colleges would be needed during the transition. He was convinced that "as we advance toward the goal of a fully integrated educational system, the role of the Fund and its member colleges becomes even more important."[19] The test of survival, according to Trent, was the measure of an institution's usefulness to society and its standard of excellence.

During the early discussions among the Fund leadership, several themes emerged: the continuing economic barriers to integration even after a positive Court ruling; the ongoing responsibility of the Fund and its member colleges to black students; the predicted increases in the country's overall undergraduate population; and the role that black colleges would play in educating this population. According to a Trent memo to the UNCF leadership, "The removal of legal prescriptions will not . . . remove the economic barriers to education, nor will it in any way lessen the responsibility of the private Negro colleges to provide the best possible education for the Negro students now enrolled in them. For an indefinite period, the major responsibility for higher education of Negroes in the South will continue to fall upon the colleges that have been serving them for the past 100 years."[20] In recognizing that black students had special needs with regard to finance and curriculum, Trent was acknowledging the role of environment in a student's educational experience and suggesting that black colleges were in a unique position to fulfill this need. However, he observed that in general college enrollment was expanding whereby the estimated number of qualified high school graduates seeking higher education each year was predicted to double overall college enrollment by 1970. Thus, according to Trent, "not only will every good college in existence now be needed, but they will have to be prepared to expand their services and new ones will have to be built."[21] Did he mean that, after integration, the expanded student population would spread out evenly among both black colleges and predominantly white institutions? Perhaps not, but the possibility of white enrollment at those institutions would, in the post-*Brown* era, emerge as a regular part of UNCF publicity.

William J. Trent Jr. was not the only person making predictions about the UNCF's future and that of the member colleges. The Negro press, curious about the future of black education, raised probing questions to some member college presidents. Specifically, in 1952 the Pittsburgh *Courier* asked, "In view of the recent Supreme Court decision on higher education, and the current NAACP campaign for equal educational opportunities on other levels, what effects will these moves have on your institution within the next five years?"[22] In terms of institutional changes, the presidents' responses ranged from "sweeping changes" to "no significant effect." However, all made the suggestion that whites might soon enter their institutions in significant numbers. For example, President A. D. Beittel of Talladega College in Alabama said, "We are convinced that we should move as rapidly as possible in the direction of a completely integrated institution. We have the endorsement of the board of trustees, faculty and students of Talladega to move in this direction. . . . We hope to increase the number of exchange students, but we are especially interested in enrolling fulltime Caucasian students at Talladega."[23]Likewise, President M. Lafayette Harris of Philander Smith College in Arkansas stated, "We propose an institution of sufficient quality and effectiveness to serve all citizens, . . . to share in the training of teachers and other community workers who will make their contributions to the over-all program of increased educational opportunity for everyone."[24]

While noting that there would be little change in the way the institution operated, Dr. J. S. Scott, president of Wiley College in Marshall, Texas, claimed that the quality of his institution would make it attractive to all students: "our policy is to make Wiley one of the first-class small colleges, so that when full integration comes, we will be able to attract students because of the quality of work that will be done in the college."[25] Unlike Trent's early response to those seeking predictions, which focused on meeting the continuing needs of black colleges in a desegregated environment, the member college presidents emphasized opening their doors to whites and expanding their institutional missions. In the aftermath of *Brown* the presidents brought these ideas together and emphasized them simultaneously. The black college presidents remained in the media spotlight after the *Brown* decision, and Trent and the UNCF leadership used their voices strategically to send a clear message about the future of the Fund.

The evening before the Supreme Court's decision on *Brown* was to be rendered, UNCF member college presidents convened to prepare an official reaction to either ruling. If the Court chose to uphold the segregated status quo legally, black colleges would not unleash a barrage of criticism; instead, they would continue to work toward equality within the confines of segregation. According to William J. Trent Jr., "each president was told to go back to [his] community and say this is the attitude of the black college presidents toward the whole thing."[26] If, the Court chose to strike down segregation, the college presidents would be cautiously optimistic about the future of integrated educational institutions. The Fund's preparation to present a united front was an important step in its evolution; it marked the first time that the organization became a mouthpiece for the entire group of private black colleges.

The Aftermath of the Supreme Court's Decision

F. D. Patterson, president of the UNCF, made a public statement: "At 1:20 P.M. on Monday, May 17, 1954, we reached the goal of our long journey toward the American ideal of equality of educational opportunity for all. At that time, in a simple but majestic announcement that went to the hearts of millions throughout the world, the Supreme Court of the United States declared segregation incompatible with the principals [sic] enunciated by our founding fathers and confirmed by our constitution."[27] After the *Brown* decision made "separate but equal" an untenable legal concept, the United Negro College Fund took immediate action with regard to its public relations and fund-raising strategies.[28] At a meeting on May 18, one day after the *Brown* decision, the Fund planned to create special publicity pieces for each of its audiences.[29] For example, the UNCF sent a statement to the white press: "The removal of legal prescriptions will not, however, remove the economic barriers to education. . . . Since implementation of the decision will involve many local actions and the change of social attitudes, the major responsibility for higher education of Negroes in the South will continue to fall for an indefinite period upon the colleges that have been serving them during the past years."[30] Thus, the Fund leadership once again focused on the barriers to education that would continue to exist and emphasized that these persistent obstacles would render the UNCF and its member colleges useful during the transitional period.[31] Was the UNCF not worried however, about creating the perception that by preparing for desegregation not to work, they were, in effect, helping it not to work? Perhaps the UNCF was concerned: indicative of

Du Bois's "double consciousness," black Fund leaders sent the black press a separate memo stressing that, although the UNCF member colleges would continue to work hard to serve black students, the organization was wholeheartedly in favor of the *Brown* decision and the need to dismantle the ugly apparatus of Jim Crow.[32] The "hard fought efforts of NAACP leaders" to bring about integration were worthwhile, and the "continued existence of UNCF colleges in no way diminished these efforts."

According to Morehouse president Benjamin Mays, the UNCF required the support of the black press—including the Pittsburgh *Courier*, the Chicago *Defender*, the Baltimore *Afro-American*, the Atlanta *Daily World*, and the New York *Amsterdam News*—during this time as well as any time the Fund was asking for support: "It was important because all Negroes were reading and they were seeing how important it was, that the Negro colleges needed the Fund. . . . You can't get along without the media."[33] As stated by scholar Robin D. G. Kelley, these black newspapers "were circulated through many hands in households, barbershops, beauty parlors, churches, and restaurants. In the hands of Pullman car porters, they found their way into the Deep South as well."[34]

William J. Trent Jr. sent memos to the UNCF presidents and the campaign directors across the country detailing the Fund's stance on the Court's decision. Throughout these communications dominant themes emerged: Not only would racial barriers take time to overcome—a message the Fund leadership eventually developed more fully—but also the openness of their black institutions extended to whites as well as blacks. Service to a wider community became a necessity because of projected population increases, increases that the UNCF leadership brought to the attention of their donors and potential donors. These themes were crucial to the UNCF's fundraising success during the immediate post-*Brown* era. According to Frederick D. Patterson, the Fund "skillfully prepared" their post-*Brown* fund-raising literature and campaign materials by focusing on the organization's goals and needs.[35]

Despite the proactive stance of the black leaders of the UNCF, some of the whites involved, including John D. Rockefeller Jr., initially felt that black colleges would no longer be needed.[36] According to his associate Lindsley Kimball, upon hearing the decision, Rockefeller Jr. said, "We won't need the United Negro College Fund or any of the member colleges. That means I won't have to serve on the board anymore and we won't have to raise any money any more."[37] Frederick D. Patterson heard this kind of response from many of the white northern donors at the time: "Immediately after the Supreme Court's decision, there was this wave of all right, we helped you up, but now this takes care of everything, and all you have to do is close the black colleges and the white colleges will receive the kids."[38] Although Rockefeller Jr. soon saw the continuing need for UNCF, in many ways his initial reaction to the *Brown* decision guided his subsequent interaction with the Fund. After 1955, the aging philanthropist had little interaction with the UNCF, except that he let it use his name for fund-raising purposes. Just six years after *Brown v. Board*, John D. Rockefeller Jr. passed away at the age of 86.

Responsibility to the Black Community

Awareness of the extent to which Jim Crow was woven into the fabric of southern life led the UNCF leadership and the member college presidents to predict that integration would come neither quickly nor easily. UNCF presidents strove to "make equality of educational opportunity an economic reality, as well as a legal one."[39] As they had seen earlier with *Sweatt* and *Sipuel*, the southern states tried various methods to postpone full-fledged integration. In the interim, however, the UNCF focused on its responsibility to a black population yearning for education.[40] In 1954, 73 percent of blacks of college age lived in the South. Furthermore, improvements in primary and secondary education resulted in more members of this population having college aspirations.[41] According to the UNCF leadership, in the short-term *Brown* effectively decreased enrollment at UNCF colleges; student attendance increased again after a few years and exceeded 24,000 by the end of the 1950s—as predicted by the UNCF leadership (see figure on p. 98).[42] Although the UNCF leadership attributed the slight decrease from 1954 thru 1956 to the impact of the *Brown* decision, as noted, most segregated white institutions, especially in the Deep South, did not open their doors to large numbers of black students until well into the 1970s.[43] More likely these numbers reflect a combination of low birthrates during the Great Depression and sagging enrollment at the tail end of the post–World War II G. I. Bill.[44]

Even when admitted to predominantly white institutions, many black students were not able to pay the tuition. The UNCF used this fact to argue for continued support of black colleges. According to J. S. Scott Sr., president of Wiley College, "As integration proceeds, these schools of the United Negro College Fund still bear the responsibility of offering this type of liberal education to countless young people who cannot afford to pay more than $700 a year for tuition, room and board."[45] In 1954, the average cost at a private black college for tuition, room and board was $238.[46] In the mid to late 1950s, the economic status of blacks in the South was so far below that of most whites that, according to Scott, "the day is not yet in sight when the masses of Southern Negroes, whose income is derived from unskilled and farm labor, will be able to select their schools without regard to cost."[47] Sociologist and Fisk University president Charles S. Johnson wrote several articles both prior to and shortly after the *Brown* decision that supported Scott's conclusions; he noted that "Negro families as of today earn on the average only one-half of the income of white families. There are, it has been pointed out, four times as many white as Negro families earning as much as three thousand dollars annually, a minimum for supporting a son or daughter in college."[48] The post-*Brown* fund-raising literature emphasized how the economic limitations of the black community hampered college choice. Moreover, the UNCF pointed to the continued need for these institutions in an era of legal integration and indirectly expressed its concern that even private black colleges would be closed as a result of *Brown*.[49]

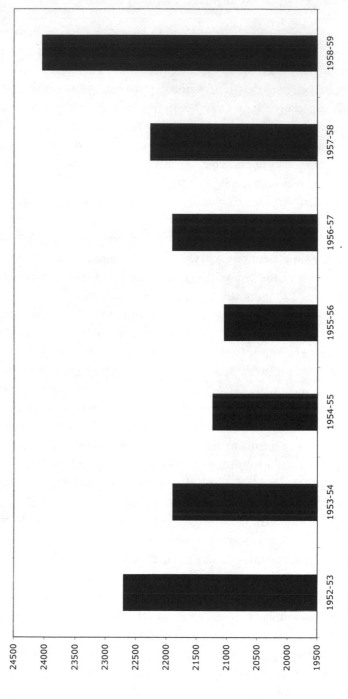

UNCF Total Yearly Enrollment, 1952–1959

In addition to the special economic needs of black students, the Fund's leadership focused on the loyalty of the black college constituency in the South and across the country.[50] According to the UNCF, although predominantly white institutions would be an option for some blacks, for others, family tradition dictated college choice.[51] In the words of Albert Manley, president of Spelman College, "many of the students who attended these colleges had parents and grandparents who had attended" as well.[52] In this way, black colleges were similar to their white counterparts. Students made their choices based on alumni influence, religious affiliation, course offerings, faculty, social environment, location, cost and, above all, where their parents went to school.[53] Many black colleges had a long tradition of nurturing and producing leaders who enriched and developed the black community. In fact, the majority of the UNCF leaders and most of the member college presidents and faculty had attended black colleges at some point in their careers.[54] For all these reasons, the UNCF claimed, many black parents in the South would continue to encourage their children to attend black colleges.[55]

Despite this seeming confidence among UNCF leaders about black loyalty to black colleges, there were conflicting views in the larger black community about how integration would affect education. Executive Director William Trent Jr. himself was concerned that it would become difficult to raise money from black people who would say "well now . . . we can go to any college we want to . . . we don't need the colleges."[56] Other black leaders had divergent ideas about how integration efforts could be helped along. Some of these leaders, including those within the NAACP, favored eliminating black colleges in a seemingly natural way to hasten the enrollment of blacks at segregated white institutions. In their view, even private black colleges gave whites an excuse to keep blacks out of white institutions. In his book *Is Separate Unequal?*, Albert L. Samuels concludes that the NAACP "deliberately decided on an approach that ultimately assigned little value to [black colleges] once it had secured for African Americans the legal right to attend previously all-white institutions."[57] In the NAACP's view, history had shown that it was impossible for black colleges, whether public or private, to be equal; arguing for their continued existence contradicted the ideals put forth by the American creed of equality for all. Samuels documents countless speeches made by NAACP executive director Walter White against black colleges during the 1950s, including one in which he questioned the motives of the black college leaders who argued for their institutions' continued existence. In White's words, "In the field of higher education, the colored people in the United States must be willing to give up their little kingdoms that have been carved out in Southern states."[58] Walter White felt that black colleges were "not only inferior to white institutions; in addition, agitation on the part of blacks for additional funds for these schools was a waste of time."[59] According to Albert Samuels, "the Court's opinion [in *Brown*] did not make clear whether the harm of the *Plessy* regime was segregation itself or the state's role in legally imposing it," thus leaving black colleges in a political quandary.[60] People of all backgrounds questioned whether "all-black" necessarily meant inferior.

Serving a Wider Constituency

Based on the federal government's education statistics, the Fund predicted that between 1954 and 1964 college and university enrollment would increase by about one-third—to more than 3 million students. Between 1964 and 1970 enrollment would double again, to more than 6 million students.[61] In the South, the number of high school graduates seeking a college education in the 1950s was greater than ever before.[62] This fact led the Fund to reemphasize its position: in addition to the current colleges and universities in the South, new colleges needed to be built to meet future enrollment demands.[63] This message, included in most publications, prefaced the Fund's main publicity emphasis, which was opening the member colleges' doors to all and embracing integration in its fullest form: "The Fund's member institutions will continue—not as colleges limiting their services to Negro students, but as *first class institutions* for *all* qualified American youth."[64]

A particular emphasis was placed on the black colleges' history of educating whites and international students and their legacy of an integrated faculty, which began with their establishment in the nineteenth century. From its inception, the UNCF claimed that it had abhorred segregation and held the belief that while Jim Crow laws had segregated its member institutions, they had not been segregating institutions in their philosophy and outlook. As private colleges, the UNCF institutions were technically not segregated; few had provisions in their charters preventing whites from enrolling. However, the pervasive and onerous hold of Jim Crow laws, both written and unwritten, had prevented even private black colleges from enrolling significant numbers of whites. In fact, many local white communities around private black colleges objected to the mere presence of whites on the campus.[65] Small violations in Jim Crow etiquette resulted in sanctions by the local whites. Likewise, state governments could threaten to revoke institutional charters (and did so in the case of Tougaloo College, for example) and tax-exempt status if a private black college did not adhere to the racial status quo.[66] Moreover, the existence of legalized segregation gave states free reign to enforce their civil codes unequally. Thus, even if the *Brown* decision was intended to cover only public primary and secondary schools, its declaration that separate was "inherently unequal" had a wider reach, a view that raised the possibility of desegregation of all public and private institutions.

In an effort to demonstrate the member colleges' willingness to accept white students, Frederick D. Patterson went so far as to write to member college presidents to ask whether their charters contained any reference to race or color; if they did, he explored what steps were taken to remove such references. In addition, Patterson inquired about the attitude of their trustees and faculty members with respect to the admission of white students.[67] In the past, some of the member colleges' white trustees demanded statements in the institutional charters that in effect "segregated" the institutions, not through law, but through policy.[68] Yet in response to his letter, Patterson found that twenty-four of the thirty-one member colleges had no reference to race or color in their original charters. Of the ones that did, some had already removed it or were considering its removal; others felt that it would in no way prevent white students from applying to the institution.[69]

Quotations from the member college presidents supporting the UNCF message that black colleges welcomed all students were used in publicity pieces to potential donors and to the white press. For example, one president said: "Our faculty, without any known exception, favors the admission of students of any race. In our catalogue of 1951–52, we inserted a positive invitation to students of other races, calling attention to our charter provisions."[70] Another president noted, "Our faculty and members of the administration are in accord with the action taken by the Board and we are conscious of an obligation to help our students, our alumni and the general public understand the implications of integration and find the best means of properly implementing that principle."[71] Again, despite the fact that these private black colleges were not segregated by law, in most cases, because of the horrors of Jim Crow, they felt compelled to act as segregated institutions until the post-*Brown* era. Similar information sent to the black press did not place such an emphasis on modifying original college charters.[72]

Statements from the member college presidents, which likewise showed their support of both the UNCF and the *Brown* decision, and their willingness to work to make the transition to integration a success were important to the UNCF leadership's fund-raising plan. The UNCF Annual Meeting in New York City included donors, potential donors, member college presidents, national campaign directors, and many influential philanthropists. During his 1955 address Benjamin Mays, president of Morehouse College, emphasized the fact that black colleges had a long tradition of accepting whites, albeit in small numbers.

The vast majority of these colleges were interracial in origin. De-voted[,] competent, saintly church people, imbued with a sense of mission, graduates of the best colleges and universities in the land[,] left their comfortable environments of the North, went into the heart of the South and founded Hampton, Virginia Union, Bennett, Fisk, the Atlanta group, Talladega, and the rest. They lived with the Negro students and taught them with great affection and love. They saw their students not as sons and daughters of slaves but as human beings of intrinsic value, wor-thy of respect and a chance to develop to the status of full grown men and women. The faculties soon became integrated and these institutions have never lost their interracial character.[73]

In referring to the interracial character of private black colleges, Mays was, for the most part, pointing to the presence of white fac-ulty and administrators on black college campuses. As I mentioned earlier in this book, white missionaries, instrumental in the found-ing of many private black colleges, typically remained at the institu-tions for many years as teachers and administrators, and there was a tradition of educators from liberal white denominations (for example, Congregationalists or Quakers) coming to teach at black colleges. Mays's message was used over and over in speeches and in the official UNCF publicity.[74]

Many people in the North especially were unaware of the inte-grated past of black colleges; presenting the history in a way that showed racial cooperation was an effective strategy for garnering funds. President Mays also offered black colleges as potential meet-ing places for the discussion of integration strategies. According to Mays, this had been a traditional role for many member colleges. "When churches were closed to interracial gatherings, . . . it was on the campuses of *these* colleges that Negroes and White people of good will and prophetic insights met to discuss their common prob-lems and to lay foundations which helped to pave the way for the momentous decision of May 17, 1954."[75] For example, at Fisk Uni-versity in Nashville, Tennessee, sociologist Charles S. Johnson held

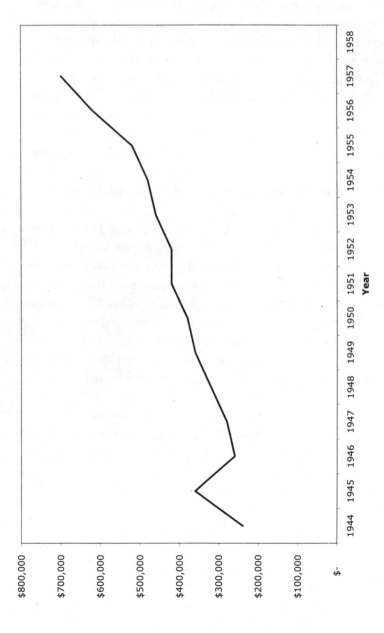

UNCF Source of Funds, Corporations, 1944–1958

internationally known race relations institutes to bring together intellectuals, government leaders, civil rights activists, and community members to find practical solutions to the nation's race problems.[76] The Supreme Court's decision set in motion the process that would eventually remove the stigma from the kind of integrated activities already taking place on these campuses. Luther H. Foster, president of Virginia State College, speaking in support of the UNCF colleges, wrote, "A college is a community force for good. The location of the UNCF institutions throughout the South has helped create an atmosphere of understanding and goodwill among all the people. It is often these UNCF colleges which have provided the only type of community contact between two groups [races] which have many aspirations in common."[77]

The Impact of the *Brown* Decision on Donor Perceptions

In June 1954, Lindsley Kimball conducted "polls" with contributing corporations to discern whether the *Brown* decision would change their giving patterns. Kimball found that "most of [those] consulted to date have expressed the belief that the decision in no way lessens the responsibilities of the colleges. Most have agreed that these institutions face an even greater opportunity for the future, and that the need for strengthening them, has, if anything[,] increased."[78] Kimball's poll was accurate in its assessment. After the Court's ruling, corporate support of the UNCF increased at a faster pace (see figure on p. 104).[79] Explaining the way corporations responded to the *Brown* decision, future UNCF president Stephen J. Wright, who was president of Bluefield State University at the time, noted that "corporate giving tends to be sophisticated. . . . They tend to see beyond the moment and put their emphasis on the long range impact of what they are doing and why."[80]

In the wake of *Brown*, however, individual donations declined. This reduction in support may have been a direct result of the *Brown* decision. Many white Americans "believed that the desire of black Americans to attend white colleges, as indicated by fierce opposition to segregation [on the part of blacks] in education, proved that there was no reason for maintaining existing black institutions."[81] In fact, according to Paul Younger, a UNCF fund-raising consultant, "The reaction to the Supreme Court decision . . . of many potential donors to the capital fund reflected doubt over the permanence of the member colleges. Many indicated a reluctance to make a capital investment in a group of institutions whose future, in their minds[,] was not clear."[82] Some individual donors wrote to the Fund asking that their names be removed from mailing lists; they noted that black colleges were no longer needed "now that the colleges have been integrated."[83] In the words of one longtime UNCF donor, "hallelujah, it's all over, and there isn't any need for black colleges . . . it's going to be just great." During this time, the UNCF was in the middle of a capital funds campaign, which had begun in 1951. Doubts about black colleges' future led to diminished returns, and the UNCF closed down the campaign early, raising only $15 million instead of the anticipated $25 million.[84]

In a statement made on behalf of the UNCF, Hollis F. Price, president of LeMoyne College in Memphis, Tennessee, noted, "It is of extreme importance that the present Negro colleges be improved and strengthened that they may become equal of any college."[85] Morehouse College president Benjamin Mays concurred that black colleges needed continued and additional support because of the demand that would be put on them in future years. In his opinion, it was a "foolish notion" to think that white students would not want to attend black colleges: "If the Negro institutions are first rate, white students will matriculate. If a Negro speaker is first rate the white people will hear him and invite him to speak. If the Negro physician is outstanding, white people will use him. If a Negro bank is first rate, white people will invest their money in it. If a Negro restaurant is first class, white people will eat in it. If a Negro College meets the standard of excellence set by regional rating boards, students will enroll there."[86] This faith in the willingness of whites to accept the accomplishments of black citizens on their own merits seemed to contradict the experience of UNCF member college leadership as expressed in some of their other statements. After all, many black college leaders, including William J. Trent Jr., noted that segregation would continue to exist for an "indefinite period."[87] If whites were truly interested in hearing a "Negro speaker," being healed by a "Negro physician," and depositing their money in a "Negro bank," why would the process of desegregation be so painfully slow?

In fact, other aspects of the fund-raising appeals did not emphasize the image of integrated campuses. Although John Lewis, president of Morris Brown College, suggested that the fund-raising solicitations be slanted away from racial identification and moved to a more regional affiliation, the Fund leadership chose not to follow that suggestion. Instead, publicity showed well-groomed *black* students at well-manicured colleges in need of building funds.[88]

The UNCF had difficulty maintaining some support from foundations, including the Ford Foundation. Shortly after the *Brown* decision, there was a distinct feeling that the leaders of the Ford Foundation were "trying to kill" the UNCF.[89] The Ford Foundation, as well as the Rockefeller Brothers Foundation, conducted independent studies during the late 1950s that attempted to gauge the future of black colleges over the next twenty years.[90] Based on this research, some foundation leaders surmised, off the record, that black colleges would not be around in the coming years. Although these foundation leaders, with the exception of Ford, did not make any public statements alluding to this idea, they did refrain from giving money for new buildings to black colleges during the early years after *Brown*.[91] The Ford Foundation, however, went even further by refusing to give money to the UNCF.[92] Although Benjamin Mays would not name specific individuals, he noted that "it was the opinion of certain Ford Foundation leaders that to support the black colleges was perpetuating segregation" and that liquidating the UNCF, the life line of the colleges, would help the cause of desegregation. Mays himself went to talk to the head of the foundation, Franklin Thomas, in 1955: "I went down to see him . . . and urged this man to get the Ford Foundation to make a significant contribution, and he would not do it."[93] Despite its refusal to back the

UNCF, the Ford Foundation did come to the aid of a few black colleges, including Atlanta University, Fisk, and Dillard. Most likely, these institutions were seen as having the potential to recruit white students, and thus, most likely to integrate.[94] In addition, leaders of the Ford Foundation believed that it was best to concentrate funding on those institutions with the greatest capacity—that is, those that were the strongest.[95]

Convincing New York City and the Nation

After multiple parties throughout the country voiced their skepticism about the value of maintaining black colleges, the UNCF member colleges and the New York leadership decided to stage a spectacular public event to rally support to their cause. The most important place in the country to target, in the Fund's opinion, was New York City because most of the money was raised there. According to Fund Secretary Betty Stebman, the Fund needed

> to do something that would make front page news in New York, that would really get across to the people in New York to make them understand that this was not an end but a beginning; that the colleges in the United Negro College Fund had never themselves discriminated but had been discriminated against and that the opportunity now was for them to open their doors, as their charters permitted them to, and to take white students without being afraid that they would lose their tax exemption . . . this was a moment in history when the private Negro colleges could fulfill their true mission as good institutions capable of educating the people in the community who came to them, black and white.[96]

Stebman took her idea to William Trent and C. D. Jackson, the chairman of the men's committee and publisher of *Fortune* magazine. The well-connected Jackson served as President Eisenhower's special assistant in the White House and as a delegate to the United

Nations. Stebman wanted the women's and men's committees to work together in an effort to make a "stir in the city," and she asked Jackson if he would consider being the chairman of this initiative. He gladly agreed.

The hardworking UNCF secretary began planning the event immediately; she rented the old Metropolitan Opera House, which seated 3,700, for an event to be held Sunday, March 20, 1955. Originally the UNCF invited President Eisenhower to be the keynote speaker, but he declined. Instead, they secured John Foster Dulles, the secretary of state. Although Dulles was the main attraction of the event, Benjamin Mays would also be on the agenda, and, according to Betty Stebman, just as at the past symposiums, he would be "the guy that they would remember when they left."[97]

Although the Women's Division itself had more than ten thousand names on its mailing list, the UNCF staff thought they would have a difficult time filling the 3,700 seats and thus decided to offer the boxes in the opera house to various groups throughout the city, including the Girl Scouts, the National Council of Negro Women, the National Council of Jewish Women, and Riverside Church. In exchange for a free opera box, Stebman asked the organizations to send invitations to their memberships, which greatly expanded the UNCF's potential donor base. As a consequence, the Fund filled all the opera house seats.

The event, which was meant to "show off" the UNCF presidents to New York City, began with a Friday morning greeting from New York's Mayor Robert Wagner to all of the presidents. Afterward Columbia University hosted a luncheon in its faculty club for the UNCF presidents, which was also attended by leaders of elite colleges in the region, including Yale, the University of Pennsylvania, and Princeton. Of course, the social stigma attached to integrated events would have made such a gathering very unlikely prior to 1954. After lunch the UNCF presidents went to the United Nations where they were briefed by a group of dignitaries, including the United States Committee for the United Nations. In the evening the presidents participated in a reception hosted by the secretary general of the United Nations, Dag Hammarskjöld of Sweden. The next day, the presidents were guests of the New York Public Library for lunch. This event was followed by a dinner at the Cosmopolitan Club dedicated to the alumni associations of all the member colleges. Black leaders being invited to a meal at that exclusive club was another breakthrough made possible by integration.

On Sunday morning, as was traditional before all of the other UNCF convocations, the presidents spoke at churches all over the city. Their sermons were featured on television and radio programs. And in the wake of the *Brown* decision, Mrs. Waddell's wish was fulfilled: members of the Women's Division were finally allowed to serve as hostesses for integrated dinners. On Sunday evening prior to the event at the Metropolitan Opera House, the UNCF arranged for "a hundred dinner parties that took place all over town." The members of the Women's Division served as hostesses for the dinners, which were "approved" in the new "legally desegregated" nation.[98] The evening included performances by the Tuskegee choir and Leontyne Price, the African American opera singer, as well as the speeches by John Foster Dulles and Benjamin E. Mays.[99] The UNCF handily achieved its goal of getting national press coverage for the UNCF. Both the *New York Times* and the *Herald-Tribune* ran front page stories on the event. In addition, all the local television and radio programs featured excerpts from the evening.[100]

Prior to the event, Betty Stebman briefed President Mays on the importance of his speech: "Dr. Mays, the future of the United Negro College Fund rests with you. This is a moment when this country needs to hear from us that the Supreme Court decision does not mean the end of the private Negro colleges. It means a whole new life for them. And you have got that responsibility. You've got to explain it to the people who are sitting in the Metropolitan Opera House and for the press that will be there that will be covering the story and across the nation. It's all in your hands."[101] Mays' speech was a huge success. He told his audience that "the American ideal of equality of opportunity for all of the people has taken on a new meaning" and further explained that the nation's black colleges

Benjamin Mays, 1965. Used with permission from the United Negro College Fund, Fairfax, Virginia.

would be instrumental in realizing that new meaning. Mays pointed out that "custom made them segregated institutions, but they have *never* been segregating institutions." Thus, the Supreme Court's decision allowed the black colleges to include all people, black and white, among their students just as it allowed the country's traditionally white institutions to now accept black applicants for admission. [102]

Moreover, Mays defined the need for black colleges in the nation's efforts to bring blacks up to speed (in many ways foreshadowing Affirmative Action): "As wonderful as the decision of the Supreme Court is, it cannot remove the fact that at present, and unfortunately for a long time to come the Negro people will be a disadvantaged economic group. This will be true long after every vestige of legal segregation has disappeared from the American scene. Whether in the North where no legal segregation exists or in the South where it does exist, the economic status of Negroes is far below that of white people."[103] Mays was correct in his assertion. As of 1950, according to the Department of Commerce, the median income for a white family in the United States was $3,445, as compared to blacks at $1,869. Thus, the average African American family had an annual income of 46 percent less than that of a white family. After discussing the dire situation that blacks faced, Mays ended on a jubilant note, foretelling the future of black colleges in the most idealistic of ways:

> Finally, it will be a great tribute to American democracy when a future historian writes that between 1854 and 1900 scores of private church colleges were established mainly to educate the sons and daughters of slaves but by a certain year in the twentieth century America had abolished all forms of segregation based on race and color and that these colleges formerly founded for Negroes had made so great an imprint on American life and were so adequate when segregation was abolished that students from the four corners of the earth, irrespective of race, were studying within their walls. It will be an exciting and thrilling story. *Where else could it happen? Nowhere—except in these United States.*[104]

Mays' prediction remained simply speculative. White Americans did not see beyond the stigma of inferiority the nation placed on black colleges, and as a result only limited numbers of white students ever enrolled in black colleges, public or private. Those who did so enrolled mainly because of convenient location or low tuition (for example, West Virginia State, Lincoln University in Missouri, and Bluefield State University).[105]

Recruiting Whites Becomes Difficult

Immediately after the *Brown* decision, the UNCF effectively persuaded donors that more money was needed to attract white students and to build the infrastructure of the member colleges. However, the actual recruitment of white students was not as easy as the Fund had stated it would be.[106] The problems exceeded the mere willingness of member colleges to accept white students. Whites faced community pressure and negative attitudes toward the black colleges, thereby creating resistance among potential white applicants. For example, a 1954 National Education Association study found that in Pennsylvania only one out of 47,000 prospective white high school graduates listed a black college as a choice for collegiate education, despite the presence of Lincoln and Cheney, two centrally located black colleges in the state.[107] Likewise, a scholarship effort completed in 1954 by the National Scholarship Service resulted in only six white high school graduates who wanted to attend black colleges, even with ample scholarship support.[108]

In 1956, the Rockefeller-affiliated staff of the UNCF in New York became concerned about the integration problems of its member colleges. In a discussion with William J. Trent Jr., Rockefeller associate Yorke Allen Jr. discovered that fifteen white students attended Fisk University in Nashville, the largest number of white students attending a UNCF college. The majority of these students were women from Ohio and Pennsylvania; not one was from Tennessee. Among the non-UNCF public black colleges that served blacks, the most thoroughly integrated institution was West Virginia State College near Charleston.[109] In the academic year 1956–1957, this institution was 50 percent white and had a faculty with 10 percent white members. However, the integration at West Virginia State reflected primarily geographical factors. West Virginia's flagship institution, West Virginia University, was located on the other side of the state. Many white students who lived near West Virginia State preferred not to travel a long distance to college. By 1956, the enrollment of West Virginia State had increased from 600 to 1,200 students; of these, 600 were white.[110] Psychologist and Howard University dean Charles H. Thompson was not optimistic about the integration of black colleges overall, and in 1959 he wrote in the *Journal of Educational Sociology*:

Despite the possibilities which this example [West Virginia State] suggests, it does not seem likely that the majority of Negro colleges will have large white enrollment in the immediate future. And there are several reasons which may account for this; one of the most important being the unwillingness of most white students to face "the stigma attached to pioneering against a taboo." Moreover in several states, even when there has been some desegregation of the white state universities, white state officials have definitely frowned upon, and in some cases, actually forbidden, the acceptance of white students by the Negro state colleges. As for the Negro private colleges, most of them are located in the deep South where little or no desegregation has taken place in anything.[111]

What if more black colleges had seriously pursued the goal of integration?[112] The Fisk University example provides some insight into this scenario. The atmosphere at Fisk in Nashville, Tennessee, during the tenure of Charles S. Johnson was unique. The fact that Fisk was able to attract more white and international students and faculty during this period was the direct result of Johnson's twenty-year effort to establish the institution as a national presence (for example, Fisk was the only black college with a chapter of Phi Beta Kappa). Johnson used foundation monies not only to subsidize basic education for the Fisk students, but also to establish nationally recognized programs in sociology, art, and mathematics which attracted both white and black students.

Implausible Suggestions, Real Possibilities

Although it was true that white students shied away from attending the UNCF colleges, it was also true that the member colleges never fully pursued white enrollment. To launch a successful appeal to a white constituency, the black colleges would have had to abandon much of what made them unique. On the surface the UNCF leadership seemed to agree about the direction of black colleges immediately after *Brown*; however, the goals set forth in that period were obviously contradictory. Before the *Brown* decision, the UNCF typically presented black colleges as the best way to educate blacks in the South.[113] The *Brown* opinion, however, held that segregated institutions were inherently unequal. Some people interpreted segregated as meaning "all black" because the "harm" done to black children in the *Brown* case took place at segregated "all black" schools.[114] Thus, it became difficult to claim that black colleges were still the best method by which to educate black students. To justify their continued existence, black colleges had to provide another argument, and integration's probable slow pace fulfilled this need. It was desirable for blacks to attend predominantly white institutions, but prejudice might in the short run prevent their enrollment. But what about the long-term future of black colleges? How would they appeal to donors to support their endowments? The official position stated that they would become integrated institutions.

As mentioned, the idea that whites would flock to black colleges was implausible in a world where integration, especially in the South, was so controversial. Were the UNCF college presidents hopelessly naive when making statements about the future integration of black colleges? Had they accepted passively the idea that their colleges would simply dissolve into the mainstream in order to continue? After spending many years building institutions that served the specific financial, social, and intellectual needs of blacks, these suggestions are unlikely. A more plausible explanation is that the black college leadership put forth statements about white enrollment as a fund-raising strategy more than an actual prediction of future enrollment patterns. By once again adhering to a "double consciousness" to make sense to white donors, the UNCF leaders emphasized complete agreement with the idea of totally integrated institutions. The UNCF presidents could not logically claim that segregation was a terrible blight on the black population and simultaneously say that permanently separated black colleges provided a beneficial learning

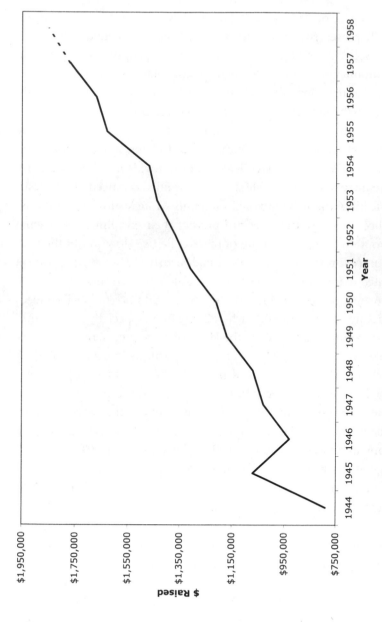

UNCF Annual Campaign Results, 1944–1958

environment. To remedy this rhetorical quandary UNCF college administrators stated that the blackness of the UNCF colleges was a temporary, but necessary, condition during a transitional period.

The blackness of these institutions was not, however, temporary; but this did not prevent the UNCF from significantly increasing its fund-raising proceeds during the years following *Brown* (see figure on p. 116).[115] Perhaps Howard professor Charles H. Thompson described the key to black colleges' success in a post-*Brown* era best:

> I make this observation primarily to emphasize, that if the Negro college in pursuit of its objectives has developed any unique values, they should not be lost in the transformation from a segregated to a desegregated institution. In making this observation, I hope that no one will misunderstand me as saying, or even implying, that the segregated Negro college *per se* should be preserved. What I am saying is, that there should be values that have been developed in or by this institution during the past 90 or 95 years, which should be just as important in a racially-integrated college as in a segregated one.[116]

Because the UNCF leadership and member college presidents could not simultaneously support both this idea and that of integration, they relied on a practiced strategy: crafting a message that was slightly different from their real intentions. If, during the pre-*Brown* era, the Fund's true interest had always been in realizing Du Bois and Johnson's ideas of the black college, they couched the reason for their existence as simply fulfilling the educational needs of blacks within a segregated society. This rationale was the only one that many white donors accepted. Similarly, the UNCF responded to the *Brown* decision by claiming that black colleges would serve their regions as part of mainstream higher education, but black college leaders meanwhile continued to believe that the black college was and would remain a unique place that should be preserved.

A bolder statement in favor of black colleges was finally expressed as the 1950s came to a close. Newly installed UNCF president Benjamin E. Mays made clear that UNCF colleges did not exist merely to fill in a gap created by the process of desegregation, but he argued that they were important in their own right. At a UNCF fund-raising banquet with a mostly white audience, Mays stated: "I can read your mind. . . . You are silently asking me, are we not perpetuating segregation when we support the UNCF colleges? I answer with a resounding 'no.' We believe that our true worth to America has never been adequately appraised. We are convinced that the private Negro colleges have done more to foster good human relations in the nation, and especially in the South, and have built more permanent bridges of interracial good will than any other agency in our nation."[117] Although this part of the Mays' speech contained some of the same themes as previous UNCF fund-raising rhetoric (for example, touting the black colleges as interracial meeting places), it was devoid of any suggestion that the black college would dissolve. Mays continued, "I am still reading your minds. You are asking me, what will happen to these colleges when segregation goes? The future of these 33 colleges will be the same as the future of the segregated white colleges in the South. When Emory University, Duke, Tulane, Vanderbilt, Agnes Scott and the other segregated white colleges cease to segregate they will continue as unsegregated colleges; so will it be with the 33 colleges that make up the United Negro College Fund. They will be desegregated."[118]

For the first time, a UNCF speech mentioned white colleges by name. Significantly, Mays used the word *segregated* three times in connection with these colleges; he stressed that the segregated nature of these elite, private, southern institutions is not a fact of law, but the sole responsibility of each institution. And, in a reciprocal challenge, Mays contended that black colleges would join the mainstream only at such time as the rest of society allowed. In other words, white society, not black colleges, held the keys to desegregation.

CHAPTER 5

Responding to the Black Consciousness Movement

With the passage of the 1964 Civil Rights Act and the 1965 Voting Rights Act, the Civil Rights Movement reached a peak, and momentum toward integration was gaining. Yet at the same time, enrollment at black colleges, both public and private, was also reaching record levels; one hundred thousand black students were attending college.[1] The changes brought by civil rights legislation offered relief to many Americans but sparked anger in others; the changing nation was tense. Riots took place in the Watts area of Los Angeles and in several other cities throughout the country, and Malcolm X, the symbol of Black Nationalism, was assassinated. At the same time, an increased sense of black consciousness among young African Americans led to an upsurge of racial pride and increased willingness to challenge status quo relations.[2]

Patricia Gurin, Edgar Epps, and Steve Biko described black consciousness as the idea that blackness is not just pigmentation but a self-concept that defines one as black. Blackness is a consciousness of being part of an oppressed group and an understanding of how white power is used against blacks living in a "colonized" world. With this realization comes a sense of empowerment that leads one to rise up and fight against oppression.[3] According to Joy Williamson, "students at [black colleges] across the South entered the Civil Rights Movement and inaugurated a period of sustained mass activism in 1960. Their brand of activism broke with the past and shifted civil rights agitation from the courts to the streets."[4] In response to the changes taking place on black college campuses, the United Negro College Fund departed from its rather conservative public stance to embrace a more black-centered style of fundraising and become much more activist in its approach to representing black colleges as a whole. However, this reaction did not come immediately; the UNCF first grappled with an appropriate response to the protest activities during the Civil Rights era.[5]

Activism on Black College Campuses

Beginning in the late 1950s, African Americans on black college campuses began to listen more closely to national and world politics; they took notice of their role in making change throughout the country. This increased awareness led many of them to challenge the status quo and contradict Jim Crow. At Howard University, where students were once labeled "Black Anglo-Saxons" by former Howard professor Nathan Hare, they began to identify with fellow blacks of other socioeconomic strata in the struggle against racism. For example, students in the Non-violent Action Group participated in sit-ins in segregated restaurants and picketed on campus to protest the exclusion of Negro workers by Jim Crow unions on a University construction job.[6] According to Charles U. Smith, White southerners regarded this "change" in the black students as an "unexpected break with traditional patterns of 'good racial relations.'"[7] Sociologist Daniel C. Thompson claims that the "white power structure instantly demanded that these colleges should reaffirm control over their students by severely disciplining those who had been recalcitrant in regard to local racial patterns." At this point, black college leaders began to see "the end of their long-established neutrality in their local communities."[8]

The U.S. Cold War efforts, and particularly its goal of preventing Soviet inroads into the developing world, set the stage for the Civil Rights Movement to succeed.[9] The existence of discriminating laws in the South became an increasingly awkward situation for U.S. presidents during the Cold War as they sought to uphold the nation's standing as leader of the free world, and this public stance hastened segregation's demise. Numerous scholars have pointed to the confrontations in Birmingham as the quintessential example of how the Civil Rights Movement seized the world stage at a critical point in history. As the world reacted in horror to Bull Conner's dogs and fire hoses, the United States was forced to act on behalf of the protesters or risk tipping the balance of world opinion toward the Soviet Union.[10]

Overall, students on black college campuses during the 1960s knew that the United States was in need of radical change and sought a truly integrated society.[11] Moreover, these same students, imbued with a sense of racial pride, felt able to overcome obstacles and face hardships. According to one black college student interviewed by Patricia Gurin and Edgar Epps during the late 1960s, racial pride meant "being a part of a group that has enormous determination and courage—nobody can miss that and I wouldn't trade places with anyone."[12] Regarding the increased level of black consciousness, another student said: "Yes, it's exciting to look around you and see all these blacks, even tenant farmers and people who have a real reason to fear repression, stand up for their rights—I always knew we were courageous people but it means something special to have the world stand back and take note."[13]

This new sense of self among black students, along with an awareness of their place in national and international politics, led students to call for a greater voice in campus governance at black colleges. Students wanted to "decolonize Black colleges, to make them truly relevant for Black people."[14] Early protests at black colleges, such as those in the 1920s at Fisk, Howard, and Florida A & M, were focused on students' treatment under southern segregation. However, these later protesters saw themselves as participating in a larger struggle against colonization.[15] The students, who believed that black people ought to control their own educational institutions, "translated their broad concerns about political nationalism into a desire to determine educational policies of Black colleges."[16] These changes manifested themselves in many ways on black college campuses. Students asked for the dismissal of conservative faculty members, disrupted lectures by invited guests, called for amnesty for protest participants, and demanded that the dean of students be a student advocate, not a hired arm of the administration.[17]

Students at public black colleges, repressed by state governments, led many civil rights–era protest activities, but those students at the private UNCF member colleges also participated.[18] For example, students from both Shaw University and Tuskegee Institute pushed for black studies programs, protested against segregated facilities, and encouraged the presence of the Black Panthers, which inevitably prompted student uprisings owing to the more radical approach of the Panthers. Specifically, on the Tuskegee campus, students formed the Tuskegee Institute Advancement League (TIAL) to show their interest in "civil rights, freedom and equality, and dignity and justice."[19] TIAL played an important role in student demonstrating against local businesses, organizing with national boycotts, and lobbying for legislative activities in the nation's capital.

The six affiliated black colleges in Atlanta—all members of the United Negro College Fund—also boasted students who were dedicated to peaceful protest and racial change.[20] With the backing of their institutional presidents in 1960, the students drafted a manifesto, "An Appeal for Human Rights," which called for the abolishment of injustice in Atlanta. Although they specifically targeted local issues, the title suggested a sense of connection to worldwide concerns. This appeal ran as a paid advertisement in the *Atlanta Journal-Constitution*.[21]

Also in 1960, students, including John Lewis and Diane Nash from Fisk University, sat at lunch counters throughout Nashville, Tennessee, requesting service and refusing to give up their seats until forced to by police.[22] Fisk president Stephen Wright recalled of this incident, "One [Friday] I had driven to Tuskegee . . . to do the speech for the Southeastern Regional Alumni Association of Fisk University, which met on the Tuskegee campus, and as I started off the platform President Foster handed me a note—a telegram—that said that 57 Fisk University students were in jail, including some 20-odd women, and it was signed by my Dean of Students."[23] Wright left on a bus that evening, and the next morning he prepared comment for the media and called a student assembly for one o'clock the same day. He wanted to head off the inaccuracies sure to be conjured up by the local white community. In one of the strongest statements of support yet by a Black college president on behalf of student protestors, Wright said, "the Fisk University students were all being reared and educated on the great scriptures of American Democracy, and . . . no one should be surprised or astonished that they are seeking to exercise them . . . as long as they conducted themselves peaceably in their demonstration I [have] no present intention of asking them to discontinue their efforts. In the meantime, I [expect] responsible protection of them from the police in the City of Nashville."[24]

Gathered for the assembly was the Nashville media along with students from Tennessee State, Meharry Medical College, the American Baptist Theological Seminary, and Fisk. They filled the entire chapel on the Fisk campus including the choir loft, applauding profusely upon hearing Wright stand up to Nashville's white community. According to Wright, until the signing of the 1964 Civil Rights Act, there were Fisk students in jail almost every week. Although there were a few occasions when Wright had to tell the students, including John Lewis, "you can't go down today [to protest]," he never had any "basic disagreements with the kids" on their efforts to fight for desegregation.[25]

Taking a Position on Protest

What was the United Negro College Fund doing to respond while activists were protesting throughout the South and garnering national news coverage? Black college protests, making some UNCF donors and potential donors uneasy, caused mixed feelings at the Fund. Donors who did not want their names linked with growing civil rights agitation put pressure on the UNCF to monitor the situation at its member colleges.[26] This kind of donor response was not atypical among black organizations and, in fact, organizations such as the National Association for the Advancement of Colored People (NAACP), the National Urban League (NUL), and the Southern Regional Council (SRC) all experienced fluctuating donations during this time.[27] However, the UNCF was a direct funding link to the very black colleges that were educating the "agitators." In a statement that reveals his inability to acknowledge the humanity of those less privileged than he, Lindsley Kimball commented on this era at the UNCF:

> Certainly, a lot of people blamed the uprising on having educated Blacks. When they lived in a hovel and didn't have any money they had no way of protesting. These colleges have helped to contribute to all of this. That was tied in with the influx of Blacks from the rural south to the cities. That had an effect on the colleges that nobody has appraised. The Black who lived in a windy hovel along the Mississippi . . . they don't have any outlook, they don't have any future. They're very peaceful, even among themselves because they squat there and want to die almost. You get them in a city and they see life all around them, automobiles whizzing by, and they want some of this. They want a part in it. That affects both favorably and negatively the colleges and their campaigns. So Civil Rights couldn't have gotten off its feet without the colleges but all the same they made it more difficult to raise money.[28]

Of course, Kimball's statement did not especially credit black consciousness; instead, he blamed civil rights agitation on the desire for material status. His statement represented the typical white viewpoint: to view the protests as questing for justice for blacks would likewise acknowledge white injustice against blacks.

In responding to the activities of the Civil Rights Movement and the corresponding surge in black consciousness, the UNCF tried to "balance its sole mission of raising funds for the black colleges with its sympathy for the objectives of the civil rights movement."[29] The organization's responses appeared in several different venues, including reaction statements, official UNCF publicity, and the UNCF administration's public speeches. These responses showed a progression from timidness and adherence to the status quo to a full-blown embrace of the ideas embodied in the black consciousness movement.

In 1963 the UNCF issued a statement explaining its stance on civil rights protest to its donors and the media. Under pressure from past donors to publicly state its position on the Civil Rights Movement's protest activities, UNCF Executive Director William J. Trent Jr. proclaimed:

> The Fund is an agency of its thirty-two member colleges organized by them to raise funds for current and special purposes . . . Its program is to raise ever increasing funds so that the colleges might do two important things:
>
> 1. Educate an increasing number of *responsible Negro leaders.*
> 2. Provide the *trained manpower* to take advantage of the rapidly increasing job opportunities in industry and government.
>
> On the central question of segregation and discrimination in American life, there is complete unanimity on the part of all of the member colleges of the Fund that these have no place in American life and must be rapidly done away with. On the matter of direct involvement in the current crisis, each college, through its administration and trustees, follows its respective desired course of action.[30]

The statement is quite restrained and in some respects conservative. Phrases such as "responsible Negro leaders" and "trained manpower" referenced a historical discussion of black education that accommodated segregation. Whites believed black leaders were "responsible" if they declined to argue against the status quo.

"Trained manpower" made reference to industrial education—the kind favored at one time by both Booker T. Washington and white industrial philanthropists. Together, these phrases suggested a submissive role for educated blacks: to be well-enough educated to find a place in the southern economy (and therefore avoid the problems created by poverty) but not so well educated as to demand political autonomy. By its implicit reference to past discourses, this phrasing addressed the widespread fear of whites: the black menace was kept in check only by education.[31]

Like previous UNCF material, however, the statement offered a dual interpretation, depending upon the reader. The black reader clung to hope with phrases like "complete unanimity" and "segregation and discrimination . . . must be rapidly done away with." But the statement offered white donors a cautionary tale as well by effectively disavowing any unanimous action to uproot segregation and discrimination: "each college, through its administration and trustees, follows its respective desired course of action." Overall, the statement's labyrinthine twists and turns (bouncing rapidly between black and white perspectives) are intelligible through the lens of Jim Crow–era race relations, which allowed for the creation of black-centered institutions only through the use of smoke-and-mirror deceptions. During this time, according to Lindsley Kimball, "you used to hear they're getting too much education, more than they can swallow, more than we want them to be educated."[32]

Initially, donors to the UNCF and other black organizations were hesitant about connections to the Civil Rights Movement, and donations diminished. Over time, however, financial contributions leveled off and, in fact, increased substantially by the mid-1960s. For example, at the UNCF, donations increased from $2,004,191 in 1960 to $4,016,495 in 1966.[33] The 1966 figure actually doubled the donations of 1960. In its upward path, the trend at the UNCF resembled the fund-raising performance of the NAACP and the National Urban League. For example, the NAACP raised $103,838 in 1960, and, although it experienced a slight dip during the time of the lunch counter sit-ins, the organization raised $597,425 in 1966.

Likewise, the National Urban League generated $257,000 in funds in 1960, experienced no dip, and, by 1966, brought in an enormous $2,201,000 in outside sources.[34]

According to sociologist Herbert H. Haines, "a portion of the nation's corporate elite recognized that it had a crucial interest in pacifying the black population, particularly in the volatile cities, and in accommodating certain manageable black demands."[35] Lindsley Kimball believed that it was easy to convince corporations to support the UNCF colleges because "they could all see that you had to have leadership if you didn't want a mob."[36] Historian David Garrow claims that whites supported the Civil Rights Movement's more moderate groups, such as the NAACP and the Urban League, "at the expense of those [groups] that were the more 'radical' cutting edge of the southern movement."[37] In fact, the "radical" behavior of black power groups actually aided more moderate groups in raising funds. In Garrow's words, these radical organizations "deserve credit for the sudden and very substantial increase in foundation support of 'responsible' black organizations." As Garrow notes, wealthy individuals and foundations had "clear 'social control' motives" in their support of black organizations during the 1960s.[38]

Fund-raising during the Black Consciousness Movement

In 1966, at the age of 72, Benjamin E. Mays retired from his post at the UNCF and made way for the next generation of African American leaders at the helm of the organization. Stephen J. Wright was a logical choice as Mays' successor during this turbulent time; Wright had considerable experience with civil rights protest and had served as president of both Fisk and Bluefield State. Wright held the post from 1966 to 1969, a time of great change for the organization.[39]

During Wright's tenure, the UNCF put forth a series of mixed fund-raising messages: one foot remained in the old approach to fund-raising, and one foot stepped in a newer, more assertive direction. For example, a 1967 brochure, "Advance Guard of a New Generation," included much business language and appealed to a cor-

Stephen J. Wright, 1954. Used with permission from the W. E. Herbert Collection, College Archives, G. Hardway Library, Bluefield State College, Bluefield, West Virginia.

porate audience. However, for the first time the brochure asked potential contributors to take a stand for equality: "If truly equal educational opportunities were available today, there would be a threefold increase in Negro college enrollment. By contributing to the Fund, you will be acting *directly and purposefully* to help overcome these existing disparities."[40]

Although the UNCF maintained its emphasis on industry, the organization changed its description of blacks from "industrious" to "intelligent."[41] One brochure, "We've Got a Goldmine Here," emphasized the academic and professional achievements of black college students noting, "UNCF colleges produce more than half of the nation's black elected officials today, 85% of our black doctors[,] and 75% of America's young black men and women now working for advanced degrees have come from these colleges. Some 40% of the students attending them will go on for graduate degrees. And among our 130,000 alumni there are mayors, judges, diplomats, col-

lege presidents, corporate officers, scholars, and government officials."[42] With this brochure, the UNCF made no apologies for its support of thinking black students and emphasized the education of
black leaders—a position advocated decades earlier by W. E. B. Du
Bois. Further along, the text reminded the potential donor of what
was to come if black colleges were not supported: "Without these
colleges, thousands of young blacks would have no alternative but
alienation, rebellion, and despair."[43] Although this message spoke
to white fears of a black menace on one level, it simultaneously and
directly addressed black fears of white control as well; the black
response to the lack of opportunities was simply human.

It is important to note that the UNCF did not support the violent
forms of activism that occurred between 1964 and 1970. According
to Stephen Wright,

> When I was President of the Fund, a different kind of activism
> began to develop at these colleges, like locking up boards of
> trustees, setting a torch to some buildings. I thought that an
> important enough development to ask the group to come to-
> gether and meet, and I handled it this way. I asked those presi-
> dents who had gone through this business to give a factual
> statement of what the situation was and how they handled the
> situation, and then to second-guess themselves on how they
> would have handled it had they had an opportunity to do it all
> over again, for the benefit of the presidents who had *not* expe-
> rienced it.[44]

According to Wright, when he was president of Fisk, no one ever
said a disrespectful word to him: "In a way I was a hero to the Fisk
youngsters during the civil rights fight, and not a target of their
wrath about anything."[45] Because of his fairness in approaching students, Wright was seen, not as part of the problem, but as an ally in
the fight against southern racism. However, after 1964 students grew
frustrated with any complacency—either real or assumed—they saw

on the part of black college presidents, who worked with students as they aimed to "decolonize" their campuses.[46] Wright described the general situation:

> It was a very different kind of tenor. . . . My guess is had I been there, since I tended to run a tight ship, I would probably have been the victim of as many things as anybody else was, so I am not exempting myself, as I wasn't running an institution at the time that this occurred. But I spoke on a number of campuses where it did occur. At Lane for example they burned down a science building and in that burning down they burned up a priceless microscope collection that went back to Leeuwenhoek, and I said in the commencement address that I did down there [as President of the UNCF] that they had committed, as far as I was concerned, an unforgivable sin.[47]

Such violent actions followed the union of the remaining members of the Student Nonviolent Coordinating Committee (SNCC) with the newly formed Black Panther Party. In their opinion the Black Panthers sought a bolder stance than previous civil rights leaders had displayed against racial oppression and the war in Vietnam. During his visits to campuses throughout the country during the mid-1960s, Stokely Carmichael, the leader of the Panthers, urged black college students to challenge the passive traditions of black college administrators. Students who embraced the idea of "Black power" were no longer willing to endure jailings and physical attacks by the police.[48] For example, in 1967, on the campus of Memphis's LeMoyne-Owen College, Martin Luther King Jr. offered support to the sanitation workers' march. One student group, The Invaders, "had a philosophy that nothing could change anything in society but violence, and they broke up Martin Luther King's first march."[49] Moreover, in the fall of 1968, not long after King's assassination, The Invaders took over the administration building with the goal of "freeing" it. Hollis Price, LeMoyne-Owen's president, commented on the events:

I went up to the building that they had taken over, and they were in there with guns and all kinds of weapons and things. My first reaction was, well, now it's up to me to protect this building, because they'll wreck this building overnight. So I just went in there. . . . I spent the night in there talking to them. They stayed, and we had a meeting around 9 o'clock, the next morning and they got out. . . . The interesting thing was that the police were up the street just a block from the school, massed up there waiting for me to call them in to put the Invaders out. . . . Now generally speaking in our community the general attitude toward the police [was] not that they are there to protect us, but to beat our heads, and if I had called those police on in there somebody might have been killed.[50]

President Price never learned the real reason why The Invaders tried to "free" the building. It was enough that this kind of activity was happening throughout the country, and his students wanted to be part of it.[51]

According to Albert Manley, president of Atlanta's Spelman College, leading a women's college was particularly tricky during this time: "in my situation, I perhaps had even additional problems, because here were girls from different parts of the country who had been sheltered and protected at home. And all of a sudden, they were in jail. And some of those jails were ill kept and poorly supervised. You didn't know whether they were going to get raped or what was going to happen to them."[52] Although at times the situation at Spelman was quite intense, Manley never tried to talk the students out of their pursuits against injustice: "I never tried to stop them. But I would meet with them. And I emphasized the great need to be non-violent and to be very careful."[53] Manley recalled a particular incident:

I remember the day when the tension on the campus reached its highest level. It was the day Martin Luther King, Jr. was assassinated. Lester Maddox was governor. The students had decided that they were going to march on the state capitol. We didn't know what was going to happen, what kind of hell would break loose, because they were bringing Martin Luther King's body from Memphis back to Atlanta that evening. And they were rioting and rioting all over the country. What was going to happen to Atlanta—not only Atlanta—but the family wanted Martin's body to lie in state in Sisters Chapel on the Spelman campus. We approved without delay the family's request. The students wanted to march on the Capitol. Lester Maddox . . . had called out the State Militia, and its members, many of whom were in an ugly mood, had surrounded the Capitol. The presidents decided to dissuade the students from marching on the Capitol. After a lengthy talk with the student leaders it was agreed that the heads of the six institutions would march with the students; a route limited to Southwest Atlanta would be followed; and the march would end at the Morehouse gymnasium where President Emeritus Benjamin E. Mays would address the group. These activities were carried out as planned and there was no riot in Atlanta.[54]

In retrospect, according to Manley, the presidents of the Atlanta colleges were skillful in their handling of a potentially dangerous situation. In the process, there was "never any major conflict between the presidents and students. The students knew they had the support of the presidents."[55]

As noted, under Wright's presidency of the UNCF, acts of violence at the member colleges were not tolerated. However, Wright did not instruct the member college presidents about their personal responses to protests and violence; Wright merely talked about these issues when asked to visit individual colleges and on occasion at general UNCF events. According to Benjamin Mays, reacting to activities during the Civil Rights Movement was a question for the "individual head of the institution and not the College Fund itself." "Nobody could tell him [the college president] what to do. It was an individual affair"[56] LeMoyne-Owen president Hollis Price concurred; he noted the "great upheaval in the colleges," but that did not translate into general UNCF policies for dealing with these incidents on the member college campuses.[57] This position was consistent with the mission of the Fund—a loosely organized consortium of individual institutions rather than a centralized agency governing black colleges as a single unit.

New Leadership: Enter Vernon Jordan

Because of a difference of opinion with white advertising tycoon David Ogilvy, the chairman of the still mostly white board of directors of the UNCF, Steven Wright left the Fund in 1969. According to Wright,

> David Ogilvy and I had differences of opinion on people to hire, people who had to be responsible to me. You can't have someone—or at least I will not tolerate any person who reports administratively to me who also feels free to report to the chairman of the board. I can't direct his duties and responsibilities and evaluate that person properly with that kind of interference. . . . I don't think that a chairman of the board ought to be involved in choosing the personnel that's going to work with you if you are going to be the chief administrative officer. . . . I made it very clear [to him].[58]

Wright was insistent upon ending the "Rockefeller-type" outside control from wealthy whites over the Fund's daily activities, but at this point he could not win the fight. Ogilvy, given other business interests, left the UNCF shortly after Wright's departure. This point in the Fund's history marked a watershed moment for the organization. From its outset the UNCF, albeit a black organization representing black colleges, was heavily controlled by wealthy whites. Beginning in the 1970s, the UNCF became more independent. However, the organization maintained its close connection to corporate America, which continued to provide a large share of its funding.

Vernon Jordan, 1970. Used with permission from the United Negro College Fund, Fairfax, Virginia.

Vernon Jordan joined the UNCF as president in 1970. The board members saw him as young, energetic, and willing to fight for a cause. A graduate of Howard University law school and protégé of Thurgood Marshall, Jordan came to the position with experience as a civil rights leader and attorney. He served as the Georgia field director of the NAACP and director of Voter Education at the Southern Regional Council. In the words of subsequent UNCF directors, including Christopher Edley and William Gray III, Jordan transformed the UNCF from a "mom-and-pop" operation controlled by a few white philanthropists into a nationally recognized fund-raising organization, both imitated and applauded.

Upon his arrival, Jordan did much to change the language and images that had become standards for the Fund, which by this time

134

represented thirty-six colleges. In a publicity piece, "A Rationale for Corporate Investment in the Thirty-Six Member Colleges and Universities of the United Negro College Fund," Vernon Jordan appealed to businessmen and asked them to broaden their constituency to include "those black people who cry out today, not for freedom and equality but for a crust of bread and a morsel of meat. Those little black children who cry out not for Black Power but for medicine for their festering sores and protection from the rats and roaches."[59] By describing extreme poverty and resulting social unrest in stomach-turning detail, Jordan forced corporate leaders to imagine themselves in the dire situation of a black person without education. Jordan's approach was particularly poignant: he showed whites a world from a black point of view. Jordan's message turned out to be more powerful than the raised fist of black power: Black consciousness is black power. His nuanced statement depicted the suffering of blacks, not as a simple appeal but as a pointed indictment. The accusatory tone noted that black living conditions were so bad that they did not have time to think about political rights; they focused on basic survival.

In 1970, the UNCF began to expand its role from that of a mere fund-raiser to a more active agent of social progress. The UNCF leadership's speeches moved beyond asking for funds to discussing social change and the crucial role of black colleges in this change. Jordan saw the UNCF as "a means of transforming lives."[60] Even the white UNCF board chairman Morris B. Abram, recruited by Jordan, spoke out in favor of black colleges' role in fostering a sense of black consciousness.[61] Abram, who had been general counsel of the Peace Corps under the Kennedy administration, delivered a provocative speech that recognized the shift within the UNCF:

American liberals, and I include myself in this group, have been slow to recognize the need for black institutional power. Yet, as we review the civil rights revolution of the past decade and a half, it is clear that the sparks to essential reform—the lunch counter sit-ins and boycotts of Greensboro, Atlanta, and Birmingham—might have been many more years in the making had it not been for the consciousness developing in black institutions across the South. Black awareness, the pride of black men in their heritage and accomplishments, is essential to the development of effective black leadership. And nowhere is this sense of self better nurtured than in the UNCF colleges.[62]

This statement foretold a new approach and a new look in UNCF publicity. Morris Abram's comments acknowledged that the Fund had entered an era in which the administration was not hiding evidence of black colleges' role in developing a unique sense of self-consciousness.

Vernon Jordan made the Fund's message even clearer by proclaiming unequivocal acceptance of black consciousness and carefully disavowing separatism. He forcefully commented on issues of black power and black consciousness during a speech before the NAACP:

It must be made clear to black and white alike in this land that black power, black consciousness, and black awareness and black institutions, are not incompatible with an open, integrated society. Nor do they mean black separation, which I unequivocally reject. For me, DuBois [sic] points the way with these words: "One ever feels his twoness—an American and a Negro; two souls, two thoughts, two unreconciled strivings; two [warring] ideals, and one dark body, whose dogged strength keeps it from being torn asunder. The history of the American Negro is the history of this strife—this longing to attain self-conscious manhood, to merge his double self into a better and truer self. [. . .] For he simply wishes to make it possible for a man to be both Negro and American."[63]

Although this speech was given for a black audience, Jordan was just as vehement when speaking in front of a room filled with white foundation executives. In fact, he chastised those foundations that did not speak out in support of civil rights and scolded them for never taking "part in this crucial arena for change."[64] Jordan took his criticism a step further and rebuked foundations that backed down when confronted by white conservative critics of their policies toward black education: "Today, I sense more caution, less initiative, and a generally more rigid attitude in some corners of the foundation world. Many foundations have been besieged by critics, both from without and from within, urging a de-emphasis of social concerns. Partly to counter this, black foundation executives have created an Association of Black Foundation Executives that has formally called for greatly increased foundation activity in helping to resolve problems afflicting blacks and the cities."[65]

Jordan's words were a turning point for the UNCF. No longer willing to submit to the agenda of white corporations, the contemporary role and message of the Fund challenged the status quo, held donors responsible, and brought to the fore the social ills of the United States. Jordan's words foreshadowed a new, more black-conscious UNCF.

CHAPTER 6

Speaking Out on Behalf of Black Colleges

As a result of the stigma placed on all-black environments in the post-*Brown* era (that is, in a time when all-black necessarily equaled inferior), during the mid- to late 1960s, scholars and foundation officials placed black colleges under a microscope. Instead of passively accepting this white scrutiny and the white influence within the UNCF chain of command, the UNCF's black leaders assumed positions of greater authority. The leaders' actions in this regard manifested themselves in several incidents: one was a response to the Ford Foundation's continuing bias against the UNCF and against black colleges in general. Another was the UNCF's involvement in studies of black colleges conducted with foundation support. In the mid-1960s, the Carnegie Foundation sponsored two studies, one by Earl J. McGrath and one by Christopher Jencks and David Riesman. Although the McGrath study was generally well received by the UNCF and some college presidents commended McGrath for his evenhanded approach, the Jencks and Riesman study was a stinging indictment of the institutions. The Jencks and Riesman study struck a severe blow to black colleges and the UNCF, but its publication, widely covered in the media, provided an opportunity for UNCF presidents to unite in a challenge against their harshest critics. The response to Jencks and Riesman was a turning point in the UNCF's evolution from a corporate fund-raising wing of industrial philanthropy to a spokesperson and promoter of black college interests.

The Shift toward Greater Agency

An early example of this change in agency among the black leaders of the Fund took place in 1962, under William Trent Jr.'s leadership, when the member college presidents used their connection with John F. Kennedy to twist the arm of the Ford Foundation. As noted earlier, throughout the 1950s Ford exhibited a marked anti–black college bias. The UNCF took a stand against the Ford Foundation during its early 1960s $100-million capital campaign. When the time came to publicly announce the campaign, the member college presidents wanted to have the backing of a prominent American, so they approached President John F. Kennedy, who had been sensitive to some African American needs and initiatives. Kennedy's attitude toward the Fund was considerably more sympathetic than Eisenhower's, who regularly declined to participate in UNCF events. Kennedy had been somewhat active in his support of African Americans in the past, including helping to free Martin Luther King Jr. from jail in 1960 and offering rhetorical support of civil rights.[1] However, even with Kennedy's support the UNCF tended to undersell its member colleges' needs.

According to Stephen Wright, president of Fisk University at the time and one of the dignitaries assigned to meet with Kennedy,

A committee of [UNCF] presidents . . . went to see Kennedy to ask him for his personal endorsement of this . . . we drafted the letter then went to him as a group, and I still remember he read it—the two pages of it—almost at a glance, because he was a speed reader, and we were so sure that he hadn't read it, and weren't sure until he began to ask us pinpoint detailed questions about what it said, because we were thinking in terms of 100 million for a variety of reasons, but that he would give his endorsement to 50, that he would call together some of America's major corporate leaders for a White House luncheon, and help launch it, which he did.[2]

Luther Foster (Tuskegee Institute), Benjamin E. Mays (Morehouse College), William Trent Jr. (UNCF), and Albert Dent (Dillard University) with President John F. Kennedy at the White House. Kennedy took an interest in the UNCF beyond the level of his Oval Office predecessors. Meeting at White House, l. to r., Luther Foster (Tuskegee Institute), Benjamin Mays (Morehouse College), William Trent Jr., Albert Dent (Dillard University), and President John F. Kennedy, 1962. Used with permission from the United Negro College Fund, Fairfax, Virginia.

Although Wright figured that Kennedy was accustomed to raising large amounts of money and thus knew the limits of the UNCF's abilities, in a 1987 interview Benjamin Mays attributed the scaled-down figure to the unwillingness of the country to put full support behind black colleges: "Even with the prestige of President John F. Kennedy behind the effort, the President of the thirty-three United Negro College Fund colleges could not get anyone to head a drive to raise a hundred million dollars for all of these colleges. The goal we had to accept was fifty million, and we raised only thirty million. The University of Chicago recently raised a hundred and sixty million dollars in three years. The Negro is truly the invisible man."[3]

Lindsley Kimball affirmed Mays' view of the attitudes of whites toward giving to black colleges:

I think they [whites] gave too little but that's part of the way they were used to doing. In other words, sure, we give $100,000 to Yale or Harvard but we'll give maybe $5,000 to the College Fund and that's about right. They were brought up that way and you can't change over night. There again I blame that on historical necessity. In other words, before you had the College Fund, when the presidents had to go it alone, they were used to taking nickels and dimes. They were not used to asking for big amounts of money. Therefore nobody was ready to give big amounts. They thought these Negro people will be very happy on peanuts. They weren't very happy but they were living on peanuts.[4]

Despite Kimball's description of the actions of whites, he placed little if any blame on prejudice or racial superiority; instead, he blamed the African Americans for their fate because they sold themselves short. Throughout the Fund's early history, in fact, the black leadership disagreed with the white leadership over the amount of money to be raised. However, according to Patterson, the black staff members were not the cause of this: "We did find in a few instances that we were not even able to attract the big money people, because they said, you're not asking for enough money. We knew we weren't asking for enough, but our dilemma was trying to harmonize the fact that we weren't asking for enough with the fact that we had to carry along [white] leadership, and leadership does not like campaigns that fail. And so they held our goal down."[5] Regardless, in F. D. Patterson's opinion, President Kennedy's support "went beyond what most Presidents do." He donated all the proceeds from his Pulitzer Prize–winning book *Profiles in Courage* (first published in 1956) to the Fund and held the campaign kick-off at the White House. According to Patterson, having the President's support was crucial: "the President will not endorse, it's my general impression, a program that is not in the interest of the general welfare, and his endorsement is really a recommendation to the nation."[6]

However, Kennedy's support of the Fund was resented as overly heavy pressure by at least one potential donor. Shortly after the start of the campaign, Frederick D. Patterson followed up on a lead with the Ford Foundation, which Kennedy had originated. Henry T. Heald, the head of the foundation, did not appreciate the UNCF's bold approach. Patterson described his conversation with Heald:

> He [Heald] became angry when Kennedy asked him. . . . he said, "Well, you didn't have to hit us over the head with the President of the United States." I said, "well, I've been in here before and nothing has happened." . . . I said, "we didn't go to the President of the United States to appeal to the Ford Foundation. That was his initiative to come to you. We went to him because we felt that this was a cause in the national interest and that nobody better than the President of the United States could bespeak that fact." And so Ford gave fifteen million dollars.[7]

Kennedy's influence on the Ford Foundation was profound. For example, the former president of Ford Motor Company, which in the 1960s still had substantial representation on the Ford Foundation board, was Robert McNamara, who served as secretary of defense during the Kennedy administration. With his connections, the young President could easily pick up the phone and persuade one of the most powerful foundations in the world to back the UNCF. The black leadership of the Fund knew of Kennedy's influence and used it to their advantage. This incident is one of the first times that the African American leadership was able to use its contacts in the white community to shape the actions of white philanthropists. Rather than being in the role of subservience to a foundation's direction and ideas, the Fund leadership began to conduct business on its own terms. In many ways, this incident and those that follow were setting up the future success of the Fund and paving the way especially for the fearless "A Mind Is a Terrible Thing to Waste" campaign.

The Carnegie Foundation–Sponsored McGrath Study

During the mid-twentieth century several concerned parties began to question the kind of education offered at black colleges.[8] Most prominent among these were the Ford, Carnegie, and the Rockefeller Brothers foundations. These organizations were interested in gauging the colleges' quality so that they could either justify continued support or rationalize reduced assistance. Although most constituents of black colleges knew disparities existed between black and white institutions in the type of education offered, no "scientific" evidence demonstrated these inequalities.[9] Among the most important of these studies was Earl J. McGrath's Carnegie-sponsored book, *The Predominantly Negro Colleges and Universities in Transition*, published in 1965. Two years earlier, the Carnegie Foundation asked McGrath to conduct the study; subsequently it made a grant to the Columbia University's Institute of Higher Education where McGrath was employed as a researcher. In preparing the study, McGrath was guided by the advice and expertise of both Stephen J. Wright and Frederick D. Patterson. He pointed out the weaknesses among black colleges but set them in context. McGrath noted that many similar conditions existed at predominantly white institutions of similar size, endowment, and operating budget.[10]

According to Benjamin E. Mays, president of Morehouse College, "there was a study done of black colleges whose methodology I think was unquestionable. This is the McGrath study of the black colleges by the title of *Negro Colleges in Transition*."[11] McGrath studied and collected data on faculty and administration, curriculum, physical plants, support services, students, and financial viability. His method included survey research and qualitative interviews via campus visits.[12] Partly because of his rigorous methods and willing-

143

ness to consult with members of the black college community, including many of the member college presidents, McGrath produced an evenhanded study. Nevertheless, McGrath's report did point to areas of weakness among black colleges—a fact that the researcher thought would aid in their improvement. In summarizing his report, McGrath noted:

> To be sure, this type of general approach which often results in the portrayal of general features rather than catalogues of individual institutional characteristics has some disadvantages. Since in many features of institutional life the averages fall below those for the colleges and universities of the nation at large, some may feel that the figures do an injustice to the better institutions, or even to all of them. This position rests on an assumption of questionable validity; namely, that if the weaknesses of some are exposed all will be commensurately depreciated and some or all of the Negro colleges will unfairly lose prospective additional financial and moral support.[13]

McGrath, believing that his report would have positive results, optimistically noted "that the revelation of the weaknesses of some and the needs of all will generally swell the flow of new support."[14] When pointing to these institutions' shortcomings, he was especially careful not to compare them to white institutions in different categories by, for example, comparing small and impecunious Dillard University to large and wealthy Harvard. In the foreword to his book McGrath wrote, "As the report repeatedly states, on any measure of faculty competence, library facilities, salaries, physical equipment, and a host of other characteristics, the predominantly Negro institutions run the entire gamut from the highest to the lowest. When compared with the predominantly white colleges they can be matched institution by institution."[15] McGrath also pointed to the problems in the way that many see black colleges "the concept of excellence can be realized, not by the application of the negative philosophy of casting out all those who do not come up to elitist standards—and this view appears to be gaining popularity among many American educators."[16] Yet, the staid and fair-minded tone of McGrath's report attracted the attention of neither policymakers nor the media.

The Carnegie Foundation–Sponsored Jencks and Riesman Study

In the winter of 1967 the *Harvard Educational Review* published "The American Negro College," written by Christopher Jencks and David Riesman.[17] Because of the prestige of the journal and the institutional affiliation of the authors (both were professors at Harvard), the article received much attention in both the academic community and the popular press (*Time, Newsweek,* and the *New York Times*). In its severe criticism of the black colleges, the article described them as "academic disaster areas." Within the black college community there was a sense of shock, dismay, and betrayal.[18] These sensations were evident in the United Negro College Fund's response to the article in a subsequent issue of *Harvard Educational Review.*[19] In 1967, the UNCF president Stephen Wright and the member college presidents took their boldest step yet, in an attempt to carve out an image of black colleges that was defined by African Americans rather than wealthy, elite whites.

During the exposure of the Jencks and Riesman article, many of the nation's leading newspapers were running stories related to black colleges. For example, in January 1966 the *New York Times* ran a series of articles—"Integrating the Negro Colleges," "Negro Colleges Recruit Whites," and "The Negro College Pleas for Donations."[20] Curiously, national newspaper articles focused on the recruitment of whites and the financial problems of black colleges, but they largely ignored the positive changes taking place on the campuses. Jencks and Riesman used a similar approach; when they began their research work in 1965, they focused on the problems and virtually ignored the successes of black colleges, their leaders, and students.

The Harvard-based authors started their research on black colleges as part of a larger book project with chapters devoted to each of the major groups of institutions; this project was eventually published as *The Academic Revolution*. Jencks, although quite young, was an editor for *The New Republic*. Riesman, already considered an eminent sociologist, had recently written *The Lonely Crowd*, which was on the *New York Times* bestseller list and is still considered one of the most influential books of the twentieth century.[21] Earlier, in 1956, Riesman had written *Constraint and Variety in American Education*, a volume that described a hierarchy among types of colleges and universities and the corresponding competition within this hierarchy.

Commenting on how they came to the idea for the black college article, and with a perspective that indicates a post-*Brown* bias against black colleges, Jencks said, "David Riesman had visited a few Black colleges and I had visited one or two of them. And the logic of the book if you were writing it in the mid-1960s was that you needed to pay attention to these institutions. The United States was going to integrate white higher education so it would also need to do something *about* historically black colleges [author's emphasis]."[22] Through its continuing earlier interest in the state of black colleges and perhaps because the sponsor was not satisfied with the results of the McGrath study, the Carnegie Foundation provided funding to Jencks and Riesman.[23] In the "The American Negro College," the Harvard sociologists attempted to identify the problems faced by these institutions and made predictions for their future.[24] Specifically, Jencks recalled, "The goal was to describe what was going on, to understand the evolution of these institutions, and to discover what kind of dilemmas they faced." Moreover, in a later statement indicating that he had a sense of the importance of the black college research, Jencks said, "[We aimed] to tell someone who knew nothing about black colleges, which was about 97% of the population, how to be thinking about them."[25]

Jencks and Riesman's opening statements in the *Harvard Educational Review* article seemed to anticipate the racial conflict that the publication was likely to spur. The authors began with a caveat that justified the article's harsh tone and preemptively dismissed charges of racism:

> Few who write about the conditions of American Negro life can entirely escape the racist assumptions which are so much a part of American culture. This applies to Negroes as well as Whites. Nor can such writers escape the fact that oppression corrupts the oppressed as well as the oppressors. Many features of Negro life are extremely ugly, and are made no more beautiful by the knowledge that they are by-products of White prejudice. Since racists use such ugliness to justify continued segregation and paternalism, writers who provide them with ammunition are bound to look like racists to many readers. . . . Nonetheless, it seems important to try to describe what we have seen as honestly as we can rather than trying to pretend that we have not seen it at all.[26]

"The American Negro College" opened with an historical overview of the development of African American society in the United States and the subsequent need for and establishment of black colleges. Jencks and Riesman did justice to the complicated political situation that blacks faced during the early to mid-twentieth century by placing most of their emphasis on the gaps in income, education level, and employment status as compared to the majority community, including the immigrant populations of the time.

In their discussion of philanthropy's involvement in the establishment of black colleges, the Harvard sociologists sided with conservative scholars, noting that "rather than assuming a Machiavellian plot to support 'Uncle Toms' like Booker T. Washington against 'militants' like W. E. B. Du Bois, we would argue that the Northern whites who backed private colleges for Negroes were moved by genuinely philanthropic motives."[27] Jencks and Riesman believed that northern whites saw no conflict between their own personal monetary gain and the gain of blacks.

In their discussion of contemporary black colleges, they relied on several sources for their data: miscellaneous interviews with a few black college faculty (black, white, and Asian American faculty), surveys, statistical data, government documents, and published books and articles. In fact, Jencks and Riesman's explanation of their methodology was quite vague and fell short of the standards of most academic research—a point they conceded in their later statements. Their unsystematic acquisition of data relied on impression and intuition far more than is typically allowed for a scholarly article. Often the authors wrote several pages without citing either any relevant literature or even their own data sources. By contrast, researchers Patricia Gurin and Edgar Epps, who wrote about black higher education at the same time (and also did not refrain from criticizing black colleges), included a clear explanation of their method and rigorous citations.[28] Likewise, Earl J. McGrath's study clearly indicated the source of the data (interviews conducted by the researcher) and explained the questionnaire used to obtain the data.

Although Jencks and Riesman pointed out that not all black colleges were alike, their explication of the topic neglected to keep this notion in mind. With the exception of the "Negro Ivy League" (Fisk, Spelman, Morehouse, Hampton, Tuskegee, and Dillard), Jencks and Riesman labeled the fifty large, public black colleges and the sixty small private black colleges (the majority of them members of the UNCF) "academic disaster areas."[29] Grand generalized statements like this were typical of the article's language.

Coming to their research with an incomplete set of facts and a deficient understanding of the historical and contemporary issues facing black colleges, the Harvard sociologists often made distorted claims about their subject.[30] For example, in reference to the Civil Rights Movement, Jencks and Riesman stated: "the Negro college campuses have not, with few famous exceptions, been the center of protest in the South, nor have they provided the shock troops for organizations like the Student Non-violent Coordinating Committee."[31] As noted earlier, there were in fact more than a few exceptions, including North Carolina A & T, Shaw, Spelman, Fisk, and Tougaloo colleges. Many UNCF member college presidents knew of these protests firsthand and had supported the expressions. Above all, black colleges had been an incubator for many of the ideas that undergirded the movement. Prior to the 1960s, Fisk University's renowned Race Relations Institutes, for example, gave a forum to Martin Luther King Jr. as well as a variety of international guests who spoke about the growing agitation against colonialism and thereby placed the southern struggles within a wider push for the liberation of oppressed peoples worldwide.[32]

In their explanations for black colleges' deficiencies, Jencks and Riesman followed a trend in research (including the Moynihan Report on the African American family)[33] by generally liberal thinkers who did a disservice to blacks by attributing all of their current problems to the legacy of slavery. This interpretation denied black agency and overlooked black accomplishments since slavery and the oppressive existence of Jim Crow.[34] Such thinking tended to see current black organizations in terms of the slave plantation and explained flawed leadership as "House Negro" or "Uncle Tom" behavior. Thus Jencks and Riesman mischaracterized black colleges as shying away from civil rights protest and black college presidents as "domineering but frightened." While any argument about blacks in U.S. society must take slavery into account, Jencks and Riesman offered only a stifling oversimplification. According to this view, black college administrators were simply protecting the small scraps of power in their possession, just as some "House Negroes" had relished their status over "Field Negroes" on the plantation. Jencks and Riesman saw black society as static, with no role for recent events in the shaping of its history; it was as if the world wars, great migration, Harlem Renaissance, and the Great Depression had never taken place. Moreover, this view ignored the contributions of blacks to their own lives.

In spite of the generally negative portrayal, Jencks and Riesman looked to a future for black colleges and their graduates in their article. Although they thought that black students would be better off at predominantly white institutions, they saw black colleges attracting the children of alumni for years to come—a viewpoint held by the UNCF leadership as well. If the intent was to offer "constructive criticism," however, the authors failed; for the picture of black colleges they had painted by the end of the article was so bleak that it undermined any positive predictions about the institutions' futures.

Responding in the Media

Given the national reputation of both Christopher Jencks and David Riesman, the content of "The American Negro College" was picked up by the popular press, placing the UNCF member college presidents in a difficult situation.[35] In the words of Morehouse president Benjamin E. Mays: "Riesman? Harvard? The *Harvard Educational Review*? [They carry] automatic endorsement for lots of people."[36] Articles in *Time* and the *New York Times* discussed the most scathing comments made by the authors, leaving out most contextual information. *Time*, for example, reported, "Despite the steady increase of Negro students at the nation's major universities, the U.S. still has more than 120 colleges that have a predominantly Negro student population. How good are they? In the current issue of the *Harvard Educational Review*, Sociologist David Riesman and Christopher Jencks, a contributing editor of *The New Republic*, deliver a soberly scathing judgment. The Negro colleges, they argue, constitute an 'academic disaster area.'"[37] The *Time* statement that the United States "still has more than 120" black colleges referenced the widely held view that these institutions were leftovers and no longer needed in a post-*Brown* era. Thus, the article was imbued with negative assumptions about black higher education.[38] Although the *Time* article was careful to note that the "facts" about black colleges were the opinions of Jencks and Riesman, its tone implied that these "facts" were authoritative. Not being an academic publication, the editors of *Time* critiqued neither the data collection methods nor the unsubstantiated claims contained in the Jencks and Riesman article. The news magazine merely reported the findings that were most inflammatory.

Time also quoted Jencks and Riesman's descriptions of black college leaders as "domineering but frightened president[s]" who "tyrannized the faculty." Moreover, according to the article, the two black medical schools (Meharry and Howard) reportedly "rank among the worst in the nation, and would probably have been closed long ago had they not been a main source of doctors willing to tend Negro patients." Summarizing the situation, *Time* noted that according to Jencks and Riesman, black colleges were "an ill-financed, ill-staffed, caricature of white higher education."[39] This coverage essentially popularized Jencks and Riesman's phrase "academic disaster areas" as an overarching description of all black colleges and thus intensified the anger and sense of betrayal felt by the black academic community. Jencks and Riesman themselves thought the *Time* magazine portrayal of their work was an "extremely one-sided summary, which quoted [their] gloomiest judgments."[40] In fact, the Harvard sociologists tried to provide a rebuttal to the *Time* article, but the news magazine refused to publish their "letter of protest." Their rebuttal would not have disavowed the material quoted, but it would have reported a more well-rounded version of their research.[41]

The UNCF Response

According to Christopher Jencks (in a much later interview), "Anyone writing about race at [this] point in history knew that these were sensitive issues."[42] James Coleman's *Equity of Educational Opportunity* and Daniel P. Moynihan's *The Negro Family: A Case for National Action* had just been released to harsh criticism from the black community. The country was in the midst of heated racial dialogue that sparked riots and protest. In response to these issues, black college presidents took a more activist stance.[43] With a new sense of black identity and purpose, these leaders banded together in support of their institutions. Jencks, in fact, was "surprised at the intensity" of the black response to the article. In his words, "I underestimated how rapidly the racial climate was changing in the United States."[44]

Determined to get a more nuanced view of black colleges into the debate taking place throughout both academic and political circles, UNCF president Stephen J. Wright (the same man who was fighting against white interference in the day-to-day operations of the Fund) called together three UNCF member college presidents to craft a response in the academic press. Along with Morehouse president Benjamin E. Mays, Hampton Institute president Hugh Gloster, and Dillard University president Albert W. Dent, Wright drafted a rebuttal to Jencks and Riesman's article and sent it to the *Harvard Educational Review*. The rebuttal, which consisted of individual letters from the four member college presidents, was published alongside a reply from Jencks and Riesman.[45]

Although certain key themes appeared in all of the black college presidents' statements, they each attacked the Jencks and Riesman study on disparate levels and with varying strategies. Some exposed the unfairness of the comparisons made in the article, some questioned Jencks and Riesman's methods and qualifications, some accused the authors of racial bias, and one drew attention to the struggles that black colleges had faced and the value of protecting their future.

Stephen J. Wright wrote the first response on behalf of all black colleges. He began by noting that the article "has had such a shattering effect upon Negro educators and those who support the colleges that it needs to be put in perspective."[46] Not only did Wright spell out the detrimental effect of the article on the black community, but he clarified for the journal's distinguished audience what he termed "four significant facts" about black colleges that "anyone who knows anything about these institutions, should know." Specifically, Wright noted that, in spite of dealing with disadvantage, black colleges produced competent graduates:

1. That they are, with very few exceptions, overwhelmingly *undergraduate* institutions and therefore cannot be seriously compared with universities;
2. That as a group, they have served and continue to serve, with some exceptions, the most culturally deprived college stu-

dents in the nation, which means that their students, in the main, do not enter with "Ivy League" preparation;

3. That with very minor exceptions, they have been, and still are, the *underfinanced* colleges of the nation, with all that this implies;

4. That despite these all but insurmountable handicaps, they have managed, somehow, to develop a very substantial number of Negroes who qualify to teach in the public schools across the nation, who qualify for admission to medical colleges and eventually pass state and national medical examinations, and who qualify for admission to graduate schools of the arts and sciences and earn doctoral degrees and even teach, in modest numbers, in the predominantly white universities—not to mention the Negro colleges.[47]

These "facts" provided a sense of the playing field at black colleges for the reader before he or she began to judge the institutions. Wright pointed out Jencks and Riesman's failure to take into account the historical disadvantages and uniquely challenging mission of black colleges.

Wright then critiqued the very core of the Jencks and Riesman article—the data collection method. Specifically, he charged, that "The article is not a report of a thorough-going scientific investigation. It is rather a reportorial essay, replete with unsupported generalizations, judgments, speculations, impressions, and a good many errors, stated or implied, and written in unscholarly language, i.e., language that makes extensive use of loaded words and phrases which are not adequately defined: 'Uncle Tom,' 'academic disaster areas.'"[48] Wright expanded on his critique: "As a reportorial essay, it reports impressions of what others are alleged to have said, and draws sweeping 'conclusions'—not reasoned judgments based on actual findings—from impressions and anecdotes. In a sense, it is not even good reporting because the authors fail to distinguish in importance between what they themselves have seen, experienced, or researched, and what they were told."[49] Wright proceeded to give many examples of the mistakes and generalizations in the article and also pointed out the most damaging aspect of the piece: it was written by men of great stature and published in a highly reputable journal; if this were not the case, an article so flawed would have received little attention.[50] In fact, Jencks and Riesman's research methods drew the greatest fire from those in the larger academic community who supported black colleges.

In concluding his attack on the methodological approaches, lack of fact checking, and overall arrogance of the Jencks and Riesman article, Stephen J. Wright took his criticism a step further and questioned the very motives of such research. Wright said, "It is difficult for me to understand, without serious question of racist motives on the part of the authors, how responsible scholars could put such damaging impressions in print without evidence, which they freely admit they do not have."[51] Here, Stephen Wright, in effect, criticized the motives of not only Jencks and Riesman but also of the white foundation sponsoring the study.

Like Wright, in his response Benjamin E. Mays was critical of the method used by Jencks and Riesman. However, he focused his assessment on their comparison of black colleges to elite white institutions and the Harvard professors' lack of equal criticism for struggling white colleges. Mays pointedly stated, "When they say, 'In part, the problem is that no Negro college's B.A. carries the same weight as one from Harvard, Oberlin, or Berkeley' (p. 47), they talk like uninformed men. Do they not know that possibly 90 per cent of all white colleges are not in a league with Harvard, Oberlin, and Berkeley?"[52] He then noted the unequal standard to which black colleges were being held: "Two years ago, there were 401 predominantly white colleges in the country too feeble in academic performance to be rated by any one of the six regional accrediting agencies, which places them below the weakest of the accredited Negro colleges. It is strange indeed that no article has been written describing these colleges as areas of 'academic disaster.'"[53]

Mays' comments were similar to those made a few years earlier by

Earl J. McGrath. In an eerily accurate prediction of the unfair comparisons made by Jencks and Riesman in 1967, two years earlier McGrath had not only commented about his own review of black colleges but he also specifically mentioned David Riesman's earlier writing: "Occasionally [educators and laymen] appear to believe that the nation's predominantly Negro colleges make up a small isolated band of institutions at the end of the American academic procession—the procession of colleges and universities that David Riesman has depicted so graphically as a snake-like line, led by experimental avant-garde institutions, followed by a multitude of colleges attempting to keep up with the first, and tapering to a long, trailing line of weaker institutions that form the tail."[54]

Although he pointed to some of the same issues as Stephen J. Wright and Benjamin E. Mays, Hampton Institute president Hugh Gloster took a special interest in exposing the racist assumptions and sense of racial superiority embedded in the article. Specifically, Gloster pointed to Jencks and Riesman's glaring exclusion of any exemplary examples of black college graduates. He exposed the Harvard scholars' obsession with the slave plantation mentality, and their tendency to highlight so-called "Uncle Tom" behavior:

It has been said that the main contribution of Negro Americans to white Americans is a lower socio-economic status that allows the latter group to have smug feelings of racial superiority. Although Jencks and Riesman are knowledgeable enough to understand that Negro disadvantage is a product of white prejudice, they also reveal symptoms of racial complacency. For example, although they do not tell a single success story concerning a Negro student or professional person in a sixty-page article, they do amusedly describe an unidentified Negro dean whose "head often itched when he talked to white men, because as a child he had habitually assumed the 'darky' pose of scratching his head and saying 'Yassir' to white men" (p. 7).[55]

Hence, Gloster explained, the problem with Jencks and Riesman is that their research accentuates the negative and submissive and ignores any examples to the contrary.

Dillard University's Albert W. Dent wrote the last response to the article. Dent, taking a very different approach from Wright, Mays, and Gloster, found an overall positive picture in an article that he claimed the authors filled with "impressions" and "moribund stereo-types."[56] According to Dent, when looked at from a slightly differ-ent and clearer point of view, black colleges had a heroic past; they had persevered in spite of disadvantages and potentially flourished in the face of current criticisms being heaped upon them:

> The real good that can possibly come from this article will de-rive from the fact that it does call dramatic attention to a group of colleges that have too long struggled against almost impos-sible odds to provide an adequate education for several gener-ations of Negroes who were denied education in other colleges. Thus it is hoped that instead of arousing damaging public con-demnation of these institutions, . . . the article will stir fair-minded individuals, philanthropic agencies, and government on all levels to see an opportunity to make a needed, lasting contribution to American higher education.[57]

Dent examined specific points made by Jencks and Riesman and provided the reader with an alternate way of viewing them. He urged the reader to acknowledge the ills of slavery and Jim Crow but to avoid letting the reporting of these ills mask the agency and efforts of black college leaders and black colleges on behalf of their students. For example, he admitted that many black colleges enroll students who might not otherwise be able to attend white institu-tions. However, he informed the reader of the steps that black col-leges were taking to compensate for the skills garnered at "inade-quate high schools."[58] Dent identified the pre-freshman programs at Dillard, Morehouse, and Spelman that had received national at-tention in 1959. These programs were designed to "bridge some

serious academic gaps between an inadequate high school education and the freshman college program."[59] He also pointed to the
federal government's Upward Bound initiative. According to Dent,
as a result of improvements in high school environments and
preparatory programs, "the future of Negro college graduates seems
brighter than ever before."[60]

Closing the UNCF and black college response to Jencks and Riesman were Dent's stinging but forward-thinking comments:

> I would expect a more factual and positive approach to the
> problems of the Negro college than that of scholars like Jencks
> and Riesman. But it may be that what they have written will un-
> derscore what Negro college administrators have insisted upon
> over the years—namely, that with the proper understanding
> and support of the American people, these colleges can make a
> distinct contribution toward establishing and maintaining the
> democratic society to which our nation is committed.[61]

Picking up on the criticisms of Jencks and Riesman by the UNCF
leaders, other scholars likewise attacked the "American Negro Colleges" article. For example, Princeton scholar John Sekora took issue
with Jencks and Riesman's portrayal of black colleges in a peer-
reviewed response in 1968. Augmenting the voices and ideas of the
black leaders, he took specific issue with the tone, method, and "bla-
tant" dismissal of already existing black scholarship. Sekora referred
to Jencks and Riesman's tone as "brittle, reductive, and dehumaniz-
ing," and described their method as using "random, selective impressions to further [their] arguments where no statistics exist."[62] He
pointed to the many scholars who wrote specifically on issues related to black colleges that the Harvard sociologists chose not to
draw upon, including Horace Mann Bond, Carter G. Woodson, Louis
R. Harlan, Charles W. Dabney, and Saunders Redding.[63]

A life-long defender of black accomplishments and author of *The
Art of Slave Narrative*, Sekora was most critical of Jencks and Riesman's portrayal of black college presidents. According to the Prince-

ton scholar, the authors failed to acknowledge both the thoughtful, inspired actions of black college leaders and any evidence to contradict the "Uncle Tom" stereotype they perpetuated.[64] The presidents of private black colleges were particularly activist. They were not under the thumb of southern legislatures and thus were more able to assist their students in civil rights efforts. Specifically, Sekora charged, "they have no room in their purview for the presidents who opened their campuses and even their homes to civil rights meetings. . . . They have no room for those presidents who for years gave half of their meager salaries to the NAACP; or for those presidents and deans who marched alongside their students in the early 1960's."[65] Most important, Sekora upbraided Jencks and Riesman for reporting the "tales of academic horror committed *by* the [black] colleges" but ignoring the "frequency of senseless violence against Negro colleges."[66] For example, in 1961, both Jackson State University and Tougaloo College students were confronted with "blockades, tear gas, billy clubs, and attack dogs" while protesting on behalf of their civil rights. The Mississippi police arrested students, worked with members of the local community to disband their organizations, and enforced stiff rules regarding student conduct.[67]

Also in 1968, a former Harvard colleague of Jencks and Riesman offered his own contrasting view of black colleges. John U. Monro was the former dean of Harvard College "who made headlines when he left a high post at Harvard to take a job at a Negro school in Birmingham [Miles College]."[68] In an interview with *U. S. News & World Report*, Monro, drawing upon a concept introduced by Jencks and Riesman, passionately stated, "The black colleges are moving away from the old ideas that they should be imitative of white colleges. . . . These colleges are trying to become distinctively Negro colleges."[69] When the *U. S. News* reporter asked "In what way?" Monro responded,

One of the problems has been that the Negro-college curriculum hasn't been attentive enough to the needs of black people. I'm just as sure as I can be that there is a black community with special problems, a special outlook, special needs of organizing to develop its institutional strength. But the Negro colleges, until lately, have seen themselves as mainly preparing people to be teachers or preachers, or to get good jobs in a middle-class white situation a thousand miles away. . . . They have offered traditional, adequate, liberal arts curricula—but that will not do anymore.[70]

More important and more to the advantage of black colleges, Monro described the institutions as "centers of black power"—not in the sense of militant groups, such as the Black Panther movement, but in the sense of "black awareness, black identity, and black pride." In a somewhat radical stance given the situation in the United States at the time, Monro explained for the "average" reader of the news magazine the concepts of white power and white privilege: "It doesn't take you very long, living in the black community, to understand about 'white power.'" Monro's portrayal, though critical of the past situation at black colleges, offered one of the most optimistic predictions for their institutional futures. Given his stature as a former dean at Harvard, the UNCF was able to influence potential donors by referring to Monro's ideas. However, Monro has not had the lasting impact of Jencks and Riesman.[71]

Jencks and Riesman's Response to the UNCF Leaders

Christopher Jencks and David Riesman took advantage of two opportunities to explain themselves and their provocative article. The first appeared side by side in the summer 1967 issue of the *Harvard Educational Review* with the rebuttal of the black college presidents. The second came with the publication of *The Academic Revolution* in 1968. When considered as a whole, their responses addressed the details but not the substance of the accusations against them. Although they diminished the importance of their own work, they later claimed a kind of moral duty to point out glaring problems that others declined to tackle. They admitted to faults, but in such a way as to deride their accusers as being "quibblers." They dodged the blame for generalizations and omissions by attributing them to the larger, racist society and to the black colleges themselves.

Blaming others for exaggerating the significance of their research, Jencks and Riesman began their *Harvard Educational Review* response with an explanation that their article was "not the result of a major research project aimed specifically at Negro colleges." The Harvard sociologists' response in this case leads the reader to wonder why the authors published work that was "not a major research project" in a major education journal. Although the professors never fully answered the question, they did inform the reader that this "chapter" was part of a larger project, *The Academic Revolution*, "which attempts to describe many different sorts of colleges and universities as products of history and current social forces."[72] *The Academic Revolution* actually won the American Council on Education's Borden Prize for Best Book on Education. In a remark difficult to read without inferring a tone of condescension, the authors pointed out that the very inclusion of a chapter on black colleges was a tribute to their increasing importance; they noted that black colleges only required two sentences in their earlier work on the American academic enterprise.[73] Although Jencks and Riesman gave themselves credit for bringing black colleges to the fore, in fact, the activist black scholars of the 1960s and 1970s (those who pushed for black studies programs) and black college presidents were largely responsible for the increased interest in these institutions.[74]

Faced with glaring errors and omissions in their work, as identified by the black college presidents, the sociologists deferred to their black college critics and tried to explain themselves when possible. In reference to the accusation that they focused on "Uncle Tom–like" behavior, Jencks and Riesman responded by splitting hairs; they admitted to incorrect characterizations in some areas but reasserted the basic truth of their claims. For example, when addressing a critique of their comments made about internalized racism and black college beauty queens (that is, that more lighter skinned women won on-campus beauty or homecoming contests), Jencks and Riesman said, "On the color of Negro college beauty queens, we defer to Dr. Wright's judgment. We note, however, that when a girl with a 'natural' hairdo [an Afro] was crowned this year at Howard University, the event was described there as unprecedented."[75] Jencks and Riesman were correct in part; conservatism prevailed on some black college campuses. Black intellectuals, such as E. Franklin Frazier, had pointed out this phenomenon years earlier in his classic *Black Bourgeoisie*.[76] However, Jencks and Riesman failed to talk about these incidents as individual cases, and they did not give credit to those black college presidents and administrators, such as Adam D. Beittel at Tougaloo College and Benjamin E. Mays at Morehouse, both of whom wholeheartedly backed the Civil Rights and black power movements.[77]

With the publication of their comprehensive volume *The Academic Revolution*, Jencks and Riesman had a second opportunity to comment on the reaction to and criticism of their original article and to make changes to the article/chapter itself.[78] This time they had more column space and more time to think about their response. The authors of *The Academic Revolution* began their commentary with a rather apologetic defense of their method, in a seeming response to widespread criticism by both blacks and whites that plagued their book well into the late 1980s.[79] Jencks and Riesman explained their method as "personal rather than impersonal":

[we] visited a number of Negro colleges for relatively short periods, talked to or corresponded with many knowledgeable insiders and outsiders, read the better-known books and articles on the subject as well as some obscure ones, listened to critics who said we were wrong on particular points, and made numerous corrections in response to their objections. Other writers who visited the same colleges, talked to the same informants, and read the same materials might well have come to different conclusions. Yet this does not strike us as a serious objection.[80]

Careful readers, however, were struck by the arrogance of Jencks and Riesman, who continued to pass off casual reporting as academic research. In a recent interview Jencks commented, "Someone once told me that sociology is slow journalism. I would describe what we did in those terms. It was not the kind of social science people do these days—including me. My current work is much more based on quantitative evidence." Looking back, "I would have been more cautious about some of the things we said. I would have made more attempts to document what we saw. However, I am not sure if that would have brought us to different conclusions."[81] Yet the author's explanation does little to deflect UNCF president Stephen Wright's original assertion: that this article is really "fast and loose journalism"; by failing to distinguish between honest impressions and hearsay, it did not rise even to the standards of good reporting, let alone academic research.

Jencks and Riesman also responded to the criticism that their outsider status made them poor candidates to undertake this study. Dismissing the idea of leaving the research to black intellectuals because it is "not our style," the Harvard professors claimed that it was "much harder for a Negro to say these things than for a white to do so." According to Jencks and Riesman, "Whoever says them will, after all, antagonize most of the Negro leadership." On this note, they claimed a kind of *noblesse oblige;* their privileged status obligated them to take on sacred cows that others were afraid to touch. As an example of the hostility potentially felt by blacks critiquing black education, Jencks and Riesman cited E. Franklin Frazier and noted that "few wish to endure the persecution he got after writing *Black Bourgeoisie.*"[82] Unlike their black colleagues, "Whites . . . can afford to make sure enemies."[83] Jencks and Riesman did not acknowledge the fact that other scholars, like Earl J. McGrath, had taken up the mantle of critically examining black colleges without drawing nearly as much fire.[84]

Justifying their research in the face of their critics, Jencks and Riesman stated, "This is a moment when Whites can do no right [in the study of black colleges]: the critics are viewed as traitors and the supporters as gullible fools to be used as best one can. Under such circumstances one might as well forget about winning friends and do what one thinks is right."[85] These comments certainly summarized the incendiary atmosphere of the 1960s, in which race and politics divided college campuses and public discourse at large. Although the two viewed their research as supportive of black colleges, many in the black community saw it as a "betrayal of the cause." The well-placed article and its resulting national media coverage made it harder to raise money and recruit faculty. Benjamin E. Mays summarized the damage: "I think whenever the image of an institution is damaged an impact is made. It isn't always easy—or it's probably never easy—to assess exactly what that impact is, but if it leads to a conclusion that these institutions are not worthy of support or even existence, in the minds of important people it can do damage over a period of time."[86]

Jencks and Riesman, doubting the potential impact of their article, offered yet another insensitive critique: "It is an insignia of the marginality of these colleges that they should assume one article of this kind, written by men who control no resources and have only the most marginal official influence, could seriously affect their future."[87] In making this statement, the authors ignored obvious facts of their situation: they were Harvard professors publishing in a highly respected journal. According to Stephen Wright, when the Jencks and Riesman article was published, he had to answer unending questions from the public: "I remember on one occasion [in 1968] soliciting across the table a 100,000 dollar contribution to the United Negro College Fund, and in that encounter every tough question that I can think of was thrown at me."[88]

In closing their chapter on black colleges, Jencks and Riesman stood behind their method and conclusions but appeared to take ownership for the "abrasive" tone that they used throughout the chapter/article. They admitted that some of the critique regarding their tone was justified: "Oppression corrupts the oppressors as well as the oppressed. Ultimate responsibility for this corruption rests with those who have power, and in the last analysis this means prominent whites." However, the authors were unable to truly reassign the blame. They ended their chapter with a final insult: "Today most of the men who exercise day-to-day power in Negro colleges are Negroes. They may not be morally responsible for their failures, but they are often administratively responsible."[89] With this statement, as noted by Princeton scholar John Sekora, Jencks and Riesman acknowledged the agency of black leaders only in regard to their failures.

Earl J. McGrath's assessment of David Riesman's earlier work was indeed prophetic. Just as the Carnegie researcher had predicted, Christopher Jencks and David Riesman produced a book, *The Academic Revolution*, which had at its core the idea that institutions of higher education could be ordered in a hierarchy whereby those at the bottom try continually and unsuccessfully to imitate those at the top. Such a premise, when applied to black colleges, had an even darker overtone: black colleges, like so many other aspects of black life in America, were pathetic attempts to imitate the white model.[90] Although its authors claimed that the chapter was but one of many in a larger work and held no greater significance, "Negroes and their Colleges," was indeed full of meaning for the black college community.[91] Many UNCF colleges, especially the smaller ones, came away from it labeled "academic disaster areas." This phrase and many of the other comments included in the publication have had a lasting impact; they continue to be used in subsequent research, to be seen as "truth" by well-meaning scholars, and shape the view that both practitioners and scholars hold of black colleges today. For example, in an October 3, 2003, article on racial censorship, conservative black scholar Thomas Sowell wrote, "Today, if you want to read an honest assessment of the black colleges, you have to go back to a 1967 article by Christopher Jencks and the late David Riesman in the *Harvard Educational Review*."[92] Sowell first made this comment in his *Black Education: Myths and Tragedies* (1972), but his reassertion thirty years after its original publication testifies to the longevity and influence of Jencks and Riesman's damaging interpretations.[93] Although the Harvard sociologists' intents may not have been tinged with racism, their lack of collaboration and consultation with black college presidents, disregard of earlier research by African Americans and whites, and failure to anticipate the media's use of their commentary led to a report that was racist in its effect.[94]

Hampton president Hugh Gloster urged Jencks and Riesman to see how their actions reeked of racial superiority. However, it was unlikely that the researchers would change their view of the situation without the black college community coming together to challenge their work. As scholars McGrath, Sekora, and Munro demonstrated, it is imperative that those doing research on black issues have a solid background in black history and culture. With this background, Jencks and Riesman might have had a better understanding of just how a report like theirs would be interpreted. Echoing the sentiment of John Monro, with greater knowledge of black culture, the authors might have understood how "white power" operated in a case like this. In a situation in which the general population possessed little knowledge of a given topic, any information that scholars offered had the potential to be interpreted as truth. This was even more likely when the scholars offering it were from Harvard, whose name for many Americans was (and still is) synonymous with solid rigorous research.

But what of black college president Albert Dent's interpretation of the Jencks and Riesman article? Was it possible for good to come from the publication? Most important, the controversy provided an occasion for the UNCF to provide a collective voice for black colleges. In doing so, the UNCF presidents laid the foundation for an alternative discourse on black colleges—one that was truly rooted in an understanding of the historical and cultural context in which black colleges operated. The ideas set forth by the black college presidents in the wake of Jencks and Riesman's article influenced several studies such as those by Daniel C. Thompson, Charles V. Willie and Ronald Edmonds, Frank Bowles and Frank A. DeCosta, and more recently, Walter Allen, and Henry Drewry and Humphrey Doermann. These later works represent products of collaborative research between scholars and black college practitioners. Significantly, this subsequent research possessed an understanding of the historical and cultural context in which black colleges operated.[95]

Although in 1967 the UNCF took an assertive stance against the meddling of others in their area of expertise, the long-term outcome of the Jencks and Riesman controversy was a draw. To this day, black colleges and the organizations that represent them have not been able to control the discourse on their institutions. The arguments set up in 1967 by Jencks and Riesman continue to be debated today and attract considerable attention from the media, scholars, and policy-makers. The real coup for the UNCF against anti–black college sentiment was to come in the 1970s with the "A Mind Is a Terrible Thing to Waste" campaign. With the combination of increased influence within the white community and a new sense of leadership on the topic of black colleges, the UNCF forged ahead to further define their institutions for the American public.

CHAPTER SEVEN

"A Mind Is a Terrible Thing to Waste"

Launched in the early 1970s to encourage Americans to support the UNCF, the slogan "A Mind Is a Terrible Thing to Waste" has helped generate more than $2 billion for black colleges. The motto, unchanged for more than three decades, has become part of the American vernacular, much like Maxwell House's "Good to the Last Drop" or Nike's "Just Do It!"[1] In fact, many causes unrelated to black education use the phrase to demonstrate the importance of education. But how and why did this slogan originate? The campaign for which it was created was the impetus for collaboration among the UNCF, the Ad Council, and the Young and Rubicam Marketing Company; these entities wanted to establish a lasting image of black colleges, tap into a growing black middle class, and attract a more sympathetic white donor. Much different from earlier UNCF publicity, which depicted a conservative and obedient African American student, the "A Mind Is a Terrible Thing to Waste" campaign was assertive.[2] The campaign asked two fundamental questions: Is anyone's mind of so little value that we should waste it? Shouldn't everyone have the opportunity to learn?[3]

When Vernon Jordan became president of the Fund in 1970, he brought his experience working with the NAACP and the Southern Education Foundation's Voting Rights Project to his position. Under his leadership, the Fund made considerable progress in diminishing white control of the organization and overcoming the "double consciousness" phenomenon in its publicity. Moreover, in his efforts to manage the day-to-day operation of the organization, he brought a self-assured attitude, especially in the way he handled problems of money management and donor relations.

At the time that Jordan took the reins, the Fund was operating at a loss and large donors, including John D. Rockefeller III, threatened to withhold their contributions. Because of his close relationship with white staff members and his family's history of control over UNCF affairs, Rockefeller III was able to gather information about the organization's internal problems, generally unavailable to the average donor.[4] According to Joe Taylor, the national campaign director, the situation with Rockefeller III was difficult but "Vernon was [up] to the task. He knew how to approach it."[5] Jordan went directly to Rockefeller, explained the situation at the UNCF, and discussed how he would rectify it; Rockefeller was not interested. According to Jordan, "He had some ideas that maybe the College Fund ought to go out of business."[6] In taking this stance, Rockefeller III was echoing the two most common post-*Brown* arguments: black colleges were no longer needed in an integrated society, and African American students were successfully entering traditionally white institutions in increasing numbers.[7] Getting an answer of "no" from Rockefeller III, Jordan said, "Fine, . . . I'll do it without you and did."[8] According to Jordan, "I think he [Rockefeller] was mad about the modus operandi of what had happened [mismanagement] and you know, after we showed him that it could be done he accepted the concept. [However,] he just chose not to sit on the board any more."[9] Rockefeller III's resignation from the UNCF board, in many ways, symbolized the fundamental change within the UNCF. The days of white meddling into the day-to-day affairs of the organization had come to an end.

Much of Vernon Jordan's success came from his many professional and social contacts. He was incredibly personable and frequently addressed influential groups throughout the country. At one point, in 1970, he was asked to be the keynote speaker at the New York City Economic Club, described as a group of "about 100 men who run

New York City."[10] Jordan's speech resulted in praise from the *New York Times*. Referring to Jordan's wisdom, the *Times* described him as having "an old head on young shoulders," and in so doing the newspaper provided increased legitimacy to Jordan's cause and leadership of the Fund.[11]

Although the Fund was successfully raising money prior to Jordan's tenure, it was not well-known outside the black intellectual and the white business communities.[12] The UNCF's transformation into a household name was shaped by Jordan's leadership. According to Christopher Edley, Jordan's successor at the Fund, "Vernon had a good friend [Joseph Mehan] in advertising, and with his help, [we were] able to persuade the Advertising Council to take on the College Fund as a client."[13] In reality, securing the "A Mind Is a Terrible Thing to Waste" campaign took a great deal of work and influence; its support by the Ad Council was unprecedented.

To secure the partnership of the Ad Council, Vernon Jordan had to first build up the publicity arm of the UNCF. He recruited Mehan to head a new communications division that replaced the outmoded two-person operation that had supported the Fund for many years.[14] Mehan had worked in journalism for twenty years, mostly as an NBC reporter. He had well-placed contacts in the television and public relations area. After securing Mehan, Jordan retained the services of Young and Rubicam, a well-respected public relations firm. Both additions to the UNCF team aided in the organization's move from small-time fundraiser to major player in American higher education.

After bringing Mehan and Young and Rubicam on board, Vernon Jordan, together with Joseph Taylor, the national campaign director, approached the Ad Council. A nonprofit organization, the Ad Council channeled services from large ad agencies to national causes every year. It has organized some of the most memorable public service campaigns since the early 1940s, including *Rosie the Riveter* (1942), *Smokey the Bear* (1944), and *Keep America Beautiful* (with Iron Eyes Cody in 1973); more recently, the Ad Council directed the *I am an American* campaign, which acknowledged the diversity in the U.S. in the post–September 11 period. The Ad Council was able to mount such campaigns by securing in-kind contributions from within the industry: ad agencies gave free design services to nonprofit clients, and television networks, newspapers, and magazines offered time and space to present the public service messages.[15]

According to Jordan, the UNCF had to argue its case vigorously with the Ad Council to garner its support during the early 1970s because the UNCF was competing with many other worthwhile causes, including the Peace Corps and American Red Cross. The major obstacle was convincing the Ad Council, which had "never in its history taken on a major campaign in the black community," that African American education was of *national* interest.[16] As demonstrated earlier in this book, many in the general public felt that *Brown v. Board* had rendered black colleges unnecessary, especially by the 1970s when most traditionally white institutions were admitting African American students, at least in limited numbers. And, as discussed in chapter 6, critics of black colleges had written extensively on the shortcomings of these institutions (both real and imaginary) in articles that appeared in the late 1960s, which led to questions from those in government, higher education, media, and even the black community.[17] In this atmosphere Jordan and his associates tried to convince the Ad Council that its support would not only aid black colleges but would also strengthen education overall and help bring about equal opportunity. The UNCF had been using this same argument since the eve of the *Brown* decision.[18] After a full day of discussion, the Ad Council agreed, and the "Mind" campaign, according to the UNCF leaders, became the first ad on national television to speak from a black perspective.

The idea of blackness that comes through in the early "Mind" ads is subtle and best seen in the context of previous images of African Americans in the media, especially advertising. Prior to the "Mind" campaign, most Americans were used to seeing stereotypical images of African Americans in advertising, such as Aunt Jemima,[19] Uncle Ben,[20] and Rastus,[21] or in the comedy of black entertainers such as Flip Wilson and Sammy Davis Jr.[22] The first television shows featuring "black" characters or families were *Sugar Hill Times* (1949) and

Amos & Andy (1951 to 1966)—both of which used stereotypes for laughs and presented one-dimensional, white-minded views of blacks.[23] The difference in the early "Mind" campaign was the deadpan seriousness of the ads. The campaign was not designed to battle stereotypes but simply to present a black-minded view of the world.[24]

Joe Taylor, the national campaign director, described the way the UNCF developed the "Mind Is a Terrible Thing to Waste" slogan:

> We sat right up there on that fifth floor [at Young and Rubicam] and argued the whole afternoon on one word. The first thing . . . Young and Rubicam brought . . . us was "A mind is a hell of a thing to waste." Somebody said, we had at that time, too many presidents who were ministers and they would object to the word "hell". Then they went back and came to a mind is "A terrible thing to waste."[25]

At first, the UNCF representatives did not like the use of "terrible" because it seemed to refer to the mind; the "mind isn't a terrible thing, a mind is a good thing."[26] But as the meeting continued, the decision was made to go with the slogan. UNCF leaders' willingness to consider words like "terrible" and "hell" in their ads attests to the seriousness that they wished to convey to the American public: black realities, stark choices.[27]

A Black Mind Is a Terrible Thing to Waste

At the time of the launch of the "Mind" campaign, "graduates from the UNCF member schools represented more than half of all black elected officials in the United States, 75 percent of the country's black Ph.D.s, and 85 percent of the country's black doctors."[28] Moreover, 90 percent of these students were the first in their families to attend college, and 70 percent came from families that had annual incomes of less than $5,000.[29] The colleges were at a crucial point of great impact and needed additional funding.

This UNCF ad was one of several that asked the viewer to consider the lost potential if the United States failed to educate its black citizens. "You Can't Cure Cancer with a Monkey Wrench." 1972. Used with permission from the United Negro College Fund, the Ad Council, and Young & Rubicam.

The UNCF combined print and television advertising to make a media splash in 1971 by placing ads in national newspapers and on the major television stations in addition to placing market specific ads for African American audiences. The first ad (both print and television) featured a young African American male sitting on a chair

in a dark room under the very large heading: A MIND IS A TERRI-
BLE THING TO WASTE. The room was nicely appointed and the
young man casually dressed. The young man seemed to be posing
for a portrait until one realized that he was vanishing, perhaps in an
allusion to Ralph Ellison's *Invisible Man*.[30] The message asks the potential donor to think about what could have been if the student
and others like him had been supported:

People are born every day who could cure disease, make
    peace, create art, abolish injustice, end hunger.
But they'll probably never get a chance to do those things
    without an education.
We're educating over 45,000 students at 40 private, four-year
    colleges every year.
You can help, too. By sending a check for whatever you can
    afford.
We can't afford to waste anybody.[31]

With the exception of the ending, which asks for support of the
UNCF, the text of the ad did not mention blackness directly. Instead,
the ad refers to blackness by subtly asking each viewer to step into
the shoes of a black person. It made a proposition with which almost
everyone would agree—no one should lack the opportunity to
be educated—and then presented a more novel proposition—that
opportunity should include black youth. The ad combined radical
and conventional ideas. First, it alluded to historical racial practices:
it was acceptable to let African Americans go uneducated; it was
acceptable to waste a "Negro." It forced whites to confront their past
actions. But it also asked the viewer to move beyond seeing blackness only and likened the young man to anyone in America who
wanted to pursue an education. Of course, the 1970s espoused the
notion of color blindness: the ideal was to see everyone as equal and
to ignore difference.[32]

A 1972 ad spoke to the lost potential of African Americans, using
the tag line, "You Can't Cure Cancer with a Monkey Wrench."

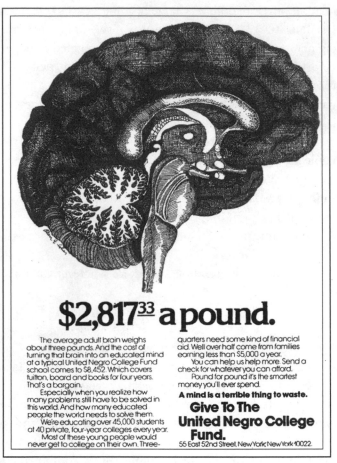

$2,817³³ a pound.

The average adult brain weighs about three pounds. And the cost of turning that brain into an educated mind at a typical United Negro College Fund school comes to $8,452. Which covers tuition, board and books for four years. That's a bargain.

Especially when you realize how many problems still have to be solved in this world. And how many educated people the world needs to solve them.

We're educating over 45,000 students at 40 private, four-year colleges every year.

Most of these young people would never get to college on their own. Three-quarters need some kind of financial aid. Well over half come from families earning less than $5,000 a year.

You can help us help more. Send a check for whatever you can afford.

Pound for pound it's the smartest money you'll ever spend.

A mind is a terrible thing to waste.

Give To The United Negro College Fund.

55 East 52nd Street, New York, New York 10022.

This ad put a price on the African American brain. It is an example of the new bold approach used under Vernon Jordan's leadership. Historically, black bodies were bought and sold on the auction block; according to the ad, one could now support black intelligence and assist African Americans in contributing to the country. "$2817.33 a Pound." 1972. Used with permission from the United Negro College Fund, the Ad Council, and Young & Rubicam.

Using a familiar strategy, the ad drew the potential donor into a scenario and begged him or her to ask "what if?" The visual image conjured up by the ad copy was directed toward those who believed everyone deserves a fair chance in America:

> Down the street from each of us there's a guy fixing cars who could be doing more than fixing cars. You know him. The only mechanic in the place who commented on the book you were carrying. You thought at the time there was a little more to him than most people you meet. But he's the guy who never went to college simply because nobody else in his family ever went. He thought about it. But more as a dream than a possibility. Now his tools are a wrench and a screwdriver and a rag, when they could have been a stethoscope or a computer or a law book.[33]

In many ways, this ad directly links the UNCF to its past, an organization that regularly featured references to industrial education in its publicity and fund-raising materials. However, this new ad alludes to the fact that blacks, black colleges, and the UNCF have moved past industrial education. It is no longer acceptable that training as a mechanic is as far as a black college graduate could go.

Eventually, the "Mind" ads became more direct. For example, some ads also spoke quite literally of the brains of the students at black colleges; for instance, a 1972 ad featured a drawing of a brain alongside the words "$2,817.33 a pound."[34] This ad made a joke, to be sure, but a dark one. It showed the black brain as a commodity, just as black bodies had been seen as a commodity on the slave block. In a sense, the UNCF was reminding people that for hundreds of years, whites had regarded blacks as raw material, and that it was time to envision a future in which blacks were valued for their knowledge.

That this kind of humor was employed is no accident when we consider that leading the UNCF at the time was a man who later titled his autobiography *Vernon Can Read*. This bit of sarcasm refers to a real-life incident in the author's life. During the mid-1950s, Vernon Jordan helped pay for college by spending his summers as a chauffeur for Atlanta's segregationist mayor, Robert Maddox. As was typical among whites at the time, Maddox knew nothing about the man whom he saw every day. One of the few pleasures Jordan had during these summers was reading in Maddox's expansive home library. Although the servants were normally expected to keep to their quarters, Jordan would sneak into the library and open a book while Maddox napped in the afternoons. One afternoon, Maddox stumbled into the library in his underwear looking for a drink, only to find Jordan reading. Startled, Maddox said, "What are you doing in the library, Vernon?" "I'm reading, Mr. Maddox," said Jordan. "Reading? I've never had a nigger work for me who could read," he said. "Mr. Maddox, I can read. I go to college." "You do what?" he asked. "I go to college." "You go to college over there at those colored schools?" "No, sir. I go to DePauw University in Greencastle, Indiana." "White children go to that school." "Yes, sir." . . . "White girls go to that school." "Yes, sir." "What are you studying to be, a preacher or a teacher?" "Actually, I'm going to be a lawyer, Mr. Maddox." "Niggers aren't supposed to be lawyers." "I'm going to be a lawyer, Mr. Maddox." Maddox finally left the library. From that point forward, whenever Maddox and Jordan were together in front of white people, Maddox would say, "Did you know, Vernon can read!"[35] Jordan leveraged these types of experiences into a powerful tool for communicating to whites and blacks alike about the importance of black higher education. His partner in publicity, Joe Mehan, also had a stinging sense of humor and employed it when vetting the ad copy for the "Mind" ads.[36]

Jordan's reshaping of the UNCF publicity materials went hand in hand with a shift in the staffing of the organization. Upon taking the position as president in 1970, Jordan noticed that not one national representative of the UNCF was black. With the goal in mind of training future black college development officers, Jordan diversified the staff.[37] Under this new leadership, the more black-centered UNCF directly confronted the issues of racism and white privilege. For example, one of the most convincing and powerful ad series used focused on the privilege that accompanies an education. Although the ads did not specifically speak directly to white people, it was obvious from the kinds of activities discussed that they were the target audience. Below are tag lines from four such ads:

FOR ABOUT WHAT IT COSTS FOR RIDING LESSONS, WE CAN SEND A KID TO COLLEGE.

FOR ABOUT WHAT IT COSTS TO STRAIGHTEN A KID'S TEETH, WE CAN SEND A KID TO COLLEGE.

FOR ABOUT WHAT IT COSTS TO SEND A KID TO CAMP, WE CAN SEND A KID TO COLLEGE.

FOR WHAT IT COSTS FOR SKIING LESSONS, WE CAN SEND A KID TO COLLEGE.

Each ad began with the phrase, "If you can afford to give your children the best, and often most expensive things in life, you're lucky." Then, the ad went on to talk about the average cost of the featured activity—be it riding horses, skiing, or camp—about $2,000. It reminded the audience that most Americans were not as fortunate, and that the UNCF, with their contribution, would help students to "break out of the urban ghettos and rural backwaters of this country and into the 20th century."[38] Here, the Fund forced middle-class white Americans to face the blunt realities that most blacks experienced.

Cognizant that white corporations and their stockholders were still very much a part of the funding structure of the UNCF, Jordan and his associates also put forth ads directed specifically at them and their interests. For example, a 1972 ad, featuring a large check written out to the UNCF, made the statement, "Don't think of it as charity. Think of it as an investment." Here, the UNCF reminded the potential donor that white Americans were better off with an educated black citizenry and that African Americans were more than a "poor" abstraction; instead, blacks were people with whom white

DON'T THINK OF IT AS CHARITY. THINK OF IT AS AN INVESTMENT.

And a good one. Because we can guarantee a substantial return for your money. It pays off in more black college graduates, with more training in more areas. People to recruit. Consumers to buy your goods and services. Just plain better citizens.

What we need is operating capital. Money we can put to work supporting forty private, four-year colleges.

These schools educate a lot of promising young kids who'd never get to college on their own. Almost three-quarters need some kind of aid. Over half come from families earning less than $5,000 a year.

With your help, we can help more.

A $5,000 donation will give four students one year at an average UNCF college. With $20,000 we can buy the machinery and equipment for a business education course. $100,000 will support an entire economics department.

We think it's one of the best investments you'll make all year. A deal?

A MIND IS A TERRIBLE THING TO WASTE. GIVE TO THE UNITED NEGRO COLLEGE FUND.

55 East 52nd Street, New York, N.Y. 10022

This ad harkens back to the UNCF's roots and ties with corporate America. It asks the viewer to consider the return on investment when one supports black education. Like many of the 1970s ads, it reminds the potential donor that the UNCF isn't asking for a handout but for an investment. "Don't think of it as charity. Think of it as an investment." 1972. Used with permission from the United Negro College Fund, the Ad Council, and Young & Rubicam.

America interacted. Specifically, the ad copy read: "we can guarantee a substantial return for your money. It pays off in more black college graduates, with more training in more areas. People to recruit. Consumers to buy your goods and services. Just plain better citizens."[39]

A Change in Leadership, a Constant Focus

In 1972, by then two years after coming to the Fund, Vernon Jordan left to become executive director of the National Urban League. Despite the Fund's best efforts to convince him to stay, Jordan thought it was best for him to leave. Speaking of his move, he said, "I think that after a while pure fund raising as a career maybe [sic] for some people is boring. Here [at the Urban League] I get to do both—program and fund raising. At the College Fund it was all fund raising, except we did some programs at the College Fund, and they were terrific and they were fun, but this was another kind of opportunity, another kind of challenge, and I took it."[40] Although his time at the Fund was limited, Jordan had a profound impact. He met the UNCF's $10-million campaign goal and added several new initiatives, such as a Summer Medical Program with Meharry medical students and college sophomores, a financial aid and recruitment workshop for black college staff members, and a direct mail program for the UNCF overall.[41] Most important, Jordan created two separate governing boards at the UNCF. Prior to Jordan's arrival, the UNCF board was made up of the member college presidents and influential power brokers, which resulted in a commingling of academic issues and fund-raising issues that did not lend itself to optimal progress. Jordan separated the board into the Board of Members (the member college presidents) and the Board of Trustees (the fundraisers). According to Charles Stephens, national campaign director from 1973 to 1976, this "was by far, the most important change that Vernon Jordan made while at the UNCF."[42]

At this same time, the candidate of choice to succeed Jordan, Christopher Edley Sr. was employed at the Ford Foundation and had "no intention of ever leaving."[43] However, Vernon Jordan and Morris Abrams, the chairman of the UNCF board, had other ideas in mind for Edley. They took him out to an intimate dinner (in which the men's wives were included as well) and after the meal "turned the conversation to black colleges, and [Edley's] thoughts about black colleges, and about the United Negro College Fund." Accord-

Christopher Edley Sr., 1975. Used with permission from the United Negro College Fund, Fairfax, Virginia.

ing to Edley, "At about 12:30 or 1 o'clock in the morning—an hour after we had gotten home—I got a phone call from Vernon Jordan saying, 'Of course you know what that was all about, don't you?' I said no, I didn't have the slightest idea. He said, 'We want you to be the executive director of the United Negro College Fund.' Well, I turned it down."[44] Jordan and Abrams ("a persistent, aggressive character"), however, were not willing to take "no" for an answer and without hesitation, called McGeorge Bundy, the president of the Ford Foundation (and former Kennedy administration insider) to ask "Can we borrow Chris Edley?"[45] In an illustration of the close relations between the Ford Foundation and the UNCF during the early 1970s, Bundy came to Edley to ask what his reaction was to the offer; Edley stated emphatically that he "wasn't ready to leave the Ford Foundation."[46] However, he was willing to take a leave of absence if the Foundation would grant him one. After two years at the UNCF, Edley decided to stay on and officially left his job at Ford.[47]

Upon arrival at the Fund in 1973, Edley "found chaos and inefficiency, but moderate success in fund raising despite that."[48] Edley had expected to find some of this based on the fact that the Fund had been led by an interim director for about a year. Also, during an interview with Morris Abrams, Edley had asked about the status of the Fund, "If I don't come to the College Fund, what will be the consequences?"[49] And the board chairman responded by saying, "Last year we raised ten million dollars. If you don't come, we probably will raise nine million dollars. The College Fund will go on. But if you come the sky would be the limit."[50] Vernon Jordan made great strides during his short stay at the Fund, but Edley found much room for improvement:

As an organization, the College Fund was sufficiently institutionalized to ensure that the central work of fund raising would go on. They might not bring in 100 percent of their potential that year, but they wouldn't be too far short of it. But there was no personnel administration; data processing was chaotic; the systems were not in place; there was no fund raising manual; the staff had not received training—management training—of any type; and supervisors had not been trained as supervisors. . . . Most of the people on the staff were in their first administrative positions or their first fund raising positions, and so on. It was an informally organized operation. There was no table of organization; the fund raisers in the field did not have supervisors. . . . There was not the management structure that you would expect to find in most organizations. The organization had a lot of political intrigue going on that interfered with efficiency; people were supervised in a capricious fashion;

nobody ever knew where he stood. . . . But the work was getting done pretty much.[51]

Edley spent much of his UNCF presidency solving these problems.

Christopher Edley came to the UNCF having served as a lawyer in Philadelphia and as the chief of the administrator of the Justice Division of the U.S. Commission on Civil Rights. He had also worked for the Kennedy administration in the Department of Housing and Urban Development and was the first black program officer at the Ford Foundation. During his tenure at Ford, the organization made a commitment to solving problems in domestic society, specifically African American leadership and businesses. Having a black presence at the Ford Foundation in a key role was a constant reminder of the problems that plagued the United States. During this time, the Foundation also gave substantial funding to the National Urban League, the NAACP, the Southern Christian Leadership Conference (SCLC), and the Congress of Racial Equality (CORE).[52] Under Edley's leadership, the Fund continued its efforts to change the way America thought about African American intelligence. According to Edley, referring to his perspective on advertising while president, "We keep recapturing it, trying to maintain it and build on it, trying to associate the College Fund with the mind, and our motto."

To build the Fund's image, the new UNCF president picked up on Vernon Jordan's enthusiasm for the "Mind" campaign and worked with the Ad Council to put forth publicity that recalled past injustices and challenged stereotypes that referred to African Americans as lazy people, living off of the government.[53] For example, the headline of one ad challenged potential UNCF supporters by reminding them of the struggles that blacks endured from the time of slavery through the Civil Rights Movement: "Once you had to put your life or liberty on the line to support black education. Today we just need your signature." The ad copy spoke directly to these issues, noting that "thousands of Americans, black and white, braved public opinion, physical violence and the law, to help blacks receive an education."[54] The most effective part of the ad was the picture that

Once you had to put your life or liberty on the line to support black education. Today we just need your signature.

Thousands of Americans, black and white, braved public opinion, physical violence and the law, to help blacks receive an education. Thanks to a continuing tradition of support for black education, the United Negro College Fund has, since 1944, helped black students fulfill their dreams and their right to an education.

Thousands have changed the courses of their lives by becoming scientists, engineers and teachers, perhaps changing the course of your life as well.

Fortunately, supporting black education won't cost your life or liberty anymore. Today, it just costs money. Please continue a great American tradition.

Give to The United Negro College Fund

500 E. 62nd St.
New York 10021   A mind is a terrible thing to waste.   A Public Service of This Magazine & The Advertising Council   Ad COUNCIL

This ad is one of a series that looks back to the days of slavery and the dangers of educating an African American. It reminds the viewer that it's quite simple to donate to the UNCF in these modern times. "Once you had to put your life or liberty on the line to support black education. Today we just need your signature." Used with permission from the United Negro College Fund, the Ad Council, and Young & Rubicam.

accompanied it: four African Americans crouched down in the darkness with the light of a single oil lamp, learning to read. In a companion piece, the potential donor was confronted with a picture of a slave with her hands tied behind her back, thick ropes lying coiled at the back of her dress.[55] Most direct in confronting past oppres-

There was a time
when supporting
black education could have
cost your freedom.
Today it just costs money.

**Give to
The United Negro
College Fund**

A mind is a terrible
thing to waste.

A Public Service
of This Magazine
& The Advertising Council

Ad
Council

This ad shows the familiar trappings of slavery—thick ropes restricting the movement of a woman. Once again, the image reminds us that supporting black education could once cost a life but now only costs money. "There was a time when supporting black education could cost you freedom. Today it just costs money." Used with permission from the United Negro College Fund, the Ad Council, and Young & Rubicam.

sion was an ad depicting a group of African American professionals standing in front of the historic Bodie plantation (now Tougaloo College). With an irony characteristic of the Vernon Jordan years, the caption read, "The Old Bodie Plantation is sending more and more people into different fields," making a play on the fact that slaves once worked in the fields but now black Americans were entering every possible professional field.[56]

Another set of ads confronted head-on the common stereotypes of African Americans, such as laziness. These ads, by combining clever text and poignant pictures, dispelled any negative notions a white audience had about African American support of black education. They showed black parents as hardworking individuals, committed to seeing their children excel. For example, a 1974 ad showed a mother down on her hands and knees scrubbing floors. The caption read, "My mother is scrubbing floors so I can become a doctor. Now my school is running out of money." As if the student were speaking directly to the donor, the ad tells the story of an individual black college student.[57] Another, even more powerful version of this ad series showed an older African American woman, exhausted and preoccupied. The caption read, "My grandmother takes in washing so I can become a teacher. Now my school is running out of money."[58] Again, the black college student was speaking to the individual donor, but in this ad the donors were informed of how hard African Americans worked for generation after generation to support their families. Another ad focused on the work of African American men. Depicting an older, tired man, the ad caption read, "My father works 12 hours a day putting down rails so I can become a lawyer. Now my school is running out of money."[59] Here, as in the other ads, the donor saw images that attest to the long work days of most African Americans.

In the words of Forest Long, an advertising executive with Young and Rubicam, the "Mind" campaign "was a plea to everybody to reject the prejudices of the past and consider the inner person. We wanted to make supporting UNCF a human issue and not a race issue."[60] Although the ads speak of the consequences of unrealized

This ad is indicative of the ironic sense of humor used in many of the mid-1970s ads. The UNCF used a bold strategy, reminding people of the nation's tragic history while showcasing its future. "The Old Bodie Plantation is sending more and more people into different fields." Used with permission from the United Negro College Fund, the Ad Council, and Young & Rubicam.

educational opportunity, they emphasize the losses to individual blacks (for example, lost talent, untapped potential) as opposed to losses to whites (loss of personal security, threat to law and order) suggested by earlier publicity, some of which ventured into racist territory. The middle ground, which suggests the extent of loss to both blacks and whites, projected the cumulative effect of talent denied to the market; without aid, good ideas will go untapped, and "we can't afford to waste anybody." By focusing on the common good, the "Mind" ads were highly successful; donations to the UNCF increased by 100 percent.[61]

The Impact of the "Mind" Campaign

During the 1970s, the Fund received approximately $10 million a year in free advertising by being a member of the Ad Council.[62] According to Christopher Edley, the value of the ads came from the "build up" resulting from their staying power: "The first time you see an ad, or the first time you hear A MIND IS A TERRIBLE THING TO WASTE, it might not catch you. In the first year you might not even hear it, but by the time we've run that for ten years [the build up] has great impact." Long-time donors have heard the ads over and over, and the message of necessary black success resonates with them.[63]

According to the Ad Council, the overall themes of the 1970s were "return on investment" and "need." The Ad Council aimed to create an image or "brand name" for the UNCF that would become part of the American vernacular and invoke a sense of urgency in the audience where none existed before. Specifically, "some public service advertisements (PSAs) reminded the public that for every student UNCF sends to college there is another equally deserving student who cannot attend because of lack of funds. Other PSAs made use of the business term 'return on investment' and noted that an investment in the UNCF yielded a successful college graduate."[64] The use of "need" and "return on investment" were not new ideas for the UNCF. Because of the Fund's connection with Rockefeller Jr. and

In 41 Black colleges today there are thousands of dedicated students who want an education. Some of them may never get it. Their schools are in desperate need of money. Your contributions can help these schools. It's important. **A mind is a terrible thing to waste.**

Give to the United Negro College Fund.
55 E. 52nd St. New York, N.Y. 10022

Photographed by Maureen Lambray

"My mother is scrubbing floors so I can become a doctor. Now my school is running out of money."

This image is one in a series produced by the UNCF in the 1970s to raise awareness of the sacrifices made by African Americans and to counter stereotypes held about them. In this case, the ad depicts the hard work of a black college student's mother. "My mother is scrubbing floors so I can become a doctor. Now my school is running out of money." 1974. Used with permission from the United Negro College Fund, the Ad Council, and Young & Rubicam.

other leading business leaders, "return on investment" was a tried and true strategy to convince wealthy whites to give, a strategy from which the UNCF benefited for many years.

The Fund had been skilled in showing need in its past publicity. For example, the 1950 publicity piece entitled "A Significant Adventure" showed the experience of living at a black college to be quite an adventure indeed. Under the heading "Poor Housing Discourages Faculty," there appeared a photo of a ramshackle two-story, wood frame house, which suggested that black college faculty were living in substandard conditions.[65] In the same publication, a photograph of two faculty members inspecting books stacked up on the floor of a basement appeared above the caption, "Limited Space Means Poor Library Service."[66] The use of "needs" as a method of persuasion was successful. However, the 1970s ads dared to remind the audience that the need applied to individual black students; rather than speaking of black students collectively, as abstractions, the ads supplied very real faces to the students. The ads offered the same effect as that of the "I am a Man" placards carried by black sanitation workers in the 1986 Memphis strike: the words demanded that the viewer face the humanity of individual black citizens.

Two faculty members inspecting books in a makeshift library. Photographs like this were used by the early leaders of the UNCF to depict institutional need to potential donors. Used with permission from the Fisk University Special Collections.

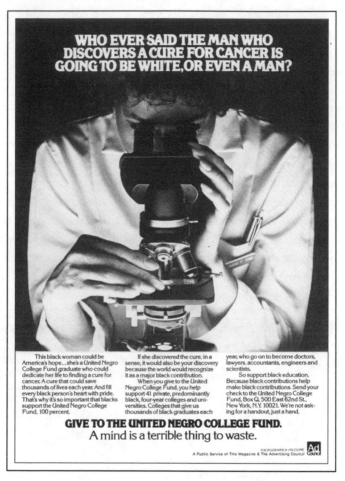

This ad is one in a series directed at the African American community. It attempts to energize the black community around the possibility of discoveries and accomplishments made by their own people. "Who ever said the man who discovers a cure for cancer is going to be white, or even a man?" Used with permission from the United Negro College Fund, the Ad Council, and Young & Rubicam.

During the first five years of the "Mind" campaign, donations to the UNCF doubled. Although the UNCF was aiming to secure donations from a wide range of people with this campaign, they were not prepared for the enormous response from African American middle-class organizations. According to Christopher Edley, the increased support from these organizations and many others can be attributed to the strong momentum toward the support of black education. In Edley's words, "There is also the possibility that success breeds success, that the College Fund had to begin to achieve certain public identity, had to become well-known, before we were deserving of this higher level support."[67]

Finally, the UNCF leadership ended its practice of selling black colleges short, a phenomenon described earlier by Lindsley Kimball. Perhaps because the need for funds was more obvious or perhaps because it used a more black-centered approach to fund-raising, the "Mind" campaign made black colleges an appealing cause for many, especially black middle-class individuals and their corresponding organizations. For example, one ad showed a black woman looking through a microscope with the caption, "Who ever said the man who discovers a cure for cancer is going to be white, or even a man?" The ad copy spoke not only of black pride and the joy that the success of one African American brings to the race as a whole but also of the obligation that blacks have to make their own successes happen. Consider this message:

This black woman could be America's hope . . . she's a United Negro College Fund graduate who could dedicate her life to finding a cure for cancer. A cure that could save thousands of lives each year. And fill every black person's heart with pride. That's why it's so important that blacks support the United Negro College Fund, 100 percent. If she discovered the cure, in a sense, it would also be your discovery because the world would recognize it as a major black contribution.[68]

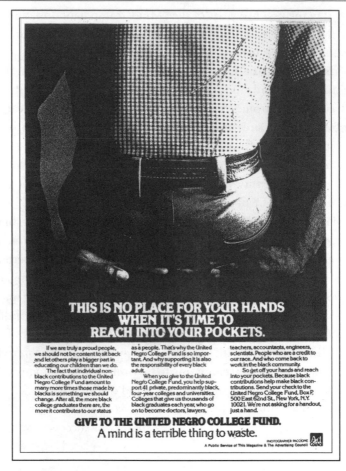

This ad series carries a pointed message to African Americans: you must support the cause of black education if you also expect others to support the cause. "This is no place for your hands when it's time to reach into your pockets." Used with permission from the United Negro College Fund, the Ad Council, and Young & Rubicam.

Another ad chided members of the black community for not contributing to the UNCF. This ad, which featured a picture of an African American man sitting on this hands and the tag line "This is no place for your hands when it's time to reach into your pockets," asked black viewers not to be content with "others" playing "a bigger part in educating" their children than they were willing to play. The ad also informed the black community that white contributions "amount to many more times those made by blacks."[69]

These ads, and many others, encouraged more individual African Americans as well as groups to give to the Fund. For example, Edley noted of The Links, an elite African American social service organization, "You know, the individual chapters have always given us $50, $100, $200. It's moving up to the grand scale that has taken time. And we are not through yet; we are still working on that; it's a big effort. I am not going to be satisfied until we are soliciting 3,000 or 4,000 black organizations a year."[70] After the success with The Links, the UNCF used similar strategies with other African American organizations, including fraternities and sororities.[71] Its most successful venture was with the Alpha Kappa Alpha (AKA) sorority in the early 1970s. During a three-year period, the AKAs raised half a million dollars for the UNCF. Not to be outdone by the AKAs, the "Alpha men—Alpha Phi Alpha fraternity—decided that they were going to make a million-dollar pledge to three black organizations," and the UNCF was one of them.[72] For years, white donors had been asking for evidence that African Americans themselves supported their educational institutions.[73] This support from the black middle-class community served as both motivation and impetus for more white corporate contributions. Of course, African Americans had been giving steadily to black education for years; however, the "Mind" campaign gave the UNCF the high-profile contributions that attract attention in the philanthropic world.[74]

The shift toward "blackness" in the "Mind" ads was subtle; the ads reminded the viewers of their subject's humanity at the same time that they appealed to the universality of themes like educational opportunity. This change not only popularized the group with blacks but also contrasted starkly with the print ads of the 1940s and early 1950s, which focused on giving money to "those people" and therefore appealed to white corporations. The urgency of the original "Mind" ads resonated with many audiences. The ads struck a delicate balance between the universal and the particular, between color-blind concerns (for example, the notion that we all lose when talent is wasted) and color-specific concerns (the fact that black suffering needs to be acknowledged and alleviated). Most important, the "mind" ads targeted the donor base as a single entity—U.S. citizens—and thus obviated the two-pronged approach used in the 1950s.

CONCLUSION

An Organization That
No One Could Argue Against

The United Negro College Fund, an institution whose main mission is to raise money, is therefore obligated to work with whomever is currently in power in the United States. Moreover, corporations in large part continue to support the UNCF. In the first three decades of its existence, important changes occurred in both the Fund's operations and its public messages.

The Fund's early publicity was thoroughly imbued with the "double consciousness" described by W. E. B. Du Bois. While not wishing to present a black-centered view of education to a public that had barely begun to grant blacks full citizenship, the Fund's leadership, mostly white, carefully presented its message in language that whites could understand. This leadership thought it essential that the donor be made to feel comfortable in supporting something that matched donor ideals. The early Fund, under the direction of John D. Rockefeller Jr., did not claim to spur change; instead, the Fund showed whites how giving to black education helped them. To maintain the UNCF's legitimacy among African Americans UNCF leaders designed separate publicity for the black community. Crafting different messages for various constituencies has been an integral part of modern fund-raising. However, this practice had a particularly painful significance for African Americans, who had to deny a part of themselves in order to sell to the white population the idea that black minds were worth the investment.

Although the organization was called the United Negro College Fund and the African American leadership had been the impetus for its creation, the inner workings of the UNCF were controlled almost exclusively by John D. Rockefeller Jr. and his white designees during its formative years. Yet if the UNCF was a fiction, it was a useful one. UNCF member colleges were much more successful at fund-raising collectively than they ever had been soliciting individually. The efficient and streamlined organization appealed to capitalist mentalities. Despite this outside control, the genius of the organization's foundation was the ability of the black leadership to make the best out of a potentially dire situation, where black colleges were slowly fading away without sufficient funding from philanthropists, their own alumni, or the government. Because the defeat of fascism in Europe and the ensuing struggle against communism placed democratic values at the forefront of the American mind, UNCF leaders saw as imperative to defeating communism that the United States fulfill at home its promise to the free world: to provide economic opportunities for all and to uphold the rights of the least advantaged citizens. By connecting the cause of black education with the tenets of the Cold War and the vision of a postwar industrial boom—ideas such as loyalty, patriotism, capitalism, and hard work—the UNCF used familiar white values to bolster the success of black colleges.

Although the white industrialists involved in the UNCF never sought social equality, the mere fact that within the organization individuals of different races worked toward the common goals of financing black colleges did aid race relations in significant ways. The UNCF served as an example of how these two populations could negotiate a mutually beneficial path on the issue of education. Of course, the African American leadership had little room to push its agenda publicly during the initial years of the Fund. However, within the black community this leadership quietly pressed for change, and, contrary to stereotypes presented by critics of black colleges, many member college presidents did support civil rights action.

With the U.S. Supreme Court's consent the white leadership was finally willing to publicly integrate the UNCF's social gatherings, but, even after the *Brown* decision, integration followed only under pressure from the wealthy white women who participated in the organization. Perhaps because of their dedication to the cause of women's colleges and their commitment to the social advancement of white women, these women saw more clearly than their male counterparts the importance of pushing the boundaries of social equality to include black men and women. The women's pivotal roles in the organization gave them a certain amount of influence with the male leadership. Furthermore, their unique position as social intermediaries afforded them the opportunity to be catalysts for change in social norms.

Under William J. Trent's leadership, the UNCF faced one of its most difficult tasks—that of redefining itself in the face of desegregation for the general public. How could an organization that represented segregated black institutions advocate for integration? How were black colleges still viable in the post-*Brown* era? Trent and his colleagues, such as Benjamin E. Mays, could convince white leadership and the public of the value of black colleges only by advocating for the integration of black institutions of higher education alongside the integration of white institutions; yet this two-way integration never materialized. The *Brown* decision inaugurated a long period (which still continues) in which skeptics asked black colleges both to defend themselves against a stigma of inferiority and to convince their critics that black institutions were moving toward being on par with comparable historically white institutions. Eventually, under the leadership of Stephen Wright, the organization claimed the territory originally set forth in its name: promoting *Negro* colleges and *Negro* education.

Wright's term as president marked an era of transition for the Fund. No longer willing to accept meddling in the day-to-day operations of the organization, Wright began to question decisions made by the white leadership. Inspired by the deep stirrings of black consciousness and the freedom movement sweeping through the black community, Wright and the African American leadership fought to define themselves and thereby the Fund. Although the Fund's publicity was still imbued with a sense of "double consciousness," the member college presidents were changing. With the support of many around the nation and the world for the cause of civil rights, it became easier for the UNCF to present itself in an honest and direct way: the organization fought for racial uplift. Still, to send the message that the black leadership desired a rational chain of command in which whites could not second-guess blacks' decisions, Wright resigned his position. Although all those involved in the Fund may not have heard this message, it proved a crucial turning point for the organization. The "changing of the guard" that began under Wright's administration went hand-in-hand with a change in the tone and purpose of the Fund's activities. Most significant was the willingness of Wright and others to engage outside critics of black colleges, such as Christopher Jencks and David Riesman; the Fund's leaders asserted the colleges' identities, no longer content to allow others to define them. The UNCF advocated visibly for black colleges: it pointed to their strengths when others would only discuss their weaknesses, and it ensured that both their successes and failures be understood in the proper context.

Vernon Jordan brought a different view to the forefront of UNCF publicity. For the first time, potential donors heard, without apologies, the story of black people from the perspective of black people. In telling that story, the UNCF defied conventional wisdom— namely, that embracing controversy scares away donors. Through the 1970s, the Fund gradually extricated itself from the pressure to accommodate and conform to a white agenda. In so doing, the Fund cultivated a new, broader donor pool. The UNCF was no longer selling black colleges short; the Fund presented the colleges as the primary incubators for African American leadership and intellect. In the 1970s Rockefeller III resigned from the board, which signaled a most important change in the Fund leadership. The departure of the name synonymous with wealth and power left a vacuum that could only be filled by potent new African American leadership. Rockefeller's resignation allowed the UNCF to embody its founding message: blacks helping blacks.

Jordan and Christopher Edley Sr. inaugurated the "Mind Is a Terrible Thing to Waste" campaign, through which the Fund's goals became broadly known. With this effort, the Fund boldly pushed forward, reminding potential donors of the needs of not only black colleges but also black people. The campaign challenged donors to give in support of their own interests and as a remedy for past injustices. Through the "Mind" campaign, the UNCF was finally willing to publicly affiliate itself with the movement for racial justice.

Since the presidency of Christopher Edley Sr. in 1990, the UNCF has had two leaders. William H. Gray III (1991–2003) and the current president, Michael Lomax (2004–). Although this book does not delve into the eras of these two men, their leadership has been hugely significant to the growth of the organization. William H. Gray, a former U.S. congressman from Philadelphia, shaped the UNCF into a model of African American philanthropy. Under his leadership, the organization raised $1.6 billion for the thirty-nine member colleges. In a move symbolic of the organization's complete break from the Rockefeller shadow, Gray relocated the UNCF's offices from New York City to the Virginia suburbs of Washington, D.C. Perhaps Gray's greatest accomplishment was securing a $1 billion gift from the Bill and Melinda Gates Foundation in 1999. Through this gift, the UNCF is able to offer scholarship opportunities to minority students in a fashion unparalleled by any other organization. Also, Gray established the Frederick D. Patterson Research Institute in 1996, a move that helped the UNCF and black colleges define themselves for researchers, policymakers, and the media. He retired in 2003 after twelve years with the UNCF.

In 2004, the former president of Dillard University in New Orleans, Louisiana, Michael Lomax, was selected to be the new president and CEO of the UNCF. Lomax came to the position with his experience as a college president and faculty member and twelve years as chairman of the Board of Commissioners in Atlanta, Georgia. Lomax is interested in both expanding many programs created under Gray's leadership and influencing the government and the public on policy issues related to black colleges. In addition, Lomax wants to build capacity at the individual member colleges, specifically to "invest in rebuilding the campuses . . . to make them not only historic but also modern."[1]

Democratic and Republican presidents come and go, but one thing remains constant: the United Negro College Fund has friends in the first family. Since Eleanor Roosevelt befriended UNCF Member College President Dr. Mary McLeod Bethune and helped make possible the flights of the Tuskegee Airmen, UNCF and its member colleges have enjoyed remarkable support from the White House. That support has cut across time and partisanship.[2]

The history of the United Negro College Fund serves as an example of what is required for African Americans to build equity in the society in which they live. The dynamics of fighting for a cause and raising money within a repressive context involves trade-offs, negotiations, and subversive acts. Despite its allegiance to white culture and white moneyed support on the exterior, the early black UNCF leaders maintained sympathies with black-centered and revolutionary ideas behind the scenes. Throughout its history, the organization has felt the tug of these opposite forces. From its inception, the UNCF had many critics: southern white detractors decried its mixed race arrangements, and blacks faulted the organization for not doing enough to overturn the white power structure. Yet, if the UNCF was founded as a collaborative effort, could anyone really expect it to perpetuate segregation? And, if the UNCF was fed by capitalism, could anyone expect it to be revolutionary? The organization's evolution may just be the logical conclusion of its founding premises: the mutual agreement on democracy and free enterprise as core American values and the understanding that education is the key to racial harmony and economic development.

Appendixes

Pittsburgh *Courier* Letter to Black College Presidents

Reprint from
"Southern Viewpoint"
Frederick D. Patterson
Pittsburgh *Courier*
Saturday, January 30, 1943

Would It Not Be Wise For Some Negro Schools To Make Joint Appeal To Public For Funds?

One of the most severe catastrophes of the present war, so far as the American people are concerned, is what is happening to our private colleges throughout the length and breadth of our nation today. They are receiving a double assault—that which comes from the loss of the majority of the male student population and that which comes through inability to receive adequate support through the taxing program now necessary to fight this war and insure the broad social programs upon which this nation has engaged for the past seven or eight years.

If this is true of private colleges in general where it may be said that these colleges have a definite constituency upon which they place a financial claim, the situation is trebly more grave with the Negro colleges of a private nature which heretofore have relied largely on gifts from substantial members of the white race for their support and maintenance. There is occasion therefore for serious alarm as to what may happen to such institutions as Atlanta, Fisk, Dillard, Morehouse, Hampton and Tuskegee to say nothing of a large number of smaller church schools.

Is Public Interested?

The handwriting is on the wall so far as substantial northern support is concerned. The question remains as to whether or not these institutions have sufficiently impressed their worth on the general public and there has been sufficient growth in the public conscience to permit the quality of widespread, if small, individual generosity that is necessary to offset the substantial gifts of the past.

The general public probably does not realize that most of substantial progress for human betterment has come through the aegis of private and charitable institutions. In the case of education the freedom to experiment and blaze new trails was a pioneering service responsible for much of the progress we know in this field today. Even now, this service is needed because of the more or less fixed pattern which governs the educational programs of most publicly supported education institutions. In not a few instances the political pot boils incessantly that anything beyond the merest traditional routine is out of the question.

Unified Appeals

Private colleges for Negroes have carried the brunt of our educational effort for the better part of this experience. They yet educate to the extent of their means nearly 50% of those who receive college training. They have provided the bulk of the educational leadership administering to colleges both public and private. They, too, have pioneered in areas, until recently, hardly possible in few if any state supported institutions.

These Negro institutions may well take a cure from the general program of organization which seems to involve most charitable efforts today. Various and sundry drives are being unified with a reduction in overhead for publicity and in behalf of a more purposeful and pointed approach to the giving public. The idea may not be new but it seems most propitious at this time that the several institutions use the funds which they are spending for campaign and publicity and that they make a unified appeal to national conscience.

How to Split Gifts

The first question which naturally arises is who will get how much of the funds collected. The only reasonable way to handle this would be to work out certain range limits of individual budgets and then see that the given percentage of a dollar that went to any institution was in terms of this range in its ratio to the whole. If there is included approximately ten institutions this should not be a too difficult mathematical problem. A given institutional range could be determined for a base period similar to that used in the cotton allotment program so as to be sure that a fair estimate of the operating budget is taken.

Negroes Should Start

Such a campaign might well begin with Negro people of America. There are few of us who have any sort of employment who haven't enough intelligence and interest, I am sure, to appreciate the importance of such a program to these institutions of higher learning. The fact that all types of education would be involved would overcome the objection which might result if a single institution were to make an appeal. In addition to this there would be the savory feeling that this contribution would be made so that a large number of individuals would benefit regardless of their educational choice.

It is also possible that by starting with the Negro people in a campaign of this kind each individual institution could continue to appeal to the donors and special friends it had developed over a period of years. The nominal contribution of one dollar per person could be sought over this wider range without any important conflict. At least during these critical times, a unified financial campaign for several Negro colleges seems to be an idea worth toying with.

United Negro College Fund
Member Colleges,
1944 to Present

Atlanta University, Atlanta, Georgia, since 1944, but has since merged with Clark University.

Barber-Scotia College, Concord, North Carolina, since 1958

Benedict College, Columbia, South Carolina, since 1945

Bennett College, Greensboro, North Carolina, since 1944

Bethune-Cookman College, Daytona Beach, Florida, since 1944

Bishop College, Dallas, Texas, since 1945

Claflin College, Orangeburg, South Carolina, since 1968

Clark College, Atlanta, Georgia, since 1944 but has since merged with Atlanta University

Clark-Atlanta University, Atlanta, Georgia, since 1944 (formerly Atlanta and Clark)

Dillard University, New Orleans, Louisiana, since 1944

Fisk University, Nashville, Tennessee, since 1944

Florida Memorial College, Miami, Florida, since 1968

Hampton University, Hampton, Virginia, member 1944–1968

Howard University, Washington, D.C., member 1944–1948

Huston-Tillotson College, Austin, Texas, since 1944

Interdenominational Theological Center, Atlanta, Georgia, since 1944

Jarvis Christian College, Hawkins, Texas, since 1972

Johnson C. Smith University, Charlotte, North Carolina, since 1945

Knoxville College, Knoxville, Tennessee, since 1944

Lane College, Jackson, Tennessee, since 1944

LeMoyne-Owen College, Memphis, Tennessee, since 1944

Lincoln University, Lincoln University, Pennsylvania, 1944–1960

Livingston College, Salisbury, North Carolina, since 1944

Miles College, Birmingham, Alabama, since 1972

Morehouse College, Atlanta, Georgia, since 1944

Morris College, Sumter, South Carolina, since 1944

Oakwood College, Huntsville, Alabama, since 1965

Paine College, Augusta, Georgia, since 1945

Paul Quinn College, Waco, Texas, since 1944

Philander Smith College, Little Rock, Arkansas, since 1944

Rust College, Holly Springs, Mississippi, since 1972

Saint Augustine's College, Raleigh, North Carolina, since 1950

Saint Paul's College, Lawrenceville, Virginia, since 1958

Samuel Huston College, Austin, Texas, since 1944

Spelman College, Atlanta, Georgia, since 1994

Stillman College, Tuscaloosa, Alabama, since 1962

Talladega College, Talladega, Alabama, since 1945

Texas College, Tyler, Texas, since 1944

Tougaloo College, Tougaloo, Mississippi, since 1944

Tuskegee University, Tuskegee, Alabama, since 1944

Virginia Union University, Richmond, Virginia, since 1944

Voorhees College, Denmark, South Carolina, since 1969

Wiley College, Marshall, Texas, since 1944

Wilberforce University, Wilberforce, Ohio, since 1968

Xavier University, New Orleans, Louisiana, since 1946

United Negro College Fund
Executive Directors and Presidents, 1944 to Present

William J. Trent Jr., executive director (1944–1963)
Frederick D. Patterson, president and founder (1944–1966)
Benjamin E. Mays, president (1955–1966)
Stephen J. Wright, president (1966–1969)
Harry V. Richardson, executive director (1969–1970)
Vernon Jordan, president (1970–1972)
Arthur Fletcher, acting executive director (1972–1973)
Christopher Edley Sr., president (1973–1990)
Virgil E. Ecton, acting executive director (1991)
William Gray III, president and chief executive officer (1991–2004)
Michael Lomax, president and chief executive officer (2004–)

United Negro College Fund
National Campaign Chairmen, 1944 to 1979

Walter Hoving, president, Lord & Taylor (1944)

Thomas A. Morgan, chairman, Sperry Corporation (1945)

Frank M. Totton, vice president, Chase National Bank (1946–1947)

William E. Cotter, counsel, Union Carbide and Carbide Corporation (1948)

John R. Suman, vice president, Standard Oil Company of New Jersey (1949)

Thomas J. Parkinson, president, The Equitable Life Assurance Society of the United States (1950–1951)

C. D. Jackson, vice president, *Time,* Inc. (1952–1953)

John W. Hanes, financial vice president, Olin Mathieson Chemical Corporation (1954)

Lindsley F. Kimball, executive vice president, Rockefeller Foundation (1955)

Lee H. Bristol, president, Bristol-Myers Corporation (1956–1957)

Stanley C. Hope, president, Esso Standard Oil Company (1958)

Bruce Barton, chairman, Batten, Barton, Durstine and Osborne, Inc., (1959–1960)

Lawrence J. MacGregor, chairman, The Summit Trust Company (1962–1963)

Carl M. Anderson, secretary, Merck and Company, Inc. (1964–1965)

Dudley Dowell, president, New York Life Insurance Company (1966; 1970)

George Champion, chairman, Chase Manhattan Bank (1967–1968)

Isaac N. P. Stokes, chairman, Phelps-Stokes Fund (1969)
Cyrus R. Vance, attorney, Simpson, Thacher, and Bartlett (1971–1973)
Thomas A. Murphy, chairman, General Motors Company (1974–1976)
A. Dean Swift, president, Sears, Roebuck and Company (1977–1978)
Lewis W. Foy, chairman, Bethlehem Steel (1979)

Archives and Oral History Collections

Charles Spurgeon Johnson Papers, Fisk University Special Collection, Nashville, Tennessee

General Collection, Manuscript Division, National Archives, Washington, D.C.

General Education Board Papers, Rockefeller Archive Center, Sleepy Hollow, New York

John D. Rockefeller Jr. Papers, Rockefeller Archive Center, Sleepy Hollow, New York

Stephen J. Wright Papers, Fisk University Special Collection, Nashville, Tennessee

United Negro College Fund Ads, Ad Council, New York, New York

United Negro College Fund Ads, Young and Rubicam Archives, New York, New York

United Negro College Fund Oral History Collection, Columbia University Oral History Collection, New York, New York

United Negro College Fund Papers, Frederick D. Patterson Research Center, Fairfax, Virginia

United Negro College Fund Papers, Manuscript Division, Library of Congress, Washington, D.C.

United Negro College Fund Papers, Robert W. Woodruff Library, Atlanta University Center, Atlanta, Georgia

United Negro College Fund Papers, Schomburg Center for Research in Black Culture, New York, New York

APPENDIX F

Oral History Interviews

James P. Brawley, interview by Marcia Goodson, transcript, March 1982, UNCF Oral History, No. 1331, Columbia University Oral History Collection.

Christopher Edley Sr., interview by Marcia Goodson, transcript, UNCF Oral History, No. 1331, Columbia University Oral History Collection.

Walter Hoving, interview by Marcia Goodson, transcript, February 1981, No. 1331, Columbia University Oral History Collection.

Christopher Jencks, telephone interview by author, digital recording, Philadelphia, 30 September 2003 (interview in author's possession).

Vernon Jordan, interview by Marcia Goodson, transcript, January 1982, UNCF Oral History, No. 1331, Columbia University Oral History Collection.

Lindsley Kimball, interview by Marcia Goodson, transcript, March 1981, UNCF Oral History, No. 1331, Columbia University Oral History Collection.

Albert Manley, interview by Marcia Goodson, transcript, May 1987, UNCF Oral History, No. 1331, Columbia University Oral History Collection.

Benjamin E. Mays, interview by Marcia Goodson, transcript, May 1987, UNCF Oral History, No. 1331, Columbia University Oral History Collection.

Frederick D. Patterson, interview by Marcia Goodson, transcript, July 1982, UNCF Oral History, No. 1331, Columbia University Oral History Collection.

Hollis Price, interview by Marcia Goodson, transcript, May 1987, UNCF Oral History, No. 1331, Columbia University Oral History Collection.

Betty Stebman, interview by Marcia Goodson, transcript, April 1982, UNCF Oral History, No. 1331, Columbia University Oral History Collection.

Charles Stephens, interview by author, digital recording, Philadelphia, 6 May 2006 (interview in author's possession).

William J. Trent Jr., interview by Marcia Goodson, transcript, February 1981, UNCF Oral History, No. 1331, Columbia University Oral History Collection.

Charles V. Willie, telephone interview by author, digital recording, Philadelphia, 2 September 2003 (interview in author's possession).

Stephen J. Wright, interview Marcia Goodson, transcript, June 1987, UNCF Oral History, No. 1331, Columbia University Oral History Collection.

Notes

Introduction. A Time for Innovation and Change

1. Lea A. Williams, "The United Negro College Fund: Its Growth and Development" (Ph.D. diss., Columbia University, 1977), 1.

2. Katrina Sanders-Cassell, *"Intelligent and Effective Direction": The Fisk University Race Relations Institute and the Struggle for Civil Rights* (New York: Peter Lang, 2005), 5.

3. Gunnar Myrdal, *An American Dilemma: The Negro Problem and American Democracy* (New York: Harper & Row, 1944).

4. John Egerton, *Speak Now Against the Day. The Generation before the Civil Rights Movement in the South* (New York: Knopf, 1994).

5. Ibid., 286.

6. Ibid., according to Egerton, although some people in the North thought of the NAACP as a more moderate or mainstream organization, in the South, from the standpoint of whites, the NAACP was considered a radical, confrontational organization during the 1940s.

7. Genna Rae McNeil, *Groundwork: Charles Hamilton Houston and the Struggle for Civil Rights* (Philadelphia: University of Pennsylvania Press, 1983).

8. Myrdal, *An American Dilemma.*

9. Of course, an even larger demonstration materialized under Randolph's leadership in 1963 with the famed March on Washington.

10. Joe William Trotter Jr., "From a Raw Deal to a New Deal?" in *A History of African Americans, from 1880*, ed. Robin D. G. Kelley and Earl Lewis (New York: Oxford University Press, 2000).

11. August Meier and Elliot Rudwick, *CORE: A Study in the Civil Rights Movement, 1942–1968* (New York: Oxford University Press, 1973).

12. Sanders-Cassell, *"Intelligent and Effective Direction,"* 5.

13. Myrdal, *An American Dilemma;* Egerton, *Speak Now Against the Day.*

14. Sanders-Cassell, *"Intelligent and Effective Direction,"* 9.

15. Penny M. Von Eschen, *Race Against Empire. Black Americans and Anticolonialism* (Ithaca: Cornell University Press, 1997).

16. Kelley and Lewis, eds., *History of African Americans,* 174.

17. Walter White, "Kinship of Colored Peoples: People, Politics, and Places," *Chicago Defender,* 3 March 1945; Walter White, *A Rising Wind* (Westport, Conn.: Negro Universities Press, 1971), 144. For a full discussion of the impact of World War II on African American politics, see Von Eschen, *Race Against Empire.*

18. Myrdal, *An American Dilemma,* 409.

19. Egerton, *Speak Now Against the Day;* Kelley and Lewis, eds., *History of African Americans.*

20. Myrdal, *An American Dilemma,* 770.

21. Ibid., 770.

22. W. E. B. Du Bois, *The Souls of Black Folks* (New York: Penguin Classics, 1996).

23. Ibid., 3.

Chapter 1. Black Colleges and the Origins of the UNCF

1. Steven Hahn, *A Nation Under Their Feet: Black Political Struggles in the Rural South from Slavery to the Great Migration* (Cambridge: Harvard University Press, 2005).

2. According to Heather A. Williams's *Self-Taught: African American Education in Slavery and Freedom* (Chapel Hill: University of North Carolina Press, 2005), the following states "prohibited teaching enslaved and/or free black people": Alabama, Georgia, Louisiana, Mississippi, Missouri, North Carolina, South Carolina, and Virginia (p. 216). Williams was not able to find such statutes in Kentucky, Maryland, Arkansas, Texas, Florida, Delaware, and Tennessee. For additional information, please see Williams's chapter 1, "In Secret Places. Acquiring Literacy in Slave Communities."

3. Ronald Butchart, *Northern Schools, Southern Blacks and Reconstruction: Freedmen's Education, 1862–1975* (Westport, Conn.: Greenwood Press, 1980).

4. Frederick Rudolph, *The American College and University: A History* (1962; reprint, with an introductory essay and supplementary bibliography by John R. Thelin, Athens: University of Georgia Press, 1990).

5. James D. Anderson, *The Education of Blacks in the South, 1860–1935* (Chapel Hill: University of North Carolina Press, 1988).

6. Ibid.

7. Ralph Christy and Ralph Williamson, *A Century of Service: Land Grant Colleges and Universities, 1890–1990* (New Brunswick: Transaction, 1992); Chris Johnston, "The 1890 Morrill Land-Grant College Act and the African-American Civil Rights Movement," http://www.tandl.vt.edu/socialstudies/hicks/cjohnsto/1890.htm.

8. Anderson, *Education of Blacks*; William Watkins, *White Architects of Black Education: Power and Ideology in America, 1865–1954* (New York: Teachers College Press, 2001).

9. The General Education Board gave a total of $325 million to education; $63 million went to blacks.

10. Anderson, *Education of Blacks*; Watkins, *White Architects*; David Levering Lewis, *W. E. B. Du Bois: Biography of a Race, 1868–1919* (New York: Henry Holt, 1994).

11. Robert Engs, *Educating the Disfranchised and Disinherited: Samuel Chapman Armstrong and Hampton Institute* (Knoxville: University of Tennessee Press, 1999).

12. It should be noted that the industrial philanthropists were not entirely opposed to the liberal arts curriculum. For a nuanced discussion of their interests, see Anderson, *The Education of Blacks in the South*.

13. Lewis, *W. E. B. Du Bois*.

14. Ibid.

15. Anderson, *Education of Blacks*.

16. Ibid., 238.

17. Ibid., 255.

18. Ibid.

19. For more information, see Marcia Goodson, ed., *Chronicles of Faith: An Autobiography of Frederick D. Patterson* (Tuscaloosa: University of Alabama Press, 1991).

20. Robert Russa Moton was an African American educator with a degree from the Hampton Institute (1890). He was the commandant of the Hampton Institute between 1890 and 1915, and, upon Booker T. Washington's death in 1915, he assumed the position of principal (and

later president) of the Tuskegee Institute. Moton held this position until 1935. During his tenure at Tuskegee, the institution was raised to national and international prominence in the area of race relations. See Robert Russa Moton, *Finding a Way Out: An Autobiography* (Maryland: McGrath Publishing Company, 1920).

21. Marybeth Gasman, "Frederick Douglass Patterson (1901–1988), College President and Founder of the United Negro College Fund," *The Encyclopedia of Philanthropy* (New York: Oryx Press, 2001).

22. Charles Stephens, interview with author, 5 May 2006.

23. Egerton, *Speak Now Against the Day,* p. 288.

24. Ibid., 288. See also, Rayford Logan, ed., *What the Negro Wants* (Chapel Hill: University of North Carolina Press, 1944), p. 288.

25. Those individuals included in the Rayford Logan volume included: Mary McLeod Bethune, Sterling A. Brown, W. E. B. Du Bois, Gordon B. Hancock, Leslie Pinckney Hill, Langston Hughes, Frederick D. Patterson, A. Philip Randolph, George S. Schuyler, Willard S. Townsend, Charles H. Wesley, Doxey A. Wilkerson, and Roy Wilkins.

26. Egerton, *Speak Now Against the Day.*

27. Charles Stephens, interview with author, 5 May 2006.

28. Scott M. Cutlip, *Fund Raising in the United States* (New Brunswick: Rutgers University Press, 1965), 296.

29. Goodson, ed., *Chronicles of Faith.*

30. Franklin D. Roosevelt, in Cutlip, *Fund Raising in the United States,* 297.

31. Frederick D. Patterson, interview by Marcia Goodson, transcript, February 1981, United Negro College Fund, Columbia University Oral History Collection, No. 1331, 7 (hereafter cited as UNCF Oral History); John Kirby, *Black Americans in the Roosevelt Era: Liberalism and Race* (Knoxville: University of Tennessee Press, 1980). According to John Price Jones, one of the leading fundraisers during the post-Depression era, it was typical to hear at this time "Why doesn't government do this?" See Cutlip, *Fund Raising in the United States,* 317.

32. Kirby, *Black Americans.* The inequities of the Roosevelt era policies were the subject of a conference entitled "The Position of the Negro in Our National Economic Crisis," hosted by Ralph Bunch at Howard University in 1935.

33. Myrdal, *An American Dilemma,* p. 754.

34. Jones, "A History of the United Negro College Fund," UNCF Papers.

35. Cutlip, *Fund Raising in the United States.*

36. Jones, "A History of the United Negro College Fund," UNCF Papers.

37. Goodson, *Chronicles of Faith.*

38. Ibid., 123.

39. Patterson, interview, February 1981.

40. John D. Rockefeller created the General Education Board in 1903 with an initial pledge of $1,000,000. When the Board ceased its "active philanthropic" activity in 1957, it had given over $60,000,000 toward black education. For more information, see Frederick D. Patterson, "Foundation Policies in Regard to Negro Institutions of Higher Learning," *Journal of Educational Sociology* 32, 6 (February 1959), 290–296. Julius Rosenwald established the Rosenwald Fund in 1917. The Fund supported the establishment of rural schools for blacks, black higher education, and many other educational and social causes. According to Patterson, "the extent of their interest [speaking of the General Education Board and the Rosenwald Fund] and the level of giving left much to be desired. For although the two foundations were among the major contributors to black colleges they made greater gifts to White colleges." Frederick D. Patterson in Goodson, *Chronicles of Faith,* 123.

41. Walter Hoving to Contributors of the United Negro College Fund Campaign, memo, December 1944, Messers Rockefeller, III2G, box 94, folder 665, Rockefeller Archive Center, Sleepy Hollow, New York (hereafter cited as RAC).

42. See General Education Board papers, RAC.

43. James P. Brawley, interview by Marcia Goodson, transcript, March 1982, UNCF Oral History, No. 1331, 59.

44. Charles S. Johnson, *The Negro College Graduate* (Chapel Hill: University of North Carolina Press, 1937).

45. Jackson Davis, General Education Board Notes, 8 March 1943, General Education Board, record group 5221–5234, series 1, sub-series 3, box 490, folder 5231, RAC. See also William J. Trent Jr., "Cooperative Fund Raising for Higher Education," *Journal of Negro Education* 24, 1 (winter 1955), 6–15.

46. Trent, "Cooperative Fund Raising." Contrary to Patterson's original intention, the UNCF has typically received less than half of its fund-

ing from the general public; the majority of its support comes from foundations, wealthy individuals, and corporations.

47. Frederick D. Patterson in Goodson, *Chronicles of Faith*, 65.

48. William J. Trent Jr. and Frederick D. Patterson, "Financial Support of the Private Negro College," *Journal of Negro Education* 27, 3, Desegregation and the Negro College (summer 1958), 398–405.

49. Williams, "The United Negro College Fund: Its Growth and Development."

50. Frederick D. Patterson, "Southern Viewpoint: Would it Not Be Wise for Some Negro Schools to Make a Joint Appeal to Public for Funds?" Pittsburgh *Courier*, 30 January 1943.

51. Jones, "A History of the United Negro College Fund," 9, UNCF Papers.

52. Frederick D. Patterson in Goodson, *Chronicles of Faith*, 135.

53. Walter Hoving, interview by Marcia Goodson, transcript, February 1981; Lindsley Kimball, interview by Marcia Goodson, transcript, February 1981, UNCF Oral History, No. 1331.

54. For more information on the fund's solicitation strategies, see record group 2, general information, reel 1511, "solicitation policy," United Negro College Fund Papers, Atlanta University Center, Atlanta, Georgia (hereafter cited as UNCF AUC Center Papers).

55. Patterson, interview February 1981.

56. Jones, "A History of the United Negro College Fund," 11, UNCF Papers

57. Hollis Price, interview by Marcia Goodson, transcript, May 1987, UNCF Oral History, No. 1331.

58. Frederick D. Patterson, "Development Programs at Negro Institutions," (speech given before the Council of Presidents of the National Association of State and Universities and Land-Grant Colleges, Chicago, Illinois, 11 November 1969).

59. Jackson Davis, General Education Board notes, 17 June 1943, General Education Board Papers, Record Group 5221–5234, series 1, sub-series 3, box 490, folder 5231, RAC; Brawley, interview.

60. Bruce Barton, William Dean Embree, and Samuel D. Leidesdorf, "A Memorandum concerning the United Negro College Fund, Inc., 1946," box 491, folder 5239, General Education Board Papers, Record Group 5235–5240, series 1, sub-series 3, RAC; Lindsley Kimball, "United

Negro College Fund, Inc., Outline Study," Messrs Rockefeller-Education, III 2G, box 96, folder 664A, RAC.

61. Hoving, to Contributors, December 1944.

62. Price, interview, February 1981.

63. Ibid.

64. Ibid.

65. Frederick D. Patterson to Jackson Davis, 28 May 1943, General Education Board Papers, Record Group 5235–5240, series 1, sub-series 3, box 490, folder 5231, RAC.

66. Frederick D. Patterson in Goodson, *Chronicles of Faith*, 131.

67. There was an acting executive director prior to William J. Trent, Charles Bynum, one of Patterson's colleagues at Tuskegee.

68. William J. Trent Jr., interview by Marcia Goodson, transcript, February 1981, UNCF Oral History, 3.

69. Jones, "A History of the United Negro College Fund," 17, UNCF Papers. Please note that an endowment is comprised of the funds that a college holds in perpetuity to support the institution as a whole. Endowment monies are typically not spent by the institution.

70. Ibid., 47, UNCF Papers

71. Williams, "Growth and Development." See also UNCF minutes, Executive Committee Meeting, 1 October 1945, 6. Please note that the resulting 25 percent of the funds collected were used for operation of the Fund itself and special initiatives designed to support the member colleges.

72. Patterson, interview, February 1981, 18.

73. Frederick D. Patterson in Goodson, *Chronicles of Faith*, 142.

74. Patterson, interview, February 1981, 83.

75. Jones, "A History of the United Negro College Fund," UNCF Papers.

76. Trent, interview, February 1981.

77. Jones, "A History of the United Negro College Fund," 25, UNCF Papers.

78. Patterson, interview, February 1981; Lindsley Kimball, interview by Marcia Goodson, transcript, March 1981, UNCF Oral History, No. 1331.

79. Betty Stebman, interview by Marcia Goodson, transcript, April 1982, UNCF Oral History, No. 1331, 12.

80. Ibid., 13.

81. Jones, "A History of the United Negro College Fund," UNCF Papers.

82. Ibid., 43.

83. Ibid., 43–44.

84. Ibid.

Chapter 2. Bringing the Millionaires on Board

An earlier version of this chapter was published as Marybeth Gasman, "A Word for Every Occasion: Appeals by John D. Rockefeller, Jr. to White Donors on Behalf of the United Negro College Fund," *History of Higher Education Annual* 22(2002/2003), 67–90.

1. Annual Report of the Executive Director of the Board of Directors of the UNCF, Inc., 8 September 1950, General Education Board, 5241–5250, 1, 3, box 492, folder 5243, RAC.

2. Frederick D. Patterson in Marcia Goodson, ed., *Chronicles of Faith: An Autobiography of Frederick D. Patterson* (Tuscaloosa: University of Alabama Press, 1991); Peter Collier and David Horowitz, *The Rockefellers* (New York: Holt, Rinehart, and Winston, 1976), 77. For an example of Rockefeller Jr.'s influence, see a letter that Prescott S. Bush wrote to him in 1946: "As a matter of fact, your original approval of the project when it started influenced me in doing something about it. I know how thoroughly you look into these important charitable matters and your endorsement really means something to me." RAC.

3. Collier and Horowitz, *The Rockefellers.*

4. Patterson in Goodson, ed., *Chronicles of Faith,* 129.

5. Kimball, Outline Study, Messrs Rockefeller-Education, III 2G, box 96, folder 664A, RAC.

6. For twenty-three years Alfred P. Sloan was president of General Motors Corporation, which was established in 1908. Harvey S. Firestone created the Firestone Tire and Rubber Company in 1900. He held the position of president in the company until 1932 when his son replaced him. Richard K. Mellon was chairman of the Mellon Bank, a conservationist, and a prominent figure in the industrial and financial life of Pittsburgh. Robert W. Woodruff was the president of the Coca Cola Company, headquartered in Atlanta, Georgia.

7. Trent, "Cooperative Fund Raising."

8. James D. Anderson, *The Education of Blacks in the South, 1860–1935* (Chapel Hill: University of North Carolina Press, 1988); Eric Anderson

and Alfred Moss, *Dangerous Donations: Northern Philanthropy and Southern Education* (Columbia: University of Missouri Press, 1999). In 1901, Ogden's guests on the "millionaire's special" included William H. Baldwin Jr. (president of the Long Island Railroad) and George F. Peabody (Wall Street businessman).

9. Anderson and Moss, *Dangerous Donations*, 43.

10. Frederick Taylor Gates (1853–1929) was a Baptist minister who from 1891 served as a trusted adviser to John D. Rockefeller in both his charitable and business endeavors. He also served as a trustee (1902–1917) and chairman (1907–1917) of the General Education Board. For more information, please see http://www.rockefeller.edu/archive.ctr/ftg.html. Wallace Buttrick (1853–1926) was a Baptist minister who served as secretary (1902–1917), president (1917–1923), and chairman (1923–1926) of the General Education Board, and as a trustee of the Rockefeller Foundation (1917–1926). For more information, please see http://www.rockefeller.edu/archive.ctr/rf_wb.html.

11. Collier and Horowitz, *The Rockefellers*.

12. Ron Chernow, *Titan* (New York: Vintage Books, 1998).

13. Collier and Horowitz, *The Rockefellers*, 132; Cary Reich, *The Life of Nelson A. Rockefeller: Worlds to Conquer, 1908–1958* (New York: Doubleday, 1996).

14. John D. Rockefeller, Jr., Biographical Notes, www.rockefeller.edu/archive, accessed March 13, 2003, RAC.

15. Collier and Horowitz, *The Rockefellers*, 157.

16. Ibid., 177.

17. Anderson, *Education of Blacks*, 256–257.

18. Ibid.

19. The Rockefellers' support of consolidation in education was reflected in GEB policy. Among the institutions that were encouraged to merge or form consortiums were not only black colleges, but also medical schools and some historically white universities. For example, Emory University, Georgia Tech University, the University of Georgia and Agnes Scott College in the Atlanta/Athens area of Georgia were encouraged to form a collegiate consortium.

20. Also see John D. Rockefeller Jr.'s radio platter on the United Negro College Fund, Inc., 23 January 1948, box 96, folder 660, Messrs Rockefeller—Education, III 2G, RAC. Also, see biographical file, record

group 3, reel 1668, United Negro College Fund Archives, Clark-Atlanta University, Atlanta, Georgia.

21. John D. Rockefeller, NBC broadcast transcript, 26 May 1944, Messrs Rockefeller—Education, III 2G, box 96, folder 660, RAC.

22. After the Civil War, some missionary and industrial philanthropists felt that it was essential to assist blacks so as to pre-empt them from becoming a menace in society. See Anderson, *Education of Blacks.*

23. John D. Rockefeller Jr. to Fowler McCormick, 6 February 1952, Messrs Rockefeller—Education, III 2G, box 95, folder 658, RAC.

24. Anderson, *Education of Blacks.*

25. Jones, "A History of the United Negro College Fund," 72, UNCF Papers.

26. When Julius Rosenwald established the Rosenwald Fund, he called for its termination in 1948.

27. John D. Rockefeller Jr. to William Nelson Cromwell, 13 April 1944, Messrs Rockefeller—Education, III 2G, box 97, folder 665.

28. Patterson in Goodson, ed., *Chronicles of Faith,* 137.

29. Hoving's position was different from Rockefeller Jr.'s position as honorary national campaign chairman. Rockefeller's name was used to garner national attention.

30. Walter Hoving is best known as the controlling share holder and president of Tiffany and Company. He began this position in 1955 and held it until 1980. Sales increased from $7 million to $100 million during that time.

31. Patterson in Goodson, ed., *Chronicles of Faith,* 131.

32. John D. Rockefeller Jr. to J. R. Warwick, 20 November 1950, Messrs Rockefeller—Education, III 2G, box 52, folder 657, RAC. This idea is present in most letters authored by Rockefeller Jr. or sent out under his signature.

33. Stebman, interview, 26–27.

34. Ibid., 27.

35. Remarks of John D. Rockefeller Jr. in a broadcast over NBC of the Negro College Fund Campaign, 26 March 1944, Messrs Rockefeller, III 2G, box 96, folder 660, RAC.

36. John D. Rockefeller Jr. to J. Howard Pew, 23 July 1946, Messrs Rockefeller—Education, III 2G, box 97, folder 665, RAC.

37. John D. Rockefeller Jr., Notes for speech, 12 June 1945, Messrs Rockefeller—Education, III 2G, box 96, folder 661, RAC.

38. Kimball, Outline Study.

39. The letters to potential local campaign chairmen exemplify this idea. They are located, primarily, in Messrs Rockefeller—Education, III 2G, box 94, folder 655A, RAC.

40. John D. Rockefeller Jr. to Bayard Pope, 28 August 1950, Messrs Rockefeller—Education, III 2G, box 95, folder 658A, RAC.

41. John D. Rockefeller Jr. to Bernard M. Baruch, 1 February 1951, Messrs Rockefeller—Education, III 2G, box 95, folder 656A, RAC.

42. Many letters to industry leaders contain the phrase "insurance against subversive influences." They are located in the Messrs Rockefeller—Education, III 2G, RAC.

43. John D. Rockefeller Jr., *I Believe*, 8 July 1941, accessed 11 April 2002 from www.Rockefeller.edu/archive.ctr/jdrjrbio.html.

44. Jones, "A History of the United Negro College Fund," 45, UNCF Papers. See also Patrick J. Gilpin and Marybeth Gasman, *Charles S. Johnson. Leadership Behind the Veil in the Age of Jim Crow* (Albany: State University of New York Press, 2003).

45. See miscellaneous letters in Messrs Rockefeller—III 2G, box 95, RAC.

46. John D. Rockefeller Jr., 10 May 1945, box 96, folder 660 ; also see, John D. Rockefeller Jr., NBC radio address transcript, 1951, Messrs Rockefeller, III 2G, box 95, folder 459, RAC.

47. "Thirty-two Steps Forward to a Better America," 1945, General Education Board Papers, Record Group 5235–5240, Series 1, sub-series 3, Box 491, folder 5238, RAC.

48. "America is Free to Choose," 1944, General Education Board Papers, Record Group 5235–5240, series 1, sub-series 3, box 491, folder 5338, RAC.

49. "A Significant Adventure," [1950], General Education Board Papers, Record Group 5235–5240, series 1, sub-series 3, box 491, folder 5240, RAC.

50. Mary L. Dudziak, *Cold War Civil Rights: Race and the Image of American Democracy* (Princeton, N.J.: Princeton University Press, 2000).

51. Leon F. Litwack, *Trouble in Mind: Black Southerners in the Age of Jim Crow* (New York: Knopf, 1998); John Egerton, *Speak Now Against the Day: The Generation Before the Civil Rights Movement in the South* (New York: Knopf, 1994); Marybeth Gasman, "Scylla and Charybdis: Navigating the Waters of Academic Freedom at Fisk University During Charles S. John-

son's Administration (1946–1956)," *American Educational Research Journal* 36, 4 (winter 1999); Ellen Schrecker, *No Ivory Tower: McCarthyism and the Universities* (New York: Oxford University Press, 1986); Cedric Belfrage, *The American Inquisition, 1945–1960* (Indianapolis: Bobbs-Merrill, 1973); David Caute, *The Great Fear: The Anti-Communist Purge under Truman and Eisenhower* (New York: Simon and Schuster, 1978); Griffen Fariello, *Red Scare: Memories of the American Inquisition. An Oral History* (New York: W.W. Norton and Company, 1995).

52. "National Mobilization of Resources," April 1952 General Education Board Papers, III 2G, box 492, folder 5241, RAC.

53. I use the term "quasi-scientific" to differentiate this presentation of data from that of scholarly social scientific research. Tables and graphs resulting from academic research might be accompanied by detailed descriptions of the methods, use a precise scale, and indicate the source of the data.

54. Kimball, interview, 16–18.

55. Patterson, interview, February 1981, 78.

56. William J. Trent Jr., interview by Marcia Goodson, transcript, October 1981, UNCF Oral History, 60.

57. Frederick D. Patterson, interview by Marcia Goodson, transcript, August 1980, UNCF Oral History, No. 1331.

58. Mobilizing Board [Harvey S. Firestone Jr., Devereux C. Josephs, Richard K. Mellon, John D. Rockefeller Jr., Alfred P. Sloan Jr., Robert E. Wilson, and Robert W. Woodruff] to Frank Abrams, 30 July 1952, Messrs Rockefeller, III 2G, box 96, folder 664, RAC.

59. John D. Rockefeller Jr. to industry leaders of Buffalo, New York, 4 May 1959, Messrs Rockefeller, III 2G, box 95, folder 659A, RAC. See also, John D. Rockefeller Jr. to Ralph Hayes, 27 July 1944 and 5 August 1946; John D. Rockefeller Jr. to Thomas A. Morgan, 7 February 1945, Messrs Rockefeller, III 2G, box 97, folder 667, RAC.

60. "America is Free to Choose," 1944, General Education Board Papers, Record Group 5235–5240, series 1, sub-series 3, box 491, folder 5338, RAC.

61. Stebman, interview, 75.

62. Charles V. Willie and Ronald R. Edmonds, *Black Colleges in America. Challenge, Development, and Survival* (New York: Teachers College Press, 1978), 91; Anderson, *Education of Blacks*, 274; Daniel C. Thomp-

son, *Private Black Colleges at the Crossroads* (Westport, Connecticut: Greenwood Press, 1973).

63. Henry Drewry and Humphrey Doermann, *Stand and Prosper: Private Black Colleges and their Students* (Princeton: Princeton University Press, 2001), 92.

64. "Appraisal of a Venture. The United Negro College Fund's First Fifteen Years, 1944–1959," John D. Rockefeller Jr. papers, RAC.

65. Goodson, *Chronicles of Faith*. While at Tuskegee, Patterson initiated many new programs related to science and technology including, commercial dietetics (1935), commercial aviation (1935), veterinary medicine (1935) and engineering (1948).

66. Anderson, *Education of Blacks*. See chapter entitled, "The Apostles of Liberal Education."

67. In the past foundations such as Phelps-Stokes, the Rosenwald Fund, and the General Education Board used images of industrial education to portray black colleges. However, these were white-led organizations operating early in the century.

68. Anderson, *Education of Blacks*; C. Vann Woodward, *The Strange Career of Jim Crow* (New York: Oxford University Press, 2001).

69. John D. Rockefeller Jr. to Governor Broughton, 28 February 1945, Messrs Rockefeller–Education, III 2G, RAC.

70. John D. Rockefeller Jr. to Colgate W. Darden, 5 December 1946, Messrs Rockefeller—Education, III 2G, box 94, folder 655B, RAC.

71. Rockefeller Jr. to Darden, 5 December 1946, Messrs Rockefeller—Education, III 2G, box 94, folder 655B, RAC.

72. Rockefeller Jr., Notes for speech, 12 June 1945, Messrs Rockefeller—Education, III 2G, box 96, folder 661, RAC. For a thorough depiction of southern gradualism, see Adam Fairclough, "'Being in the Field of Education and Also Being a Negro . . . Seems . . . Tragic': Black Teachers in the Jim Crow South," *Journal of American History* 87, 1 (2000).

73. Benjamin Mays, interview by Marcia Goodson, transcript, May 1987, UNCF Oral History, No. 1331; Patterson, interview, August 1980.

74. Kimball, interview, March 1981, 36.

75. David Garrow, *Philanthropy and the Civil Rights Movement* (New York: Center on Philanthropy and Civil Society, 1987).

76. Stebman, interview, 54.

77. Ibid.

78. Kimball, interview, 37.

79. Mays, interview, 21.

80. Kimball, interview, 17–18.

81. Ibid., 18–19.

82. Ibid., 22.

83. Stebman, interview, 29.

84. Ibid., 30.

85. Ibid., 31.

86. William J. Trent Jr., interview by Marcia Goodson, transcript, November 1980, UNCF Oral History, No. 1331.

87. "27 Negro Colleges in $1,500,000 Drive," *The New York Times*, 4 May 1944, 36.

88. Buford G. Lincoln to John D. Rockefeller Jr., 3 June 1944, Messrs Rockefeller—Education, III 2G, box 96, folder 6620, RAC.

89. John D. Rockefeller Jr. to Buford G. Lincoln, 22 June 1944, Messrs Rockefeller—Education, III 2G, box 96, folder 6620, RAC.

90. Rockefeller Jr. to Lincoln, 22 June 1944, Messrs Rockefeller—Education, III 2G, box 96, folder 6620, RAC.

91. Jones, "A History of the United Negro College Fund," 37, UNCF Papers.

92. Rockefeller Jr. to Lincoln, 22 June 1944, Messrs Rockefeller—Education, III 2G, box 96, folder 6620, RAC. Rockefeller received similar letters from William J. Woody from Savannah, Georgia and W. Carson Adams of Coal & Coke, Birmingham, Alabama, located in Messrs Rockefeller—Education, III 2G, box 96, folder 6620, RAC.

93. In most cases, black characters were portrayed by whites in black face.

94. Kenneth W. Goings, *Mammy and Uncles Moses: Black Collectibles and American Stereotyping* (Bloomington: Indiana University Press, 1994).

95. "America is Free to Choose," 1944, General Education Board Papers, Record Group 5235–5240, series 1, sub-series 3, box 491, folder 5338, RAC.

96. "The Mobilizer," June 1953, Messrs Rockefeller—Education, III 2G, box 96, folder 664, RAC.

97. Kimball, interview, 31.

98. The Mobilizer, June 1952, Messrs Rockefeller—Education, III 2G, box 96, folder 664, RAC.

99. Cutlip, *Fundraising in the United States.*

100. Collier and Horowitz, *The Rockefellers.*

101. Aristotle, *Rhetoric*, trans. W. Rhys Roberts (New York: Modern Library, 1984).

Chapter 3. Flirting with Social Equality

1. Kathleen D. McCarthy, ed., *Lady Bountiful Revisited: Women, Philanthropy, and Power* (New Brunswick: Rutgers University Press, 1990).

2. McCarthy, *Lady Bountiful.* Sondra Shaw and Martha Taylor, eds., *Reinventing Fundraising: Realizing the Potential of Women's Philanthropy* (San Francisco: Jossey-Bass, 1995); Andrea Walton, ed., *Women and Philanthropy in Education* (Bloomington: Indiana University Press, 2005). See also Teresa Odendahl, *Women and Philanthropy: Gender and Career Patterns* (New York: Russell Sage Foundation, 1988); Kathleen D. McCarthy, *Women, Philanthropy, and Civil Society* (Bloomington: Indiana University Press, 2001); Sarah Deutsch, "Learning to Talk More Like a Man: Boston Women's Class Bridging Organizations, 1870–1940," *The American Historical Review* 97, 2 (April 1992), 379–404; Maureen A. Flanagan, "Gender and Urban Political Reform: The City Club and the Woman's City Club of Chicago in the Progressive Era," *The American Historical Review* 95, 4 (October 1990), 1032–1050; Anne M. Boylan, "Women in Groups: An Analysis of Women's Benevolent Organizations in New York and Boston, 1797–1840," *The Journal of American History* 71, 2 (September 1974), 372–393.

3. Stebman, interview.

4. Hoving, interview.

5. "Mrs. Waddell, 63, was Civic Leader," *The New York Times,* 14 December 1961, 43.

6. Jones, "A History of the United Negro College Fund," 141, UNCF Papers.

7. Stebman, interview, 110.

8. Kimball, interview; Patterson, interview, August 1980, 74.

9. William J. Trent Jr., interview by Marcia Goodson, transcript, October 1980, UNCF Oral History Collection, No. 1331.

10. Ibid.; Stebman, interview,.

11. Dorothy G. Becker, "Exit Lady Bountiful: The Volunteer and the Professional Social Worker," *The Social Service Review* 38, 1 (1964), 63–64.

12. Becker, "Exit Lady Bountiful," 71.

13. Stebman, interview, 78. Descriptions of Catherine Waddell's visits to Spelman College and her service on the Board of Trustees were used in letters sent to potential female donors. See Catherine Waddell to Miss/Mrs. [generic salutation], 20 October 1948, and Catherine Waddell to Mrs. [generic salutation], 21 June 1948, UNCF Papers, Manuscript Division, Library of Congress, Washington, D.C., Reel 3082.

14. The colleges that make up the "Seven Sisters" include: Wellesley (Wellesley, Mass.), Bryn Mawr (Bryn Mawr, Pa.), Smith (Northhampton, Mass.), Mount Holyoke (South Hadley, Mass.), Barnard (New York City), Radcliffe (Cambridge, Mass.) and Vassar (Poughkeepsie, N.Y.).

15. Stebman, interview.

16. Lynn Homan and Thomas Reilly, *The Tuskegee Airmen* (Columbia, S.C.: Arcadia Publishing, 1999). See also Stebman, interview.

17. Stebman, interview.

18. It was common for the Women's Division to use lists from other organizations, such as the Museum of Modern Art, to generate their own lists of potential donors. See Reel 3115, UNCF Papers, Manuscript Division.

19. Stebman, interview, 83.

20. "America's Town Meeting of the Air," *The Jerry Lee On-Line Photo Archive at the Library of American Broadcasting*, www.lib.umd.edu, control number, 56.053, 12 April 1945, accessed 21 June 2005.

21. Stebman, interview, 84.

22. Ibid., 85.

23. Ibid.

24. Ibid., 86.

25. Ibid., 86–88.

26. In her 1948 fund-raising letters to those women who contributed the year before, Mrs. Waddall referred to segregation as obnoxious and longed for a day when "these institutions can be strengthened . . . when young white men and women can—if they wish . . . attend Hampton, Fisk, or Tuskegee and young Negroes can go to the colleges of their choice." See Catherine Waddell to Miss Tucker [sample letter], 24 September 1948, UNCF Papers, Manuscript Division, Reel 3077. In letters to potential donors in 1949, Mrs. Waddell discussed the "weak spot" in America's vision. See Catherine Waddell to Mrs. Ainslie [sample letter], 14 June 1949, UNCF Papers, Manuscript Division, Reel 3095.

27. Chauncey Waddell to John D. Rockefeller Jr., 23 November 1947, Messrs Rockefeller—Education, III 2G, box 94, folder 655C, RAC.

28. John D. Rockefeller Jr. to Chauncey Waddell, 11 December 1947, Messrs Rockefeller—Education, III 2G, box 94, folder 655C, RAC.

29. Rockefeller Jr. to Waddell, 11 December 1947, Messrs Rockefeller—Education, III 2G, box 94, folder 655C, RAC.

30. Stebman, interview, 222.

31. Ibid., 91.

32. Interestingly, the Davis Polk Law Firm was the firm of John W. Davis, who coincidentally was the same person who argued the *Brown v. Board of Education* case and lost it to Thurgood Marshall in 1954. See Stebman, interview.

33. Stebman, interview, 92.

34. Ibid., 93.

35. Cameron Binkley, "'No Better Heritage Than Living Trees': Women's Clubs and Early Conservation in Humboldt County," *Western Historical Quarterly* 33 (summer 2002), 201.

36. Stebman, interview, 93.

37. Ibid.

38. Trent, interview, October 1980.

39. Becker, "Exit Lady Bountiful," 71.

40. Stebman, interview, 92–94. Although Stebman is correct in her assessment of the "elite" nature attached to lunching at Mrs. McCullough's home, there were some women who refused to attend, preferring to give to the UNCF on an anonymous basis. They were afraid to have their names associated with the UNCF. See Reel 3095 for letters written by Catherine Waddell to "anonymous" donors, UNCF Papers, Manuscript Division.

41. Stebman, interview, 94.

42. Ibid.

43. Beverly Gordon, *Bazaars and Fair Ladies: The History of the American Fundraising Fair* (Knoxville: University of Tennessee Press, 1998).

44. David Levering Lewis, *When Harlem Was in Vogue* (New York: Penguin Books, 1997).

45. Kimball, interview, 53.

46. "Mrs. Hall Park McCullough" Honorary Program copy, n.d., UNCF Papers, Manuscript Division, Reel 1636. For lists of those who attended the luncheons see Reel 3091, UNCF Papers, Manuscript Division.

47. Stebman, interview, 106.

48. "Lady Bountiful," *Cambridge International Dictionary of Idioms* 2003; Binkley, "No Better Heritage," 179–202; Barbara Lowney, "Lady Bountiful: Margaret Crocker of Sacramento," *California Historical Society Quarterly* 47, 2 (1968), 99–112; Gregory Nosan, "Women in the Galleries: Prestige, Education, and Volunteerism at Mid-century," *Museum Studies* 29, 1 (2003), 46–71; Gordon, *Bazaars and Fair Ladies.*

49. Mrs. Hall Park McCullough to Mrs. [generic salutation], 8 March 1948, UNCF Papers, Manuscript Division, Reel 3083.

50. Kimball, interview, 54–55. For a more contemporary explanation of these differences, see Sondra Shaw and Martha Taylor, *Reinventing Fundraising: Realizing the Potential of Women's Philanthropy* (San Francisco: Jossey-Bass, 1995).

51. Trent, interview, October 1980.

52. Kimball, interview, 55.

53. "Greater New York Women's Division of the United Negro College Fund," 1948 Campaign, UNCF Papers, Manuscript Division, Reel 3082, 2.

54. Kimball, interview, 57.

55. Ibid., 56.

56. Stebman, interview, 96. The Social Register was, at one time, a book detailing who was a member of "polite society" in a given American city. For example, the *New York Social Register,* first published in 1887, consisted largely of the descendants of English or Dutch settlers, the merchant class who had built New York City. The *Social Register* pointedly excluded Jews and most Roman Catholics.

57. The Golden Rule Foundation is dedicated to "the American Dream of Self-Help" and continues to exist today.

58. Stebman, interview, 98.

59. Ibid., 99.

60. Ibid., 100. When interviewed in 1982, Betty Stebman noted of the event at the Colony Club, "I think if I wanted to do something like that, I'd have to go through the same thing at the Colony Club [today], because I don't think they've moved an inch since that time. I hope I'm wrong!" (p. 101).

61. Price, interview, 63.

62. Ibid., 63.

63. See Kathleen D. McCarthy, "Women and Philanthropy: Three

Strategies in an Historical Perspective," (working paper 22, Center on Philanthropy and Civil Society, City University of New York, winter 1994) and David C. Hammack, *Making the Nonprofit Sector in the United States: A Reader* (Bloomington: Indiana University Press, 1999). For a beautifully written synthesis of this perspective, see Walton, ed., "Introduction," in *Women and Philanthropy in Education*.

64. Vernon Jordan, interview by Marcia Goodson, transcript, January 1982, UNCF Oral History, No. 1331, 26–27.

Chapter 4. A Stigma of Inferiority

An earlier version of this chapter was published as Marybeth Gasman, "Rhetoric vs. Reality: The Fundraising Messages of the United Negro College Fund in the Immediate Aftermath of the *Brown* Decision," *History of Education Quarterly* 44, 1 (winter 2004), 70–94.

1. *Brown v. Board of Education of Topeka, Kansas*, 347 U.S. 483 (1954). For more information on the *Brown* decision in the primary- and secondary-school settings, see James T. Patterson, *Brown v. Board of Education: A Civil Rights Milestone and Its Troubled Legacy* (New York: Oxford University Press, 2001); Richard Kluger, *Simple Justice: The History of Brown v. Board of Education and Black America's Struggle for Equality* (New York: Knopf, 1976); Constance Baker Motley, "The Legacy of *Brown v. Board of Education*," *Teachers College Record* 96, 4 (summer 1995): 637–643; and Charles J. Russo, J. John Harris, and Rosetta F. Sandidge, "*Brown v. Board of Education* at 40: A Legal History of Equal Educational Opportunity in American Public Education," *Journal of Negro Education* 63, 3 (summer 1994): 297–309.

2. The UNCF's commitment to these goals is evident in both their internal correspondence and their publicity. See the UNCF AUC Center Papers.

3. Within the UNCF Papers there are countless letters between the UNCF leaders and the member college presidents detailing their immediate reaction to *Brown v. Board* as well as the organization's strategies for "spinning" the organizations' response in the years after the decision. When looking back at the decade after *Brown*, we can see the slowness of response by both the state and federal government. However, within the UNCF papers, there is a sense that the existence of black colleges, including private black colleges, must be defended.

4. Albert L. Samuels, *Is Separate Unequal? Black Colleges and the Challenge to Desegregation* (Lawrence: University of Kansas Press, 2004).

5. W. E. B. Du Bois, *The Education of Black People, Ten Critiques, 1906–1960*, ed. Herbert Aptheker (New York: Monthly Review Press, 1973), 66. Du Bois originally delivered this as a speech in 1930.

6. William J. Trent Jr. to UNCF Campaign Leadership, 1954, memo entitled "Questions and Answers Concerning the Effect of the Supreme Court Decision on the UNCF and its Member Colleges," box 16, microfiche 2295, 2296, UNCF AUC Center Papers.

7. Henry Drewry and Humphrey Doermann, *Stand and Prosper. Private Black Colleges and their Students* (Princeton: Princeton University Press, 2001). Although today the UNCF boasts 40 member colleges, in 1954, there were only 31. Membership in the UNCF required being a private institution with an "A" rating (assigned by the Southern Association of Negro Colleges and signifying that the institution offered a quality educational program). For more detailed information, see Shuana K. Tucker, "The Early Years of the United Negro College Fund, 1943–1960," *The Journal of African American History* 87, 4 (fall 2002), 416–432.

8. The Court's call for the dismantling of segregated schools with "all deliberate speed" actually came in the *Brown II* case, *Brown v. Board of Education of Topeka, Kansas*, 349 U.S. 294 (1955).

9. Michael Klarman, *From Jim Crow to Civil Rights: The Supreme Court and the Struggle for Racial Equality* (New York: Oxford University Press, 2003); Mark Tushet, *NAACP's Legal Strategy against Segregated Education, 1925–1950* (Chapel Hill: University of North Carolina Press, 1987).

10. These cases were *Missouri ex rel. Gaines v. Canada, Registrar of the University of Missouri, et al.*, 305 U.S. 337 (1938); *Sipuel v. Board of Regents*, 332 U.S. 631 (1948); *Sweatt v. Painter*, 339 U.S. 629 (1950); *McLaurin v. Oklahoma State Regents*, 339 U.S. 637 (1950). The first case, in 1938, involved Lloyd Gaines, a black, high school valedictorian who wanted to attend the University of Missouri Law School. When the law school discovered that Gaines was black they denied his admission but offered to pay his tuition in another state. In this instance, the Court declared that states must either furnish separate and equal educational institutions within the respective state or admit blacks to the all-white institutions. In effect, *Gaines* called for the provision of an equal education for all of a state's residents. Although important and effective in foreshadowing the Court's future decisions, the *Gaines* case is not discussed in detail in

this book. Taking place in 1938, six years prior to the creation of the UNCF, the case, although promising to the Fund's leadership, did not have an impact on their fund-raising strategies. The *Sweatt* and *Sipuel* cases, which offered greater hope to the Fund leadership, are discussed in the body of the chapter.

11. *Plessey v. Ferguson*, 163 U.S. 537 (1896).

12. Klarman, *From Jim Crow to Civil Rights*; Tushet, *NAACP's Legal Strategy Against Segregated Education*.

13. Tushet, *NAACP's Legal Strategy against Segregated Education*.

14. Charles S. Johnson, "Some Significant Social and Educational Implications of the U.S. Supreme Court's Decisions," *The Journal of Negro Education* 23, 3 (summer 1954), 354–371.

15. Richard Kluger, *Simple Justice: The History of Brown v. Board of Education and Black America's Struggle for Equality* (New York: Knopf, 1976).

16. Vanessa Siddle Walker provides a thorough analysis of the values of segregated schools at the elementary and secondary level in Vanessa Siddle Walker, "Valued Segregated Schools for African American Children in the South, 1935–1969: A Review of Common Themes and Characteristics," *Review of Educational Research* 70, 3 (fall 2000): 253–295. See also Johnson, "Some Significant Social and Educational Implications."

17. Frederick. D. Patterson, "The Private Negro College in a Racially-Integrated System of Higher Education," *The Journal of Negro Education* 21, 3 (summer 1952), 368.

18. John S. Lash, "The Umpteenth Crisis in Negro Higher Education," *Journal of Negro Education* 22, 8 (November 1951), 432.

19. William J. Trent Jr. to Reuben Maury, 16 March 1954, box 16, microfiche 2295, UNCF AUC Center Papers. This letter was written prior to the *Brown* decision.

20. William J. Trent Jr., to UNCF Leadership, n.d. [pre-*Brown*], memo entitled "Objectives of the United Negro College Fund," box 16, microfiche 2295, UNCF AUC Center Papers.

21. Ibid.

22. "Feel Integration will Spur Race Colleges to Excel," Pittsburgh *Courier*, 15 March 1952, located in box 16, microfiche 2296, UNCF AUC Center Papers.

23. Ibid.

24. Ibid.

25. Ibid.

26. Trent, interview, 71–72.

27. Frederick D. Patterson, "Report to Friends and Contributors of the United Negro College Fund," 27 May 1954, box 16, microfiche 2295, UNCF AUC Center Papers.

28. Stephen J. Wright, interview Marcia Goodson, transcript, June 1987, UNCF Oral History, No. 1331. See also Price, interview.

29. C. H. Raullerson to William J. Trent Jr., 1 June 1954, memo entitled "Materials prepared as a result of the Supreme Court Decision," box 16, microfiche 2295, UNCF AUC Center Papers.

30. William J. Trent Jr., "Official Statement of the United Negro College Fund Regarding the Supreme Court Decision of May 17, 1954," 1954, UNCF publication, box 16, microfiche 2295, UNCF AUC Center Papers.

31. Ibid.

32. William J. Trent Jr. to Negro Newspapers, open letter entitled "Night Letter," box 16, microfiche 2295, UNCF AUC Center Papers.

33. Mays, interview, 29.

34. Robin D. G. Kelley and Earl Lewis, eds., *To Make Our World Anew: A History of African Americans, From 1880, Volume II* (New York: Oxford University Press, 2005), 175.

35. Patterson, interview, 62.

36. Ibid.

37. Kimball, interview, 42.

38. Patterson, interview, 56.

39. Patterson, "Report to Friends and Contributors," 27 May 1954, box 16, microfiche 2295, UNCF AUC Center Papers.

40. United Negro College Fund, Memorandum of Information, 1954, box 16, microfiche 2295, UNCF AUC Center Papers.

41. "Statement by Dr. F. D. Patterson, President and Founder of the United Negro College Fund on the Decision of the United States Supreme Court on Segregation in the Public Schools of the South," box 16, microfiche 2296, UNCF AUC Center Papers.

42. "Appraisal of a Venture. The United Negro College Fund's First Fifteen Years, 1944–1959," Messers Rockefeller, Education, III 2G, box 96, folder 661A, RAC. For graph information, see UNCF Fact Sheet, United Negro College Fund, UNCF AUC Center Papers; Williams, "Growth and Development," 107.

43. *True* desegregation did not occur until the 1970s. Although only a

few blacks were admitted to historically white institutions through the early 1970s, some small gains were made prior to that time in northern states, border states, and on occasion in a state in the Deep South. Consider the following: In 1948, the University of Arkansas admitted a black student to their medical school. In the same year, the University of Delaware allowed blacks to take classes if the classes they needed were not offered at Delaware State College for Negroes, and in 1950, upon court order, the institution admitted black students "without restriction." Likewise, the University of Kentucky started to admit blacks to its graduate programs in 1949. Even Louisiana State University began admitting blacks, as a result of a court order, in 1950. In 1954, the University of Maryland opened its undergraduate program to blacks, having opened their graduate programs, by force of law, in 1950. By 1954, all colleges and universities in the state of Missouri desegregated. The University of Oklahoma was desegregated in 1948 by court order, and the state's other public institutions followed suite within the year. The court ordered the University of Virginia's law school to desegregate in 1950, and by 1953 four other state institutions desegregated voluntarily. All of West Virginia's eleven state institutions were desegregated by 1954. By 1956, three southern states opened all of the public institutions to blacks. These were Kentucky, Maryland, and Oklahoma. The same was the case in the state of Tennessee, where blacks were attending all but one of the state's public institutions. Of course, the exceptions were the states in the Deep South, including Alabama, Florida, Georgia, Mississippi, and South Carolina. For more information, see Henry Allen Bullock, *A History of Negro Education in the South from 1619 to the Present* (Cambridge: Harvard University Press, 1967). See also James S. Coleman, *Equality of Educational Opportunity* (Washington, D.C.: Government Printing Office, 1966) and various issues of *Southern School News*.

44. John Thelin, *A History of American Higher Education* (Baltimore: Johns Hopkins University Press, 2005).

45. J. S. Scott Sr., [1954], "The Supreme Court Decision and the United Negro College Fund," box 13, microfiche 1875, UNCF AUC Center Papers.

46. Jones, "A History of the United Negro College Fund," UNCF Papers.

47. Scott, "The Supreme Court Decision and the United Negro College Fund."

48. Charles S. Johnson, "Next Steps in Education in the South," *Phylon* 15, 1 (1st Quarter, 1954): 7–20, 10; Johnson made similar statements after the *Brown* decision in Johnson, "Some Significant Social and Educational Implications."

49. Albert Manley, interview by Marcia Goodson, transcript, May 1987, UNCF Oral History, No. 1331.

50. Press Release, Board Meeting in Atlanta, Georgia, 4 October 1954, box 16, microfiche 2296, UNCF AUC Center Papers.

51. Benjamin E. Mays, "In view of the recent Supreme Court decision, what do you consider the most effective arguments for continued support of the UNCF?" [1954], box 13, microfiche 1875, UNCF AUC Center Papers.

52. Manley, interview, 30.

53. "National Mobilization of Resources for the United Negro College Fund," 18 January 1955, Messers Rockefeller—Education, III, 2G, box 96, folder 664A, RAC. See also Charles S. Johnson, *The Negro College Graduate* (New York: Negro Universities Press, 1969); Robert C. Weaver, "The Private Negro Colleges and Universities—An Appraisal," *The Journal of Negro Education* 29, 2 (spring 1960), 113–120; E. C. Harrison, "On Reorientation of College for Negroes," *The Journal of Higher Education* 26, 6 (June 1955), 297–299, 342.

54. *African American Who's Who*, 1944–1960.

55. William J. Trent Jr. to UNCF Campaign Leadership, "Memorandum and Fact Sheet," 24 May 1954, box 16, microfiche 2295, UNCF AUC Center Papers.

56. Trent, interview, October 1980, 65.

57. Albert L. Samuels, *Is Separate Unequal? Black Colleges and the Challenge to Desegregation* (Lawrence: University of Kansas Press, 2004), 26.

58. Walter White, in Samuels, *Is Separate Unequal?*, 55.

59. Samuels, *Is Separate Unequal?*, 55.

60. Ibid., 68.

61. Patterson, "Report to Friends and Contributors," 27 May 1954, box 16, microfiche 2295, UNCF AUC Center Papers. See also, Johnson, "Next Steps in Education in the South," 7–20. Johnson made similar statements after the *Brown* decision in Johnson, "Some Significant Social and Educational Implications."

62. Daniel C. Thompson, *Private Black Colleges at the Crossroads* (Westport, Conn.: Greenwood Publishing, 1973).

63. Patterson, "Report to Friends and Contributors," 27 May 1954, box 16, microfiche 2295, UNCF AUC Center Papers.

64. Trent to UNCF Campaign Leadership, "Memorandum and Fact Sheet," 24 May 1954, box 16, microfiche 2295, UNCF AUC Center Papers.

65. See Patrick J. Gilpin and Marybeth Gasman, *Charles Spurgeon Johnson. Leadership Behind the Veil* (Albany: State University of New York Press, 2003) and Katrina Sanders, *Intelligent and Effective Direction* (New York: Peter Lang, 2005).

66. Joy A. Williamson, "'Quacks, Quirks, Agitators, and Communists': Private Black Colleges and the Limits of Institutional Autonomy," *History of Higher Education Annual* 23 (2003): 49–81; Joy A. Williamson, "Public Black Colleges and the Civil Rights Movement in Mississippi." In *Higher Education and the Civil Rights Movement*, edited by Peter Wallenstein (Gainesville: University of Florida Press, forthcoming). Most private predominantly white institutions were also effected by segregation laws. For example, prior to the advent of Jim Crow laws, Berea College was a biracial institution. However, nearly half a century before *Brown v. Board*, the institution was forced to become non-black. For more information, see Shannon H. Wilson, *Berea College: An Illustrated History* (Lexington: University Press of Kentucky, 2006).

67. United Negro College Fund, Official Publication, [1954], box 16, microfiche 2295, UNCF AUC Center Papers.

68. Ibid. See also James D. Anderson, *The Education of Blacks in the South, 1864–1935* (Chapel Hill: University of North Carolina Press, 1988).

69. United Negro College Fund, Official Publication, [1954], box 16, microfiche 2295, UNCF AUC Center Papers.

70. Ibid.

71. Ibid.

72. Ibid.

73. Benjamin E. Mays, "Our Colleges and the Supreme Court Decision," 20 March 1955, box 22, microfiche 3218, UNCF AUC Center Papers.

74. See Benjamin E. Mays speeches in the UNCF Papers at the Robert Woodruff Library, Atlanta University Center, Atlanta, Georgia.

75. Mays, "Our Colleges and the Supreme Court Decision," 20 March 1955, box 22, microfiche 3218, UNCF AUC Center Papers.

76. For more information, see Gilpin and Gasman, *Charles S. Johnson;* and Richard Robbins, *Sidelines Activist: Charles S. Johnson and the Struggle for Civil Rights* (Oxford: University of Mississippi, 1996).

77. L. H. Foster, "Suggestions for 1955 UNCF Campaign," 8 September 1955, box 13, microfiche 1875, UNCF AUC Center Papers. Although not a member of the UNCF, Luther Foster, as well as several other public black college presidents, banded together with the private institutions in their response to the Court decision.

78. Lindsley F. Kimball to John D. Rockefeller Jr. and the Members of the Mobilizing Board, 10 June 1954, Messrs Rockefeller—Education, III 2G, box 95, folder 659, RAC.

79. Details of the reduction in individual donors and increase in corporate donors are included in York Allen Jr. to File, 13 December 1956, Messers Rockefeller–Education, III, 2G, box 95, folder 659A, RAC. Graph data found in UNCF Papers, Library of Congress, Washington, D.C.

80. Wright, interview, 39.

81. Drewry and Doermann, *Stand and Prosper,* 103.

82. Paul Younger in Drewry and Doermann, *Stand and Prosper,* 94. For more information, see Alma Rene Williams, "A Research History of the United Negro College Fund, Inc., 1944–1987" (manuscript, United Negro College Fund, 1988).

83. Trent, interview, 88.

84. Stebman, interview, 166.

85. Hollis F. Price, "The Supreme Court Decision and the Private Negro College," 7 July 1954, box 13, microfiche 1875, UNCF AUC Center Papers.

86. Mays, "In view of the recent Supreme Court decision" [1954], box 13, microfiche 1875, UNCF AUC Center Papers.

87. William J. Trent Jr. to UNCF Leadership, "Objectives of the United Negro College Fund," n.d., box 16, microfiche 2295, UNCF AUC Center Papers.

88. Description is based on "Tomorrow's Generation," 1954, lateral file, UNCF AUC Center Papers.

89. The Ford Foundation was never in full support of the UNCF and, in fact, refused in 1944 to provide seed money when asked by Frederick D. Patterson and John D. Rockefeller Jr. See Mays, interview, and Kimball, interview. It's interesting to note that in the transcriptions of both

Mays's and Kimball's interviews, their comments about the Ford Foundation are blacked out. Marcia Goodson let each of those UNCF leaders read the transcriptions and decide what they wanted to keep and what they wanted to delete. The transcriptions were completed on a typewriter and thus from time to time there are blacked out areas.

90. Kimball, interview, 43.

91. Trent, interview, October 1980.

92. Mays, interview, 58.

93. Ibid.

94. Ibid.

95. Kimball, interview.

96. Stebman, interview, 167.

97. Ibid., 171.

98. Ibid.

99. Convocation Program, United Negro College Fund, Metropolitan Opera House, New York, New York, 20 March 1955, UNCF Papers, Manuscript Division, Reel 3217.

100. Stebman, interview.

101. Ibid., 181.

102. Benjamin E. Mays, United Negro College Fund Convocation, 20 March 1955, 1, UNCF Papers, Manuscript Division, Reel 3217.

103. Ibid.

104. Ibid.

105. See Marybeth Gasman, "From the Coffee Table to the Classroom: A Review of Recent Research on Historically Black Institutions," *Educational Researcher*, October 2005, and Marybeth Gasman, "The Higher Education Legacy of *Brown v. Board*," *Diversity Digest*, September 2004, for an in-depth discussion of the current state of black colleges, including the presence of white students on their campuses.

106. Martin D. Jenkins, "The Future of the Desegregated Negro College: A Critical Summary," *The Journal of Negro Education* 27, 3 (summer 1958), 419–429; Patterson, "Private Negro College," 363–369; Felton G. Clark, "The Development and Present Status of Publicly-Supported Higher Education for Negroes," *The Journal of Negro Education* 27, 3 (summer 1958), 221–232; Frederick D. Patterson, "Colleges for Negro Youth and the Future," *The Journal of Negro Education* 27, 2 (spring 1958), 107–114.

107. United Negro College Fund, Official Publication, [1954], box 16, microfiche 2295, UNCF AUC Center Papers.

108. Ibid.

109. Charles S. Thompson, "The Prospect of Negro Higher Education," *Journal of Educational Sociology* 32, 6 (February 1959), 309–316, 311.

110. Allen to File, "United Negro College Fund," 13 December 1956, Messers Rockefeller, Education, III, 2G, box 95, folder 659A, RAC.

111. Thompson, "The Prospect of Negro Higher Education," 311–312. Thompson also discusses these ideas in "The Negro College: In Retrospect and in Prospect," *The Journal of Negro Education* 27, 2 (spring 1958), 127–131.

112. Gilpin and Gasman, *Charles S. Johnson*. Charles S. Johnson died unexpectedly in 1956 at the age of 63. After his death, Fisk University and its new president Stephen J. Wright had a very difficult time sustaining Johnson's programs and ideas. Other black colleges also pursued efforts to integrate, including Lincoln University in Jefferson City, Missouri. According to its university history, "In 1954, the United States Supreme Court handed down its ruling in *Brown v. Board of Education*, and Lincoln University responded by opening its doors to all applicants meeting its entrance criteria" (see www.lincolnu.edu/~lupres/history.htm). Currently, Lincoln University is approximately 50 percent African American. Likewise, Howard University in Washington, D.C., has been successful in recruiting both whites and Asians to its campus. Howard University was briefly a member of the UNCF but is not currently. Lincoln University in Missouri, as a public institution, has never been a member.

113. Marybeth Gasman, "A Word for Every Occasion: Appeals by John D. Rockefeller Jr. to White Donors on Behalf of the United Negro College Fund," *History of Higher Education Annual* (2002).

114. Derrick Bell, *Silent Covenants: Brown V. Board of Education and the Unfulfilled Hopes for Racial Reform* (New York: Oxford University Press, 2005).

115. Graph data from UNCF Papers, Library of Congress, Washington, D.C.

116. Thompson, "The Negro College," 130–131.

117. Benjamin E. Mays, "United Negro College Fund Address, Buffalo New York," 5 May 1959, UNCF AUC Center Papers.

118. Mays, "United Negro College Fund Address, Buffalo New York,"

5 May 1959, UNCF AUC Center Papers. Mays' stance on the future of black colleges is also present in "Appraisal of a Venture. The United Negro College Fund's First Fifteen Years, 1944–1959," John D. Rockefeller Jr. Papers, III 2G, box 95, folder 659A, 1959, RAC. The number of UNCF member colleges increased to 33 in 1958 with the inclusion of Barber-Scotia College in North Carolina and St. Paul's College in Virginia.

Chapter 5. Responding to the Black Consciousness Movement

1. A. J. Jaffe, Walter Adams, and Sandra G. Meyers, *Negro Higher Education in the 1960s* (New York: Frederick A. Praeger Publishers, 1968).

2. Lawrence Levine, *Black Culture and Black Consciousness* (New York: Oxford University Press, 1989); Daniel C. Thompson, *Private Black Colleges at the Crossroads* (Westport, Conn.: Greenwood, 1973).

3. Patricia Gurin and Edgar Epps, *Black Consciousness, Identity, and Achievement: A Study of Students at Historically Black Colleges and Universities* (New York: John Wiley and Sons, 1975); Steven Biko, *I Write What I Like: Selected Writings* (Chicago: University of Chicago Press, 1978); Steven Biko, "The Definition of Black Consciousness," *SASO Leadership Training Course,* South Africa, 1972.

4. Joy A. Williamson, "Student Activists, Activist Students: Black Colleges and the Civil Rights Movement" (paper presented at the History of Education Society Annual Meeting, Chicago, Illinois, 2003), 6.

5. Mario Diani, "The Concept of Social Movements," *The Sociological Review* (1992).

6. Charles U. Smith, "The Sit-Ins and the New Negro Student," in *Student Unrest on Historically Black Campuses,* ed. Charles U. Smith (Tallahassee: Florida Agricultural and Mechanical University, 1994).

7. Smith, xi.

8. Thompson, *Private Black Colleges at the Crossroads.*

9. Mary L. Dudziak, *Cold War Civil Rights: Race and the Image of American Democracy* (Princeton: Princeton University Press, 2000); Thomas Borstelmann, *The Cold War and the Color Line* (Cambridge: Harvard University Press, 2001); and John D. Skrentny, "The Effect of the Cold War on African-American Civil Rights, 1945–1968," *Theory and Society* 27, 2 (April 1998), 237–285.

10. See also Melvyn P. Leffler, "The Cold War: What Do 'We Now Know,'" *The American Historical Review* 104, 2 (1999), 501–524; Jonathan

Rosenberg and Zachary Karabell, *Kennedy, Johnson, and the Quest for Justice* (New York: W. W. Norton, 2003); Gary Gerstle, *American Crucible: Race and Nation in the Twentieth Century* (Princeton: Princeton University Press, 2001).

11. Gurin and Epps, *Black Consciousness*. Of course, black students at predominantly white institutions also had these concerns. See Joy A. Williamson, *Black Power on Campus* (Urbana: University of Illinois Press, 2003).

12. Ibid., 199.

13. Ibid.

14. Ibid., 204.

15. Biko, "The Definition of Black Consciousness"; Franz Fanon, *A Dying Colonialism* (New York: Grove Press, 1965).

16. Gurin and Epps, *Black Consciousness*, 204.

17. Ibid., 207; Lisa Wolf-Wendal, Susan Twombly, Kathryn Tuttle, and Kelly Ward, *Reflecting Back, Looking Forward: Civil Rights and Student Affairs* (Washington, D.C.: NASPA, 2004).

18. Benjamin Muse, *The American Negro Revolution: From Nonviolence to Black Power* (Bloomington: Indiana University Press, 1973); Raymond Murphy and Howard Elinson, *Problems and Prospects of the Negro Movement* (Belmont, Calif.: Wadsworth Publishing Company, 1966).

19. Smith, ed., *Student Unrest on Historically Black Campuses*, 16.

20. These institutions were Morehouse, Atlanta, Clark, Morris Brown, Spelman, and the Interdenominational Theological Center.

21. Robert H. Brisbane, *Black Activism: Racial Revolution in the United States, 1954–1970* (Valley Forge: Judson Press, 1974).

22. Clayborne Carson, *In Struggle: SNCC and the Black Awakening of the 1960s* (Cambridge: Harvard University Press, 1981); Juan Williams and Dwayne Ashley, *I'll Find a Way or Make One: A Tribute to Historically Black Colleges and Universities* (New York: Harper Collins, 2004).

23. Wright, interview, 45.

24. Ibid., 47.

25. Ibid.

26. United Negro College Fund, *United Negro College Fund Finders' Guide to the Archives* (Ann Arbor: University Microfilms International, 1985).

27. Herbert Haines, "Black Radicalization and the Funding of Civil Rights: 1957–1970," *Social Problems* 32, 1 (October 1984), 31–43.

28. Kimball, interview, 61–62.

29. United Negro College Fund, *Guide to the Archives*, xiv.

30. "The United Negro College Fund and the Present Civil Rights Crisis," 29 July 1963, UNCF Papers, Manuscript Division. Emphasis added.

31. James D. Anderson, *The Education of Blacks in the South, 1860–1935* (Chapel Hill: University of North Carolina Press, 1988); William Watkins, *The White Architects of Black Education. Ideology and Power in America, 1865–1954* (New York: Teachers College Press, 2001).

32. Kimball, interview, 58.

33. "Advance Guard of a New Generation," 1967, UNCF Papers, Manuscript Division, microfiche, 2532.

34. Haines, "Black Radicalization," 31–43.

35. Ibid., 31–43, 42.

36. Kimball, interview, 59.

37. David Garrow, *Philanthropy and the Civil Rights Movement* (New York: Center on Philanthropy and Civil Society, 1987), 1.

38. Ibid., 10.

39. Although Wright came to the Fund as president (the title that Frederick D. Patterson held), he was really replacing William J. Trent Jr. as the full-time executive director. The title of executive director was no longer officially used after Trent left.

40. "Advance Guard of a New Generation," 1967, UNCF Papers, Manuscript Division, microfiche, 2532 (emphasis added by author).

41. Also see, "A Rationale for Corporate Investment in the Thirty-Six Member College and Universities of the United Negro College Fund," 1968, UNCF Papers, Manuscript Division, microfiche, 2540.

42. "We've Got a Goldmine Here," 1969, UNCF Papers, Manuscript Division, microfiche, 2511. Another brochure is entitled "Black Youth, Black Pride, Black Colleges," but it does not place any emphasis on "black pride," instead it has a business focus. See "Black Youth, Black Pride, Black Colleges," 1970, UNCF Papers, Manuscript Division, microfiche, 2538.

43. "We've Got a Goldmine Here," 1969, UNCF Papers, Manuscript Division, microfiche, 2511.

44. Wright, interview, 50–51.

45. Ibid., 51.

46. Gurin and Epps, *Black Consciousness*.

47. Wright, interview, 50.

48. Williams and Ashley, *I'll Find a Way or Make One*; Juan Williams, *My Soul Looks Back in Wonder: Voices of the Civil Rights Experience* (New York: AARP/Sterling, 2004).

49. Price, interview, 85.

50. Ibid., 86–88.

51. Ibid., 86. For a thorough and varied discussion of these issues, see Joel Rosenthal, "Southern Black Student Activism: Assimilation vs. Nationalism," *The Journal of Negro Education* 44, 2 (spring, 1975); Joy Williamson, "'Quirks, Quacks, Agitators, and Communists': Private Black Colleges and the Limits of Institutional Autonomy," *History of Higher Education Annual* 23 (2003); Diane Ravitch, "From Berkeley to Kent State," in *The Troubled Crusade: American Education, 1945–1984* (New York: Basic Books, 1980).

52. Albert Manley, interview by Marcia Goodson, transcript, June 1987, UNCF Oral History, No. 1331, 24.

53. Ibid., 24.

54. Ibid., 24–25.

55. Ibid., 25.

56. Mays, interview, 60.

57. Price, interview, 85.

58. Wright, interview, 119.

59. "A Rationale for Corporate Investment in the Thirty-Six Member College and Universities of the United Negro College Fund," 1970, UNCF Papers, Manuscript Division, microfiche, 2540.

60. Vernon Jordan, interview by Marcia Goodson, transcript, March 1987, UNCF Oral History, 208.

61. Morris B. Abram, a native of Georgia, was the president of Brandeis University and a partner in the law firm Paul, Weiss, Goldberg, Rifkind, Whorton and Garrison of New York. He was also a member of the Morehouse College board of trustees. For details on the recruitment of Abrams, see Jordan, interview, March 1987.

62. Morris B. Abram in "Is the United Negro College Fund to Limp into This Decade as an Irresistible Anachronism? I am Confident it is Not," 1970, UNCF Papers, Manuscript Division, microfiche, 2540.

63. Vernon E. Jordan, "Address to Youth Freedom Awards Dinner," speech given at 61st Annual NAACP Convention, 2 July 1970, Cincinnati, Ohio, UNCF Papers, Manuscript Division, Microfiche 1757, 13. The quotation from W. E. B. Du Bois is given here essentially as Jordan de-

livered it at the convention, with some changes to punctuation. However, Jordan's version is not technically accurate, as he introduced some changes in wording, possibly to enhance the spoken effect. The original wording can be found in Du Bois, W. E. B., *The Souls of Black Folk* (Chicago: A.C. McClurg & Co.; [Cambridge]: University Press John Wilson and Son, Cambridge, U.S.A., 1903); Bartleby.com, 1999. www.bartleby.com/114/. [accessed September 25, 2006]. Note that the original phrase "warring ideals," changed in Jordan's version to "worn ideals," has been restored here.

64. Vernon E. Jordan, "The Foundation and Society," speech given to Foundation Luncheon Group, New York City, 13 June 1972, UNCF Papers, Manuscript Division, microfiche 1758, 2.

65. Ibid., 2.

Chapter 6. Speaking Out on Behalf of Black Colleges

1. Taylor Branch, *Parting the Waters: America in the King Years, 1954–1963* (New York: Simon and Schuster, 1988). Not until 1963 did Kennedy offer any substantive support to civil rights. In June of that year, Kennedy gave a speech that endorsed the civil rights agenda and called for federal legislation to end segregation in public accommodations and racial discrimination in employment. For more information, see Nick Kolz, *Judgment Days: Lyndon Baines Johnson, Martin Luther King, Jr., and the Laws That Changed America* (New York: Houghton Mifflin Company, 2005), and Jonathan Rosenburg and Zachary Karabell, *Kennedy, Johnson, and the Quest for Justice: The Civil Rights Tapes* (New York: W.W. Norton & Company, Inc., 2003).

2. Wright, interview, 73.

3. Mays, interview, 21.

4. Kimball, interview, 21.

5. Patterson, interview, February 1981, 69–70.

6. Ibid., 89.

7. Ibid., 91.

8. Over the course of their existence, black colleges were the subject of many studies seeking to understand their role in American higher education. See Thomas Jesse Jones, *Negro Education: A Study of the Private and Public Higher Education Schools for Colored People in the United States* (New York: Arno Press, 1969); W. C. John, *Agricultural and Mechanical Colleges, 1917–1918* (Washington, D.C.: U.S. Government Printing Office, 1920);

Arthur Klein, *Survey of Negro Colleges and Universities* (New York: Negro Universities Press, 1969); Phelps-Stokes Fund, *The Twenty-Year Report of the Phelps-Stokes Fund, 1911–1931* (New York: The Phelps-Stokes Foundation, 1932); U. S. Office of Education, *National Survey of the Higher Education of Negroes* (Washington, D.C.: U.S. Government Printing Office, 1942). Although not specifically focused on black colleges, Abraham Flexner conducted a study, "Medical Education in the United States and Canada," which literally provided the plan to eliminate all but two of the black medical schools. Within several years of Flexner's Carnegie-sponsored report, only Meharry and Howard medical schools remained. See Abraham Flexner, "Medical Education in the United States and Canada," Carnegie Foundation Bulletin, No. 4, (1910). For more information, see Thomas Bonner, *Iconoclast: Abraham Flexner and a Life in Learning* (Baltimore: The Johns Hopkins University Press, 2002). At the turn of the century, black intellectuals like W. E. B. Du Bois wanted to verify the existence and success of a liberal arts curriculum at these institutions. For more information, see W. E. B. Du Bois, *The College Bred Negro* (Atlanta: Atlanta University, 1900), and W. E. B. Du Bois, *The College Bred Negro American* (Atlanta: Atlanta University Publications, 1910).

9. Jane E. Smith Browning and John B. Williams, "History and Goals of Black Institutions of Higher Learning," in *Black Colleges in America*, ed. Willie and Edmonds.

10. Earl J. McGrath, *The Predominantly Negro Colleges and Universities in Transition* (New York: Institute of Higher Education, Teachers College, Columbia University, 1965).

11. Mays, interview.

12. Lea E. Williams, "Public Policies and Financial Exigencies. Black Colleges Twenty Years Later, 1965–1985," *Journal of Black Studies* 19, 2 (December 1988), 135–149.

13. McGrath, *Predominantly Negro Colleges*, vi.

14. Ibid., vi.

15. Ibid., vii.

16. Ibid., 10.

17. Jencks and Riesman, "The American Negro College."

18. The sense of betrayal was felt by those members of the black college community that cooperated with Jencks and Riesman and then felt that they were misrepresented.

19. Stephen J. Wright, Benjamin E. Mays, Hugh M. Gloster, Albert W.

Dent, Christopher Jencks, and David Riesman, "'The American Negro College: Four Responses and a Reply," *Harvard Educational Review* 37, 3, (spring 1967).

20. "Integrating the Negro College," *The New York Times,* 18 January 1966; "Negro Colleges Recruit Whites," *The New York Times,* 16 January 1966; and "The Negro College Pleas for Donations," *The New York Times,* 21 January 1966.

21. Christopher Jencks, telephone interview by author, tape recording, Philadelphia, 30 September 2003.

22. Emphasis added in quote. Jencks, interview. See also Marybeth Gasman, "Convincing Words: Fundraising Language Used by the United Negro College Fund in the Aftermath of the *Brown* Decision," *History of Education Quarterly* 44, 1 (winter 2003).

23. Jencks and Riesman, "The American Negro College."

24. The process of accepting articles at *Harvard Educational Review* involves the board as a whole voting on the articles to be published. Then, the articles are assigned to two co-editors, who manage the content and process of one specific journal.

25. Jencks, interview.

26. Jencks and Riesman, "The American Negro College," 4.

27. Ibid., 16.

28. For examples, see Patricia Gurin, "Social Class Constraints on the Occupational Aspirations of Students Attending Some Predominantly Negro Colleges," *The Journal of Negro Education* 35, 4 (autumn 1966), 336–350, and Patricia Gurin and Edgar Epps, "Some Characteristics of Students from Poverty Backgrounds Attending Predominantly Negro Colleges in the Deep South," *Social Forces* 45, 1 (September 1966), 27–40.

29. Note that Jencks and Riesman were critical of many small white colleges as well, but these colleges were not used as comparison in the "The American Negro College" article. Jencks and Riesman's critique was published in an individual chapter ("anti-university colleges") of the *Academic Revolution.*

30. Although Jencks and Riesman did justice to their discussion of the political and economic situation for African Americans during the Jim Crow era, they were not familiar with the specific plight of black colleges.

31. Jencks and Riesman, "The American Negro College," 27.

32. Patrick J. Gilpin and Marybeth Gasman, *Charles S. Johnson: Leadership Beyond the Veil in the Age of Jim Crow* (Albany: State University of New York Press, 2003); Katrina Sanders, *"Intelligent and Effective Direction": The Fisk University Race Relations Institute, 1944–1969* (New York; Peter Lang Publishers, 2005).

33. Daniel P. Moynihan, "The Negro Family: The Case for National Action," in *The Moynihan Report and the Politics of Controversy*, ed. Lee Rainwater and W. Yancey (Boston: M.I.T. Press, 1967). In the case of Daniel P. Moynihan, a report that might have been well-meaning was dangerous to the African American community and served to undermine the structure of the African American family. Not only did Moynihan's work blame the victim rather than the oppressor for the black families in situations of poverty, but it also vilified black women and pitted them against black men. If Moynihan had consulted members of African American families and been familiar with African American history and culture, he might have crafted a richer study that was less susceptible to misinterpretation and misuse. In addition, his research might have been not only more accurate but also more useful to the very community he claimed to want to help.

34. Sterling Stuckey, *Slave Culture: Nationalist Theory and the Foundations of Black America* (New York: Oxford University Press, 1987).

35. Christopher Jencks is a professor of social policy at Harvard University. From 1961 to 1963, Jencks served as an editor of the *New Republic*, and then from 1963 to 1967, he was a fellow the Institute for Policy Studies in Washington. Shortly after writing the *Harvard Educational Review* article, Jencks took a post at Northwestern University. His research pertains to economic inequality, inherited economic advantages, welfare reform, the homeless, and standardized testing. In addition to *The Academic Revolution*, Jencks has published several other books, including *The Homeless* and *The Black White Test Score Gap* (with Meredith Phillips). A cold war–era sociologist, David Riesman died at age 92 in 2002. A lawyer by training, Riesman taught at Harvard University for most of his career. Along with Reuel Denney and Nathan Glazer, he published a bestselling book, *The Lonely Crowd*, which was a "condemnation of consumerist passivity." Riesman also wrote *Constraint and Variety in American Education* (Lincoln: University of Nebraska Press, 1956). (See Paul Buhle, "David Riesman," *The Guardian*, 13 May 2002).

36. Mays, interview.

37. *Time,* 31 March 1967, 64.

38. Marybeth Gasman, "Convincing Words: Fundraising Language Used by the United Negro College Fund in the Aftermath of the *Brown* Decision," *History of Education Quarterly* 44, 1 (winter 2003).

39. *Time,* 31 March 1967, 64.

40. Christopher Jencks and David Riesman, "Negroes and Their Colleges," in *The Academic Revolution* (Chicago: University of Chicago Press, 1968): 475.

41. Ibid., 457.

42. Jencks, interview.

43. James S. Coleman, *Equity and Educational Opportunity* (Washington, D.C.: Department of Health, Education, and Welfare, 1966); Daniel P. Moynihan, *The Negro Family: The Case for National Action* (Washington, D.C.: The Department of Labor, 1965).

44. Jencks, interview.

45. Initial remarks, "Four Responses." Stephen Wright contacted the editor of the *Harvard Educational Review* and asked if the journal would publish a rebuttal to the provocative article. The editors, Davenport Plumer and Janet J. Sanfillipo, agreed to publish the UNCF-led response in its entirety. *Harvard Educational Review* dedicated fourteen pages to the black response, asked Jencks and Riesman to comment on the response, and also included eight pages of letters to the editor on the topic (more than one page of letters on any issue was unusual). According to the Journal's editorial board, "'The American Negro College,' . . . has been the subject of widespread discussion and some misleading publicity. We are pleased to print the following four responses to the article, each written by a leader in Negro education, together with a reply by the authors. We urge interested readers to refer once again to the original article, as well as to the additional responses to it published in the 'To the Editors' section of this issue," 451.

46. Wright, "Four Responses," 451.

47. Ibid., 451–452.

48. Ibid., 452.

49. Ibid.

50. Ibid.

51. Ibid., 454.

52. Mays, "Four Responses," 456.

53. Ibid.

54. McGrath, *Predominantly Negro Colleges,* 5.

55. Gloster, "Four Responses," 458.

56. Dent, "Four Responses," 461.

57. Ibid., 462.

58. Dent described the segregated high schools as inadequate and pointed to unequal funding, poor laboratories, crumbling libraries, overcrowding, and teachers with little or no training. See ibid., 461–464.

59. Ibid., 462.

60. Ibid., 463.

61. Ibid., 464.

62. John Sekora, "On Negro Colleges: A Reply to Jencks and Riesman," *Antioch Review* 28, 1 (1968): 7.

63. Ibid.

64. For a deeper exploration, see Joy A. Williamson, "Student Activists, Activist Students: Black Colleges and the Civil Rights Movement" (paper presented at the History of Education Society Annual Meeting, Chicago, Illinois, 2003).

65. Sekora, "On Negro Colleges," 19.

66. Ibid., 18–19.

67. Williamson, "Student Activists," 25.

68. "Negro Colleges—Their Outlook," *U. S. News and World Report* (3 June 1968): 74.

69. Ibid.

70. Ibid.

71. Like Monro, A. J. Jaffe, Walter Adams, and Sandra G. Meyers published a study on the diversity among black colleges and between black college students. Unfortunately, it too had limited impact. These researchers from the Bureau of Applied Social Research at Columbia University completed their 1968 study of black colleges in cooperation with Stephen J. Wright of the UNCF. Although their study was not entirely supportive of sustaining the "poorest" black colleges, it was based on empirical data (using survey, census, and testing instruments). In addition, despite the prestigious institution from which its authors hailed, the tone of the essay was more encouraging. It should be noted that in an earlier report, sponsored by the Bureau, the authors emphasized the need for this kind of empirical research rather than mere random observation as in the case of the Jencks and Riesman article. See A. J. Jaffe, Walter Adams, and Sandra G. Meyers, "The Sharply Stratified World of

the Negro Colleges," Publication no. A-482 (New York: Columbia University Bureau of Applied Social Research, 1968).

72. Jencks and Riesman, "Four Responses and a Reply," 465–468, 465.

73. Ibid.

74. Patricia Gurin and Edgar Epps, *Black Consciousness, Identity, and Achievement: A Study of Students at Historically Black Colleges and Universities* (New York: John Wiley and Sons, 1975); Nathaniel Norment Jr., *The African American Studies Reader* (Durham, N.C.: Carolinas Academic Press, 2001).

75. Jencks and Riesman, "Four Responses and a Reply," 467.

76. E. Franklin Frazier, *Black Bourgeoisie* (New York: Free Press, 1957). Even some modern critics, such as film director Spike Lee (*School Daze*), have called into question the black college students' attraction to Greek life, societal trappings, and the hazing process.

77. See Williamson, "Student Activists"; Clayborne Carson, *In Struggle: SNCC and the Black Awakening of the 1960s* (Cambridge: Harvard University Press, 1981); and Aldon Morris, *Origins of the Civil Rights Movement: Black Communities Organizing for Change* (New York: Free Press, 1984).

78. Jencks and Riesman, "Negroes and Their Colleges." It is important to note that Jencks and Riesman did make some changes to their article when it appeared in *The Academic Revolution*. These changes were based on criticism from the black community.

79. See John R. Thelin, John T. Casteen III, and Jane M. Bailey, "After *The Academic Revolution:* A Retrospective Forum," *The Review of Higher Education* 12, 1 (autumn 1998): 1–16; Sekora, "On Negro Colleges," 5–26.

80. Jencks and Riesman, "Negroes and Their Colleges," 476.

81. Jencks, interview.

82. Jencks and Riesman, "Negroes and Their Colleges," 477. See also Frazier, *Black Bourgeoisie*. In this text, Frazier, extremely critical of the black middle class, pointed to their wearing of furs, socializing, and joining elite groups as aiding the downfall of the race. As a result, he was ostracized by some members of the black community.

83. Jencks and Riesman, "Negroes and Their Colleges," 477.

84. Earl J. McGrath, *The Predominantly Negro Colleges and Universities in Transition* (New York: Institute of Higher Education, Teachers College,

Columbia University, 1965). See also Benjamin E. Mays, "The Achievements of the Negro Colleges," *The Atlantic Monthly,* February 1966.

85. Jencks and Riesman, "Negroes and Their Colleges," 477.

86. Mays, interview, 112.

87. Jencks and Riesman, "Negroes and Their Colleges," 477.

88. Wright, interview, 113.

89. Jencks and Riesman, "Negroes and Their Colleges," 477.

90. Charles V. Willie, telephone interview by author, tape recording, Philadelphia, 2 September 2003.

91. Jencks, interview.

92. Thomas Sowell, "On Racial Censorship and Rush Limbaugh," *Jewish World Review* (3 October 2003), accessed 5 October 2003. See also Thomas Sowell, "Rush not Guilty of Overt Racism," *Lenawee Connection* (7 October 2003).

93. Sowell, *Black Education.*

94. In 1960 and 1962, black scholars and administrators contributed to the conversations taking place about the status of black colleges in an organized way. In 1960, *The Journal of Negro Education* published a special issue on black colleges, "The Negro Private and Church-Related College." Editorial Note, "The Negro Private and Church-Related College," *The Journal of Negro Education* 29, 3 (Summer 1960), and Editorial Note, "The Negro Public College," *The Journal of Negro Education* 31, 3 (Summer 1962).

95. Willie and Edmonds, eds., *Black Colleges in America;* Daniel C. Thompson, *Private Black Colleges at the Crossroads* (Westport, Conn.: Greenwood Press, 1973); Frank Bowles and Frank A. DeCosta, *Between Two Worlds: A Profile of Negro Higher Education* (New York: McGraw-Hill Book Company, 1971); Walter Allen, *Colleges in Black and White: African American Students in Predominantly White and Historically Black Public Universities* (New York: State University of New York Press, 1991); Henry Drewry and Humphrey Doermann, *Stand and Prosper: Private Black Colleges and their Students* (Princeton: Princeton University Press, 2001).

Chapter 7. "A Mind Is a Terrible Thing to Waste"

1. For a discussion of the Fund's "A Mind Is a Terrible Thing to Waste" slogan, see United Negro College Fund, *United Negro College Fund Archives: A Guide and Index to the Microfiche* (Ann Arbor: University Microfilms International, 1985).

2. Marybeth Gasman and Edward Epstein, "Creating an Image for Black Higher Education: A Visual Examination of the United Negro College Fund's Publicity, 1944–1960," *Educational Foundations* 18, 2 (Spring, 2004).

3. Marybeth Gasman, "A Word for Every Occasion: Appeals by John D. Rockefeller, Jr. to White Donors on Behalf of the United Negro College Fund," *History of Higher Education Annual* (2002); Gasman and Epstein, "Creating an Image."

4. Wright, interview.

5. Joseph Taylor, interview by Marcia Goodson, transcript, UNCF Oral History, 47.

6. Jordan, interview, March 1987, 11.

7. Gasman, "Rhetoric vs. Reality."

8. Jordan, interview, March 1987, 11.

9. Ibid., 13.

10. Taylor, interview.

11. Ibid., 47.

12. Christopher Edley, interview by Marcia Goodson, transcript, UNCF Oral History.

13. Ibid., 30.

14. Taylor, interview, 47.

15. Ad Council Papers, www.adcouncil.org, New York, New York.

16. Taylor, interview. Arguing that African American issues were of importance to the whole country was incredibly difficult, especially since the black population was located in select pockets of the United States and not spread out across the country. For a detailed description of this argument, used by the federal government to deny Black organizations access to the Combined Federal Campaign in the late 1950s, see Linda King, "The Federal Government and Black Fundraising," *Black Scholar* 9, 4 (1977).

17. Jencks and Riesman, "The American Negro College."

18. Gasman, "Rhetoric v. Reality."

19. Edith Wilson, an actress, portrayed Aunt Jemima on television, in print, and on the radio from 1948 to 1966. Beginning in 1950, Ethel Harper portrayed Aunt Jemima in various media outlets as well.

20. The Uncle Ben image was used in both print and television ads. The legend has it that Uncle Ben was a highly successful African Ameri-

can rice grower in the South. People thought highly of his product and would say, "as good as Uncle Ben's."

21. Rastas was the Cream of Wheat chef and was created in 1890. His image (that of a Chicago waiter paid $5 to pose) has been used in various media forms since the 1890s.

22. Marilyn Kern-Foxworth, *Aunt Jemima, Uncle Ben, and Rastus: Blacks in Advertising, Yesterday, Today, and Tomorrow* (Westport, Conn.: Greenwood Press, 1994); Herman Gray, *Watching Race: Television and the Struggle for the Sign of Blackness* (Minneapolis: University of Minnesota Press, 1997); Sasha Torres, *Living Color: Race and Television in the United States* (Durham, N.C.: Duke University Press, 1998); Donald Bogle, *Primetime Blues: African Americans on Network Television* (New York: Farrar Straus Giroux, 2001); Fred J. MacDonald, *Blacks and White TV: African Americans in Television since 1948* (New York: Wadsworth Publishing, 1992); M. M. Manring, *Slave in a Box: The Strange Career of Aunt Jemima* (Charlottesville: University Press of Virginia, 1998).

23. *The Hollywood Reporter*, "TV Milestones," 385, 30 (September 2004). It should be noted that most of the popular televisions shows of the 1970s that dealt with blackness didn't appear until the mid-1970s after the "Mind" ads. (*The Jeffersons*—1975; *Sanford and Son*—1972; *Welcome Back Kotter*—1975; *Good Times*—1974; *What's Happening*—1974). *All in the Family* (1971) appeared simultaneously with the airing of the first "Mind" ad.

24. Barbara Savage, *Broadcasting Freedom: Radio, War, and the Politics of Race, 1938–1948* (Chapel Hill: University of North Carolina Press, 1999).

25. Taylor, interview, 48

26. Ibid.

27. Charles Stephens, interview with author, 6 May 2006.

28. "United Negro College Fund," Historic Campaigns, Ad Council Archives, www.adcouncil.org, New York, New York.

29. Ibid.

30. The ad is arranged in a way that looks much like many of James Whistler's paintings, such as *Portrait of the Painter's Mother* and *Portrait of Thomas Carlyle*. Ralph Ellison, *Invisible Man* (New York: Vintage, 1995).

31. "A Mind is a Terrible Thing to Waste," 1971, Historic Campaigns, Ad Council Archives, New York, New York. According to Charles Stephens, the UNCF national campaign chair from 1973 to 1976, some

people found this ad to be too depressing. The idea of a black man fading away was too dire (interview with author, 6 May 2006).

32. Lewis Killian, "Race Relations of the Nineties: Where are the Dreams of the Sixties?" *Social Forces* 69, 1 (1990), 1–13.

33. "You Can't Cure Cancer with a Monkey Wrench," 1972, UNCF Papers, Manuscript Division, microfiche, 2622.

34. "$2,817.33 a pound," 1973, UNCF Papers, Manuscript Division, microfiche, 2673.

35. Vernon Jordan, *Vernon Can Read* (New York: Basic Books, 2001). For a more detailed explanation, see pages 6–9.

36. Charles Stephens, interview with author, 6 May 2006.

37. Jordan, interview, March 1987.

38. "For About What It Costs," Ads, 1973, UNCF Papers, Manuscript Division, Reel 2623.

39. "Don't Think of it as Charity," 1972, UNCF Papers, Manuscript Division, Reel 2622.

40. Jordan, interview, January 1982, 31.

41. Ibid., 17–18.

42. Charles Stephens, interview with author, 6 May 2006.

43. Please note that there was an interim director at the UNCF between Jordan and Edley. A man named Arthur Fletcher covered the position during the transition. See Edley, interview, 20.

44. Ibid.

45. Ibid.

46. Ibid.

47. Ibid.

48. Ibid.

49. Ibid., 22.

50. Ibid.

51. Ibid., 22–23.

52. See "Ford Foundation Annual Reports," 1963–1973, www.fordfound.org, accessed 12 May 2005.

53. The "Mind" campaign is most often associated with Christopher Edley Sr. rather than Vernon Jordan. However, Jordan helped created the original campaign, but Edley took the campaign to the masses.

54. "Once you had to put your life or liberty on the line," UNCF Papers, Manuscript Division, microfiche, 1677.

55. "There was a time when supporting Black education could have

cost your freedom," UNCF Papers, Manuscript Division, microfiche, 1677.

56. "The Old Bodie Plantation," UNCF Papers, Manuscript Division, microfiche, 1677.

57. "My mother is scrubbing floors," 1974, UNCF Papers, Manuscript Division, Reel 2623.

58. "My grandmother takes in washing," 1974, UNCF Papers, Manuscript Division, Reel 2623.

59. "My father works 12 hours a day putting down rails," 1974, UNCF Papers, Manuscript Division, Reel 2623.

60. "UNCF history," www.uncf.org, 5 May 2005.

61. "United Negro College Fund," Historic Campaigns, Ad Council Archives, New York, New York.

62. Edley, interview, 31.

63. Ibid., 31–32.

64. "United Negro College Fund," Historic Campaigns, Ad Council Archives, New York, New York.

65. UNCF's "A Significant Adventure," [1950], General Education Board Papers, Record Group 5235–5240, Series 1, sub-series 3, box 491, folder 5240, RAC.

66. Ibid.

67. Edley, interview, 36.

68. "Who ever said . . . ?" UNCF Papers, Manuscript Division, microfiche, 1677.

69. "This is No Place for Your Hands," 1978, UNCF Papers, Manuscript Division, microfiche, 1677.

70. Edley, interview, 36. For more information on The Links support of the UNCF, see Kijua Sanders McMurty and Nia Woods Haydel, "The Links, Incorporated: Advocacy, Education, and Service in the African American Community," in Marybeth Gasman and Katherine V. Sedgwick, eds., *Uplifting a People: Essays on African American Philanthropy and Education* (New York: Peter Lang, 2005).

71. Charles Stephens, interview with author, 6 May 2006.

72. Edley, interview, 35.

73. Gasman, "A Word for Every Occasion."

74. See Anderson, *Education of Blacks in the South.*

Conclusion. An Organization
That No One Could Argue Against

1. Ronald Roach, "Taking it to the Next Level," *Black Issues in Higher Education*, 9 September 2004.

2. United Negro College Fund, "Friends in High Place," Website (http://www.uncf.org/webfeature/archives/webfeature_01282005_First_Families.asp, accessed 5 May 2005).

Index